GHOSTS OF ATLANTA

GHOSTS OF ATLANTA

CULTURAL GENTRIFICATION OF THE BLACK MECCA

RHANA GITTENS WHEELER

UNIVERSITY PRESS OF MISSISSIPPI / JACKSON

The University Press of Mississippi is the scholarly publishing agency of
the Mississippi Institutions of Higher Learning: Alcorn State University,
Delta State University, Jackson State University, Mississippi State University,
Mississippi University for Women, Mississippi Valley State University,
University of Mississippi, and University of Southern Mississippi.

www.upress.state.ms.us

The University Press of Mississippi is a member
of the Association of University Presses.

The collage illustration on the cover was derived from images from various sources. The original photo of Big Bethel AME Church is by Keizers via Wikimedia Commons. The *Heart of Blandtown* billboard was created by visual artist and Blandtown activist Gregor Turk, whose work can be found at www.gregorturk.com. All other images were sourced from iStock. All have been altered from their original versions. Design by Jennifer Mixon.

Manufactured in the United States of America

∞

Library of Congress Cataloging-in-Publication Data

Names: Gittens Wheeler, Rhana, author.
Title: Ghosts of Atlanta : cultural gentrification of the Black Mecca /
Rhana Gittens Wheeler.
Description: Jackson : University Press of Mississippi, 2024. |
Includes bibliographical references and index.
Identifiers: LCCN 2024031198 (print) | LCCN 2024031199 (ebook) |
ISBN 9781496853370 (hardback) | ISBN 9781496853363 (trade paperback) |
ISBN 9781496853356 (epub) | ISBN 9781496853349 (epub) |
ISBN 9781496853332 (pdf) | ISBN 9781496853325 (pdf)
Subjects: LCSH: Gentrification—Georgia—Atlanta. | Gentrification—Social
aspects—Georgia—Atlanta. | Neighborhoods—Georgia—Atlanta. |
Urban renewal—Georgia—Atlanta. | Community development—Georgia—Atlanta. |
Sociology, Urban—Georgia—Atlanta. | Atlanta (Ga.)—History. |
Atlanta (Ga.)—Social conditions. | Atlanta (Ga.)—Economic conditions.
Classification: LCC HT177.A8 G58 2024 (print) | LCC HT177.A8 (ebook) |
DDC 307.7609758/231—dc23/eng/20240802
LC record available at https://lccn.loc.gov/2024031198
LC ebook record available at https://lccn.loc.gov/2024031199

British Library Cataloging-in-Publication Data available

FOR WAKANDANS

CONTENTS

ACKNOWLEDGMENTS

This book would not exist without the support and inspiration of many. To Brian, my husband, thank you for our uncountable conversations and debates surrounding this book and the ideas behind it. Your insight was an invaluable contribution. Thank you for walking with me as I navigate this world. To Linda, my mommy, thank you for being my biggest fan and having patience with me. I know that your silent prayers have been a gift showing up in ways I may never fully know. To Kevin, my dad, the more I write, the more I see you within me. Your fight for Black humanity is flowing through my veins. To Jamil, my big brother, your determination and drive have inspired me to never give up even when the process gets tough. Thank you for reminding me I'm worthy. To Janae, Jayla, Imogene, Gertrude, Alethea, Michael, Juanita, and Lee, thank you for being my family. And to my amazing friends, thank you for doing life with me.

Several people have played a role in the production of this scholarship. Patricia G. Davis has believed in me and the possibilities of this research from the start. Her help cannot be underestimated. To James Darsey, Jacqueline Royster, and Holley Wilkin, thank you for your valuable suggestions, unparalleled knowledge, and patient critique. To Carolyn Walcott, my friend, I am so grateful for your review of my work, encouragement, and unwavering support when I'm in the thick of it. To Heloisa Lanca Guilherme, thank you for your creativity and map designs, which can be found throughout this book. To the reviewers of this manuscript, while I may never know who you are, I am so grateful for you. Your constructive feedback and detailed messages helped bring this book to another level. To Allante and Star, thank you for your early feedback on my ideas.

I am particularly thankful to members of the local community who supported this research. To Gregor Turk, I'm especially grateful to you for extending your network of connections to me and contributing to the advancement of the history of Blandtown. Thank you to my many interviewees, named and unnamed, whose stories form the heart of this book.

To Wallace Bibbs, Johnny Lee Green, Alison Johnson, and Shanequa Gay, thank you for your passion for your neighborhoods, your city, and its people.

Finally, I am grateful for the institutional support from Georgia State University, where I first completed my research. Additionally, I'd like to extend my gratitude to Oglethorpe University faculty and staff for supporting my continued study. A special thank you goes to my students, who have inspired me in robust discussions and reminded me of why I do this. To the Atlanta History Center, Fulton County Deeds and Records Room, and Georgia Archives, thank you to the various archivists and researchers who were available to answer questions and aid me during this project.

Finally, I want to thank God for gifting me courage, wise words, and grace. With God, all this is possible.

GHOSTS OF ATLANTA

INTRODUCTION

> Hi, boys and girls! It's your old pal, Mr. Robinson. So much has changed since we last spent some time together. My neighborhood has gone through so much. It's gone through something called gentrification. Can you say "gentrification," boys and girls? It's like a magic trick. White people pay a lot of money—and then poof! All the Black people are gone. But where do they go, boys and girls? Back to where they come from, of course—Atlanta.
>
> —EDDIE MURPHY[1]

We are living in a time of rapid and violent urban gentrification. This has inevitably led to inquiries about how to identify and qualify the complexities of what people are seeing and experiencing. A recurrent question of the gentrification of predominantly Black communities is, Can affluent Black people be gentrifiers? The reason people ask this question is because of the prevalent association of gentrification with class. What the question misses is the cultural implications of gentrification, the reality that "poof! All the Black people are gone." The economic and class-based experiences of gentrification are real and need to be researched. But the focus of *Ghosts of Atlanta: Cultural Gentrification of the Black Mecca* is the Culture,[2] which is to say Black culture. The concern is the Culture's displacement from home. The home at the root of this book is Atlanta.

"If blacks and whites are sincere in their announced intentions, Atlanta might well turn out to be the town that taught a nation how to live," professed Phyl Garland in her 1971 article in *Ebony Magazine*, heralding Atlanta as the "Black Mecca of the South."[3] Nearly fifty years later, Eddie Murphy satirically informed the world in his 2019 special return to *Saturday Night Live* that Black neighborhoods were gentrifying and Black people were returning to "where they come from, of course—Atlanta." Both the Black journalist and comedian were making a statement about

Atlanta that marked the city as an origin for Black culture and economic and political progress, as well as a destination—a place where Black lives go when we've been displaced everywhere else. It designates Atlanta as a singular point of failure, where any obstacles to the creation of Black communities there could have national consequences. While the larger audience may see these expressions as entertaining, imaginative, mythical, and fictive, for many African Americans and people across the African diaspora, Atlanta as the Black Mecca is a statement of Black possession of a space—a homeplace. Conceivably, for a people without a place, it is the most critical affirmation of their collective existence. Yet we have not come to grasp the fullness of Atlanta's identity as a Black Mecca.

Indeed, the reason we haven't entirely conceived of Atlanta as a homeplace for African Americans is because we are attempting to rationalize "home" under modern white conceptions of a sense of place. Scholars attest that orienting spatially and temporally is essential to the human condition. A "sense of place" is a Western concept to describe the metaphysical sense of belonging individuals have to a location and time.[4] For Western colonizers, the idealized sense of place was characterized as a bounded and private location inhabited by coherent and homogenized communities.[5] The Westernized sense of place conceived of land in terms of a "kingship." This position allows a single person to own land and makes attaining personal property and authority over a place a cultural striving.

For African nations, the concept of land rights is diverse. It is expected that instead of bounded and private locations, spatial and temporal orientation can be determined by "whatever a people deem their social fabric."[6] Social fabric is the connection that makes one person a part of a whole. It is a communal orientation. Under this conception of home, "the living hold the land in trust . . . for both the dead and the unborn"; therefore, "what matters is who, among the living, can persuade others to think their ancestors pioneered a place."[7] Consequently, "kinship," at times determined by maternal lineage, is an institutional glue binding African selves to a community. Origins are determined by blood and ancestral connection to land, which creates a system premised on land rights, not ownership. Roots are stabilized in the land through heritage, making spatial and temporal separation from kin a violent separation from the origin and the physical present.[8] During modern enslavement, Africana peoples were brutally separated from their kin. And while the dominant ideology in the United States conceives of "home" under Western experiences of property ownership, because of violent displacement, the concept of "home" for the sons and daughters of the enslaved has not been experienced under these same circumstances. And this displacement has not ceased. Threats of dispossession consistently subsume Black physical locations.

Thus, "home" for Black people must be conceived of differently from both the African and the American conceptions. More than five hundred years of displacement make it impossible for us to return to our African kin origins. And racism has made kinship and kingship in the United States nearly impossible. Therefore, "home" comes to us less often from physical ancestral evidence and is more often informed by a social fabric stitched by legend-like stories, proclamations, traumas, and lost histories. There is a difference between these conceptions of place. We see that in the reasoning behind Atlanta's label as a Black Mecca. Via physical evidence, the Black Mecca could be visible and apparent, like a deed to land in Atlanta, proving homeownership. It could appear in voting for a Black mayor to city leadership and be visible when the state tips the scales for a Democratic presidential win and a Black and Jewish state senator. It can be as apparent as majority-Black neighborhoods. Yet Black homeplace is more often hidden in a feeling as rhythmic as a T.I. song and as spiritual as Ebenezer Baptist Church. It could even appear in the passion of a Black Lives Matter march or a heartened proclamation of "Wakanda forever." We might go as far as to touch it in the crevices of Stone Mountain, the abandoned tracks of city railways past, the gates of Fort McPherson, the grounds of Oakland Cemetery, or the trace of a street name. The point is that the Black Mecca is sometimes recognizable in objective and quantifiable data, like land ownership, but most often, it is in the social fabric. You will only find it if you "slip into the breaks and look around."[9] I'm most concerned with what might happen if our senses stop, if the Black Mecca is culturally gentrified, or if we just no longer perceive it there. We have not come to grasp the fullness of its identity as a homeplace. And we are not prepared to grieve its loss.

Ghosts of Atlanta explores why and from what conception of home and origin Atlanta is considered a homeplace and through what means it, like so many other homes we've carried, can be lost to us. Examining various ways Black lifeworlds are presented in gentrified or gentrifying spaces in the city, I consider how the culture can remain visible in a world where the hegemonic structure leans toward its erasure. To combat the cultural gentrification of the Black Mecca, we must first explore the different ways, physically and metaphysically, that the Black Mecca can be sensed. From there, we may learn how the Black Mecca can be retained.

THE BLACK MECCA AND FOLLOWING A HAUNTING

The descriptor "Black Mecca" is an ironic statement. There are at least two dimensions to this irony. The first is that "Mecca" implies a specific group's birthplace, origin, and center. The city of Mecca in Saudi Arabia is the birthplace of the Prophet Muhammad and the symbolic birthplace of Islam. However, the birthplace of African Americans does not have such apparent specificity. Who can mark the space and time when we first stopped being wholly African and started being African and American? Nonetheless, we choose Atlanta to mark our origins.

My experience with the city of Atlanta from the time I was a teenager reflects the metro area's existence as a Mecca, connecting African Americans to a metaphoric origin that at once recognizes the group's past, present, and future in an idealized home. In the summer of 2004, my family chose Atlanta as our destination for collective remembrance of our familial history. Arriving from Florida, New York, and California, we met up at the base of Stone Mountain for our biennial family reunion. We sat inside the hotel banquet hall listening as my cousin read out our family tree, beginning in 1815. He presented our lineage, describing how we were all connected by blood to Handy and Palace Brown McClendon, who once resided just two hours south of Atlanta. It didn't dawn on me until years later that the circumstances of slavery added unique challenges to tracing my ancestry back to its origins as, before the ratification of the Thirteenth Amendment in 1865, my slave ancestors were likely nameless tallies in a master's property ledger. Stone Mountain, a tangible symbol of Civil War history and its Confederate legacy, represented the racist ideas that left Handy and Palace's forebearers in bondage and the victory that allowed them to gain contested freedom in these united states. This turned out to be not an arbitrary or random positioning of my family reunion at Stone Mountain but rather an almost sermonic way of conceptualizing our family's birth at the base of the haunting history of the Civil War and Reconstruction period. If my family's narrative and the Confederate narratives are formed by space, then choosing Stone Mountain as the location of collective remembrance fashioned our familial identity into the stories that make Stone Mountain meaningful to the Confederacy, the Union, and the enslaved. It also designated our story as part of a more significant collective identity with those who draw their family lineage from the collective trauma of slavery and find their origins at the culmination of the Civil War and the ratification of the Thirteenth Amendment. Such a conceptualization asks that we constantly consider the interconnections of space, place, and memory. It asks that we critically assess how the labels we attach to a place force other people to look at that world our way and with our memories.

Atlanta is more than a site of cultural trauma. We remember it also as a recognizable bastion of the Culture—the aesthetic, art, and music that symbolizes Black lifeworlds and responses to anti-Black racism and white supremacy.[10] In the 1990s and early 2000s, we all heard about Atlanta through the cultural grapevine, a city with five-bedroom homes selling for $200k; streets buzzing with dancing, music, stepping, and parades during the annual college spring-break Freaknik festival; and Black businesses, entrepreneurship, and the best southern soul food. Even if we had never taken a drive around I-285 circling the city, we had all been there through the music of the Dungeon Family and So So Def Recordings. We saw the city for ourselves when Ludacris and Jermaine Dupri welcomed us and took us on a tour-bus ride in their infamous "Welcome to Atlanta" music video. On my first visit, we went to the Underground Atlanta shopping center, popular in the 1990s for Black consumerism, where I ran into my teen crush Allen Iverson at the Foot Locker. We traveled to the King Center and the historic Ebenezer Baptist Church. Atlanta seemed to be a city we were naturally drawn to; everywhere we turned, we saw ourselves—our music, our art, our speech, and our culture. Atlanta has been a significant anchor to the symbols and traditions that brought life to the postslavery Black experience, and it seemed to be saying to me, "You fit here."

At the same time, this family reunion at Stone Mountain reminded me that our permission to be in that space, at that time, as "free people" rendered us "out of place." After the trip, my mother posted a picture of my dad, brother, and male cousins on the mantelpiece. The image is a paradox. The photo is a staged portraiture of my dad, in the middle, with his arms wrapped around the shoulders of the boys, Stone Mountain in their backdrop. Behind my father's head are the images of the three Confederate figures carved into the mountain, President Jefferson Davis, General Robert E. Lee, and Lieutenant General Thomas "Stonewall" Jackson. I become unsettled by this family photo because I recognized that one of these groups was out of place. But at first, I wasn't sure if it was my Black family, showing up where they shouldn't, or the Confederates, remaining where war and time should have released them. Who had permission to be there? Permission and exclusion are the second dimensions of the ironic statement that Atlanta is the Black Mecca of the South. The phrase implies Black ownership, possession, or permission to a place, yet my idyllic family photo unsettles this element of the metaphor.

It could simply be a family photo. But the figures in the background pierce through. They draw me into the moment, and placed together, these living Black men in the foreground and deceased white men in the background become the object of my inquiry. I'm not sure what to make of it. I know what our therapist would ask: How does this make you feel? I'm unsure if I should be proud, justified that my people freely visited a space marked out for someone who didn't want us there in that capacity. Yet I feel mocked, as though the Confederates lost the war but won the mountain as our money fed back into a system that retains racist practices. Sometimes, I feel stupid to have been there and continue to visit. Other times, I'm proud. Mostly, I feel both all at once. I learned that I can't depoliticize or dissocialize these feelings, placing them in the realm of personal therapy. To do so would be to deemphasize how the experience of space, or spatial conditions and their narratives, communicates identity and fate. So, I continue to ponder this unsettling feeling.

This photo disrupts my singular view of our family reunion as being "just us." The photo captures what else was there as a "seething presence."[11] It presents a tension of two lifeworlds coming together: the Confederate lifeworld of imperialist ambition, gruesome defeat, and unrelenting consistency to the doctrine of Black inferiority and inhumanity (someone who is not human but property himself cannot possess property), on the one hand, and the Black lifeworld of double consciousness, freedom longing, and spiritual recognition of our whole, ordinary humanity, on the other. Time is in tension. The two different eras, almost 150 years apart, come together circularly. In this photo, we can see the past alive in the present and the present alive in the past. I recognize we can't divide these two lifeworlds, nor can we separate their time periods. I argue that keeping them separate creates what W. E. B. Du Bois called the "veil," a separation of Black and white lifeworlds to the point that they are like two incongruent realms, occurring synchronously.[12] But still, I wonder, Who is out of place?

Sociologist Avery F. Gordon argues that this unsettled feeling I'm having is a sign of the manifestation of ghosts. A ghost is a presence that shows up where they are not intended to be. She urges scholars, "If you let it, the ghost can lead you toward what has been missing, which is sometimes everything."[13] So I followed the ghosts in my family photo. And they led me to this question of "permission." Who allowed the mountain to be blasted with images of Confederate figures? Who permitted them to stay here? And what permissions do these faces open for some and close for others? For me? These questions of "permission" also bring up inquiries of "exclusion." And suddenly, I was spiraling, wondering, Are the Confederate figures the ghost haunting me, or is my family the ghosts haunting them? These questions of permission and exclusion led me to Handy and Palace Brown McClendon and to the plight of the enslaved after they were "freed": the convict-leasing system, Black codes, Jim Crow segregation, redlining, eminent domain, stop-and-frisk laws, police brutality, disfranchisement, and more. This "freedom" feels awfully contained, which leads me to a space in between "permission" and "exclusion"—a space that mirrors the current condition of Black life where we are both present and invisible, both giving off physical form that reflects existence in a place and being muted and constrained. It's in this condition of both being present and invisible, permitted and excluded, that Black culture forges itself into a collective identity and orients itself spatially and temporally. In this condition, we've found our physical presence in places like Atlanta as the Black Mecca, where our placemaking efforts are sometimes apparent in the physical evidence but many times in the form of a feeling of the metaphysical sort. The problem with the condition of being present and invisible is that you are often displaced by those with permission and visibility (i.e., privilege). And so one of the goals of *Ghosts of Atlanta* is to make our culture visible.

I say all this to express to you that the identity of Atlanta as the Black Mecca is complicated and complex. And it's as complicated as all placemaking and personhood for African Americans are. As Du Bois expresses, our personhood is complicated by a "double-consciousness," the constant sensation of "looking at oneself through the eyes of others, of measuring one's soul by the tape of a world that looks on in amused contempt and pity."[14] Similarly, placemaking is complicated by permissions and exclusions that render us legally allowed to own and be present while also systematically denying us full citizenship rights. *Ghosts of Atlanta* begins with a discussion of my family reunion, my childhood recollections of an idealized Black city, and my father and the boys' family photo with Confederate soldiers in their backdrop in order to transition thoughts from the physical to the metaphysical and introduce the concept of haunting. Haunting, as defined by Gordon, is "an animated state in which a repressed or unresolved social violence is making itself known, sometimes very directly, sometimes more obliquely."[15] My family photo signals the social violence on Black lives left unresolved after the Civil War. When a haunting is sensed, it calls to the passersby that there is "something left undone here" and "there is something left to do here." For Black folk in America, a haunting can also signal our presence in a state between permission and exclusion. In this way, a haunting can enliven us to something we must do to retain the Culture. Our Black Meccas, then, are sites of haunting.

Ralph Ellison's book *Invisible Man* signals this haunting too. Published in 1952 and winner of the 1953 National Book Award for Fiction, the book introduces the unnamed protagonist as an invisible man, a seething presence in the lives of white people. Ellison discusses a moment when the protagonist bumps into a "tall blond man," and after the man called him an "insulting name," the protagonist headbutted him and kicked him, demanding an apology. When the apology didn't come, the protagonist took out his knife and "prepared to slit his throat" until he realized he wasn't getting a response because "the man had not seen" him. He let the man go. As the man lay on the ground, the protagonist notes feeling "disgusted and ashamed." The man must think he's in a nightmare; he'd almost been "killed by a phantom." Ellison describes the protagonist as a "phantom" and an "invisible man." Yet he is only invisible to those who "refuse to see" him.[16] In the introduction to the novel, Ellison explains this invisibility further, arguing that the Black pigmentation of African American bodies doesn't make them hypervisible, as sociologists once suspected, but rather renders them "un-visible."[17] Racist treatment doesn't occur because Black people's skin makes them highly visible but rather is due to how white Americans look at reality. This description of the perception of Black bodies as invisible, turning them into phantoms, reflects on the complex experience of haunting inherited from the Middle Passage, slavery, and Reconstruction. Ellison is considering haunting from the Black perspective, causing him to use "invisibility" to describe the feeling of being both present and perceived by others as not there.

While Ellison describes haunting from the perspective of Black people as the invisible phantom, Toni Morrison, in *Playing in the Dark*, considers how white Americans perceive the American haunting. In assessing early American literature from Marie Cardinal, Edgar Allan Poe, Willa Cather, Ernest Hemingway, and Mark Twain, among others, Morrison best articulates how white Americans responded and came to terms with their haunting. She explains that the American haunting became a lingering shadow that is a companion to whiteness. Unconsciously or consciously, white American writers have almost always patterned the power of whiteness with an accomplice—the "representations of Black or Africanist people who are dead, impotent, or under complete control."[18] Blackness became the shadow that moved the narrative along and empowered whiteness. Morrison uses haunting to describe the puzzling existence of an American as encountering life with a semblance of solitude yet having gathered onto oneself the mask of impoverished others.[19] The shadow is akin to a haunting that whiteness cannot be rescued from because it has built its identity on it, reflecting the contradictions of the American dream of freedom and the bitter institution of slavery and post-Reconstruction segregation.

Ellison also describes this haunting from a white perspective. In Ellison's passage in *Invisible Man*, Mr. Norton, a white philanthropist funding a Black college, is asked by a Black veteran, "Why have you been interested in the school, Mr. Norton?" And Mr. Norton responds, "Out of a sense of my destined role. . . . I felt, and I still feel, that your people are in some important manner tied to my destiny . . . the success of my work, of course." The story's unnamed protagonist, the invisible man, is a student at the college that Mr. Norton funds. The Black veteran tells Mr. Norton that the invisible man is the "successful" result of his work. He says of the invisible man, "Already he's learned to repress not only his emotions but his humanity. He's invisible, a walking personification of the Negative, the most perfect achievement of your dreams sir! The mechanical man."[20] What Ellison tries to get at here is that Mr. Norton gives to the Black school to make himself feel morally superior, and the invisible man is the outcome of that process. The invisible man is Mr. Norton's shadow, gathered onto Mr. Norton's person as an oppositional comparison that helps define Mr. Norton's identity as a superior man. This is compatible with the position of communication scholars Thomas K. Nakayama and Lisa N. Peñaloza. They argue that "whiteness as a racial category does not exist except in conflict with others"—that is, it is defined by what it is not.[21] As a character of domination, whiteness is limited not by its purity but rather by being compared to what the dominant group defines as impure others. And as Ellison illustrates, the invisible Black man is a creation of whiteness that sustains white identity. Together, Morrison and Ellison reveal the white perception of that Black presence in America as a shadow of humanity buttressing white identity—a sad necessity. As such, these Black ghosts drive the narrative of white lives with "fear and longing."[22]

Ghosts of Atlanta takes up haunting as a rhetorical device that materially "moves the hearts and texts" of America's spaces with "fear and longing."[23] My texts are places or representations of places that manifest "repressed or unresolved social violence" on Black people in Atlanta. I investigate the haunting by following the ghosts, also referred to as phantoms, seething presences, or the invisible. I apply the rhetorical device of haunting to space to understand two things. First, I seek to establish how white fear and desire incite the displacement of Black language, tradition, and history, leaving Black people invisible. Second, I ask how the veil separating Black and white lifeworlds can be pulled away, revealing a humanized people rather than invisible phantoms. I suppose that removing the veil would bring Black and white lifeworlds together in these shared spaces, reflecting a new American geography as a culture of cultures.

I consider this by examining Atlanta's gentrifying spaces through different symbols of power, including neighborhood naming, public history, and the built environment. These attributes get at various ways we design public spaces and how that impacts how private people sense their community identity and connection to it. Neighborhood naming, public history, and the built environment carry narratives forged into our public spaces that reveal something about the ghosts and what needs to be done to take them out of the shadows. I explore these narratives in different periods (the Reconstruction period, the civil rights movement, and the contemporary period of "Black urban dislocation"[24]) in a circular, rather than linear, fashion in constant consideration of how the present is in the past and the past is in the present. This approach to criticizing space and circumstances of Black spatial narratives in Atlanta incorporates archival documents, informative interviews, news articles, photographs, music, naming, and numerous mediums of cultural language, symbols, and performance with critical rhetoric, literature, sociology, and geography theories. Gordon's *Ghostly Matters* is a valuable resource for this research. Part of the thesis offered here is that we can find demonstrations of haunting in areas of Black placemaking, such as neighborhoods in Atlanta where African Americans sought to create a home out of the landscape in post–Civil War America. Following the haunting, we can uncover "abusive systems of power" that hinder that placemaking.[25] In coming to this, I'm indebted to Black scholars like Toni Morrison, Ralph Ellison, and W. E. B. Du Bois. They explain what happens to American identity and geography in a historically racialized society and, more importantly for me, what happens to Black collective identity because of it. A commonality among these writers is the explanation of the complicated and complex realities of being Black in the United States through the lens of feeling, abstractions, shadows, and hauntings. Gordon has synthesized the concept of "haunting" as a theory of social life. And I extend it in this book as a method of criticizing gentrified and gentrifying spaces.

When I first came to this conception of the "ghost," I thought it a bit outside of myself to use it to understand issues of the living. However, with the complexities of modern life experiences, particularly the racialized conception of existence in the United States, ghosts and hauntings are particularly fitting as Gordon used this sociological theory to wrap her mind around the complicated dimensions of society and the complexities of personhood.[26] This theory helps us understand parts of our social life that are so complex that they fall outside the realm of rational explanation. The haunting helps clarify things that make us feel "some kind of way," even though we can't quite put a name to the feeling.[27] This unnamable unease could be a sign that a haunting may be present. Gentrification is like that for me. Gentrification has been discussed rationally, as an issue of dollars and cents, taxes and property value, and the worth of neighborhood renewal versus a resident's lifetime in a place. However, the rationale doesn't fully encapsulate the loss. As Brandi Thompson Summers argues in her telling of H Street Corridor's gentrification in Washington, DC, "most scholars and the general public can abstractly account for feelings of neighborhood change. When revitalization and reinvestment strategies are accompanied by gentrification, the overall impact on communities becomes more complicated, since most residents see the benefits of improved physical and economic conditions and services."[28] Thus, we must let go of the conclusion that Black people are simply standing in opposition to revitalization that increases property costs as it leads to stereotypes of poor Black residents as lazy and not invested in taking care of where they live.[29]

This reasoning comes from a Western conception of placemaking rather than a Black perspective. We need to talk more about the origins of place dominant in African American rhetoric, which conceives of place as kinship, kinship as collective identity, and collective identity as power.[30] This discussion requires, according to Stuart Hall, an account of the articulation of African, American, and European presences that make up the conception of home for African Americans. bell hooks's description of African American homeplaces accounts for this. According to hooks, "tenuous and fragile" homeplaces are constructed by Black women as safe spaces where Black people can "freely confront the issue of humanization" and where we can resist and heal "the wounds inflicted by racist domination."[31] The role of Black women in constructing these spaces to affirm Black humanity is reflective of an African presence in that some tribes connected origins to matrilineage, and ancient African women had greater authority to lead armies and rule nations. For African Americans, the mother is not only based on blood connection; the mother is often based on the positionality of the woman in the formation of safe spaces for Black people. Further, what hooks describes as the "tenuous and fragile" existence of homeplace reveals an American presence. According to Hall, the American presence shows up as the provocateur of migration and displacement as white desires for land provoke the dislocation of nonwhite others. Finally, hooks notes the home as a place where resistance, healing, and humanization occur. These activities happen in response to the domination and exclusionary practices of the European presence in our modern age. Together, these three appearances (African, American, and European) influence Black collective identity and conceptions of place and origin.

Considering the uniqueness of Black placemaking, I contend that African Americans oppose revitalization efforts not simply because of a fear of physical displacement but because of the substantive need to protect collective identity, humanize the ghost, and make themselves visible. Urban redevelopment gives a feeling of enjoyment of the new construction and safer places, yet it also leads to uneasy, noxious feelings. While some good is happening, something not so good persists. It's not just right or wrong, good or evil, proud or ashamed. Instead, we tend to have to carry within us two opposing things at the same time, the magnificent and the maleficent, the African presence and the Western presences. Ghosts are found in that connection, and following the ghosts is a method for excavating the complex, and studying the haunting is a way we can theorize the complicated. African Americans have created narratives to communicate Black spaces as areas inclusive of Black life. White Americans have done the same for themselves. Ultimately, following the ghosts of gentrification reveals that the issue isn't with revitalization itself but with how ethnically shared places, like cities, are culturally and collectively conceived in the United States.

Through Gordon and Morrison, I understand our idyllic family photo that made me feel "some kind of way." It is a photo that captured my attention once I learned who the figures in the background were. Looking at those three white men, I recognized that their white identity blasted into a granite mountain as a symbol of honor was bolstered by the racial system that castigated African Americans. The Confederate figures represent what Toni Morrison characterizes as "the highly problematic construction of the American as a new white man."[32] This new white man stands in contrast to the old white man of Europe. The old white man experienced powerlessness and oppression in Europe. The new white man was free from the British monarchy but still maintained a fear of subjugation and desire for power—power being held in land ownership. The new white man's fears were counteracted by the enslaved Black person. The new white man could replace their fear of subjugation with subjugation of another. As Morrison puts it, "For in that construction of blackness and enslavement could be found not only the not-free but also . . . the projection of the not-me."[33] Considered this way, the seven Black men in my family photo project a contrast with the Confederate figures, the new white man. The record of these Black men at a location dedicated to the Confederates' commemoration empowers the American new white man identity, which found its potential by constructing Blackness as inferior. Thus, there were haunting figures over our mantelpiece, proleptic reminders of the endless chains and oppression in a painful fate for African Americans.[34] However, as fraught with trauma as that history may be, when we chose Atlanta as our space for kinship, we also forged a reckoning, a meeting up of Confederate visions with ghosts of our own. That history that had been suppressed was brought to life; however frightening it may be, it produces "a something-to-be-done." As Gordon writes,

> Haunting, unlike trauma by contrast, is distinctive for producing a something-to-be-done. Indeed, it seemed to me that haunting was

> precisely the domain of turmoil and trouble, that moment (of however long duration) when things are not in their assigned places, when the cracks and the rigging are exposed, when the people who are meant to be invisible show up without any sign of leaving, when disturbed feelings won't go away when easily living one day and then the next becomes impossible, when the present seamlessly becoming "the future" gets entirely jammed up. Haunting refers to this socio-political-psychological state when something else, or something different from before, feels like it must be done, and prompts a something-to-be-done.[35]

Thus, my idyllic family photo of seven Black men at a location where ancestors of our kind were lynched stands as witness to my family's presence in a place we were never intended to be. The photo is a recognition that we were there. We are the ghosts in our family photo. And by "ghost," I don't mean the dead. I take the term "ghost" from Gordon, who describes it as a "social figure" who by their seething presence in places they weren't dreamed to be gives you a sign that "a haunting is taking place."[36] The ghosts are the "free" Black bodies traversing the park in a way they were never meant. African Americans' continued presence in Atlanta, like ghosts, produces a haunting. Though we are real ghosts, we are also haunted by Davis, Lee, and Jackson, the visible Confederate presence at Stone Mountain. Haunting is the manner of the ghost. And scrutinizing the haunting can bring us to "understanding what has happened or is happening."[37] But I want to tell you that I don't want to be a ghost and I don't want to be haunted. Therefore, my hope with *Ghosts of Atlanta* is that investigating Black presence in spaces intended for white enrichment and Black impoverishment will exhume Black lives from places of subjectivity, abstraction, and invisibility to humanization. And so this book is also about my own humanization in the city I call home: Atlanta.

To set the stage for the haunt's excavation, in this chapter, I will review cultural gentrification as a process that produces ghosts. Then, I will briefly explore the Atlanta BeltLine project, a significant change in the city of Atlanta driving fast-paced gentrification of the Black Mecca. I will conclude by explaining the methods I utilize to excavate the ghosts. The ghost hunt aims to understand how white fear and desire lead to Black displacement and to listen to the Black phantoms' stories. In them, we may find ways to pull away the veil, maintain a Black Mecca, and produce a city that is reflective of the diverse historical trajectories of its cultures.

ATLANTA'S CULTURAL GENTRIFICATION

Ten years after our family reunion in Atlanta, I found myself living in the metropolitan area, identifying with the urban-sprawl reactionary culture of driving for nearly two hours a day during the daily work commute in and out of the city. Though I was caught in the present rush of city life, Atlanta has a mysterious dialectic that forces you to slow down and take witness. It's evident in the aura of commemorative memorials to the Confederacy across the city, as well as the civil rights monuments and museums and in the discourse and public memory of the people. There is that continued haunting that forces you to pause momentarily. It seems people in this city have had consistent ghosts urging them to "do something." So Atlantans are the "do-something" types, supporting the image of a "city too busy to hate" devised by Mayor Ivan Allen's administration. In comparison to other southern urban cities during the 1960s, Atlanta appeared forward-thinking in its busyness with economic and business endeavors, but the city's Black neighborhoods faced harsh socioeconomic conditions,[38] making their lives "tenuous and fragile."[39] The neoliberal slogan "city too busy to hate" creates a false dichotomy—a dichotomy that continues to this day.

One of the most recent "do-something" initiatives is the Atlanta BeltLine, twenty-two miles of walking trails, trolleys, and light rails, which, once completed, will unite the forty-five different neighborhoods that make up Atlanta proper and will hopefully decrease the traffic and subsequent pollution caused by urban sprawl. Over more than 150 years, the city of Atlanta has expanded from its central urban core into a metropolitan area encompassing twenty-nine counties.[40] In 1999, environmental justice scholars predicted Atlanta would rapidly replace Los Angeles as the "sprawl capital of the nation."[41] They found that people in the area traveled an average of thirty-four miles a day, which, at the time, was more than anywhere else on earth and 50 percent more than people in Los Angeles. That same year, Ryan Austin Gravel ideated the BeltLine to bring a city that had been majorly dispersed to the suburbs back to a tighter community in the urban city center.[42] While the original hope was that mixed-income communities would decrease concentrated poverty and diversify segregated neighborhoods in the city center, high private investment and purchasing of low-cost properties in majority-Black neighborhoods are poised to displace African Americans. I consider gentrification as an activity that increases the proliferation of Black haunting. We become ghosts in the places from which we are displaced—places that are reborn as white space.

In this section, I will provide an overview of essential phrases and concepts relevant to the issues raised in this book, including defining "cultural

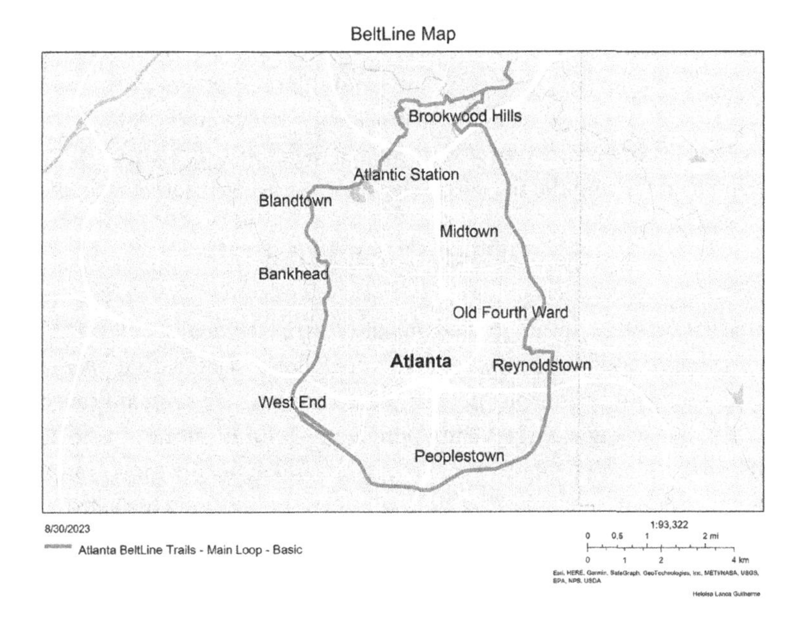

Map of the planned Atlanta BeltLine's twenty-two-mile route by Heloisa Lanca Guilherme. Copyright © 2023 Esri and its data contributors. All rights reserved.

gentrification." This is not intended to be a comprehensive review of the study of gentrification scholarship. Instead, I plan to address the book's interconnected concepts of culture and gentrification and demonstrate how *cultural gentrification* produces a haunting. We can think of Eddie Murphy's set, quoted in the opening of this chapter, as a performance of the Black collective consciousness that deems Atlanta home with an endemic permanence. Even with all that we know of this nation and the city's fraught and complex relationship with African Americans, I still find the Black collective asking, Who is this city really for? Is it for white people or Black people?[43] As urban geography scholar James C. Fraser attests, "a part of the revitalization of neighbourhood and urban space is the on-going struggle to define the meaning of a city and for whom it exists."[44] For the Black Mecca, this question reflects a pragmatic concern with the continued existence of African American culture. It hinges on the problematic actions that hinder the Culture by encroaching on spaces of Black collective memory and Black lifeworlds, violently separating Black people from kin and land. To be clear, Atlanta is an ethnically diversifying city; however, the focus of this book is its existence as a Black Mecca and the current spatial relationship between the descendants of enslaved Black people in this nation and the dominant white hegemony. It will hopefully lay the groundwork for scholars to study the spatial relationship of white hegemony with groups marginalized by class, race, ethnicity, gender, sexuality, and intersectional identifications. In this section, I will explore the tensions, oppositions, and contradictions between the supremacist-powered neoliberal logics that construct America's spatial narratives and the lived experiences of African Americans in space.

GENTRIFICATION AND CULTURAL GENTRIFICATION

Gentrification often occurs in tandem with tearing down and building back up to revitalize and renew a space. And what follows that is a disappearance. Consider how Eddie Murphy defines "gentrification." He satirically accepts that "it's like a magic trick. White people pay a lot of money—and then poof! All the Black people are gone."[45] At the same time, the most common understanding of "gentrification" is that it is the process of which "the gentry," or higher classes, move into and revitalize a lower-class area. This can result in increased property value, taxes, and rents, which inevitably leads to the displacement of lower-class residents. The issue with the popular use of the term is that it focuses solely on class, missing the effects on groups marginalized by race, ethnicity, gender, and sexuality. Specific to this study, it misses that "all the Black people are gone." So scholars also have to come to understand "gentrification" as the "displacement of lower-income Blacks and other people of color with white newcomers who possess higher incomes."[46] These understandings of gentrification rightly consider the intersections of class and race that lead to the disappearance of Black bodies in a space. In this book, I'd like to go further. At focus here is not just the displacement of Black bodies but also the disappearance of the Culture and its ultimate effects on the humanization of Black people. The displacement of Black culture—the aesthetics, stories, memory, and performance of Blackness—is not just an unfortunate outcome of gentrification.[47] Gentrification targets Black culture for violent removal and threatens Black homeplaces, spaces formed by kin for our humanization and resilience against racist environments. As Akira Drake Rodriguez attests, "We are in a new era of Black urban dislocation."[48]

Conventional gentrification discussions in local government planning deliberations have privileged the economy's role in determining social relations,[49] but *cultural gentrification* focuses on the more nuanced aspects of our struggle for space. The critical term of interest here is "culture." This book not only considers symbols of culture but also recognizes the process by which the dominant hegemony can homogenize culture. This is necessary for understanding one way that Black identity stays behind the veil. Further, it recognizes the discursive processes by which cultures can be transformed. This is important for prognosticating what America could be if we drop the veil and humanize the ghosts.

Much of the understanding of culture in this text is inspired by Stuart Hall's work in cultural studies. In the communication discipline, culture is theorized as the symbols that individuals and communities use to express their points of view. Taken further, culture is a group membership, "defined by shared language, custom, religion, and belief."[50] Groups use aesthetics, language, performance, and other modes of expression to create and preserve collective identity. Culture, therefore, is a symbolic action that maintains social relations among a collective. Hall observes two modes of cultural formation. The dominant mode places closed limits around cultural identities, and the secondary mode considers the liminality of culture. Contemporary hegemonic viewpoints of culture began at the "flash points" of the making of modern society; these flash points are the Atlantic slave trade, colonialism, and contemporary migrations. During these critical moments, the meeting up of groups with differing others led the movement to close boundaries around group belonging and culture.[51] Yet Hall attests, in reference to his observations of Caribbean culture, there is another way to understand the discursive formation of symbolic communities. In this second mode, cultural identity is not a "collective 'one true self'" that "people with a shared history and ancestry hold in common."[52] While cultures have histories, they are also always becoming, always transforming. By observing how people who are dislocated from kin and soil recreate and transform culture by articulating their identity with and through the presence of other cultures, we have the opportunity to learn "how to live with others and otherness."[53]

Cultural gentrification occurs when we operate inside the hegemonic position of culture that is closed and "grounded in a geographic sense of place that excludes what is foreign or alien."[54] The hegemonic viewpoint of culture has become naturalized as common sense in the American ideology. According to Karl Marx and Frederick Engels, this occurs as the ruling class's domination is translated into the realm of ideas.[55] Dominant codes, or hegemonic viewpoints, come to define the universe of possible meanings in a society or culture. The hegemonic viewpoint also carries a stamp of legitimacy, giving the ruling class the privileged position to define events and narrate history.[56] In this way, the construction of culture as group identity has been used to control social order through a cultural continuum, placing the wealthier class of Western tastes and ideas as "high culture" and marginalizing other groups as "low culture." The dominant culture retains hegemony by having a controlling interest in the economic and ideologic realms of societal influence.[57] Thus, today's dominant ideologies of neoliberalism and racism have become a naturalized form of thinking about and processing space in America. They instigate continued displacement of those considered "foreign or alien." It will help, then, to deconstruct the neoliberal and racist ideologies that reproduce displacement.

Today, spatial power is located within Western and North American hegemony. Their conception of power is based on the capitalist marketplace, which compresses space, creating an inside and outside, an "us" versus "them."[58] The Western experience of globalization and capitalism determines our understanding and experience of space and disregards the influence that race and gender have on that experience. From the hegemonic perspective, space and time are conceived as the linear human progression through time under one narrative of continued increases in power and control over nature—the path of the capitalist West. This is evident in the dominant form that the history of North, Central, and South America is captured and taught in the United States. As Doreen Massey explains, the modern story of this hemisphere is told from the European perspective of "voyage and discovery," of Spanish conquistadors "conquering spaces," and, I'll add, of the Portuguese taming the savage and of the British and French cultivating the frontier. The dominant narratives of modern history can "lead us to conceive of other places, people, cultures simply as phenomena 'on' this surface." Massey argues this is not an "innocent maneuver." The West equates space with land and sea and conceives of others who may be at an earlier stage of the single narrative of human progression as "lie[ing] there, on space, in place, without their own trajectories," without "potential for their own, perhaps different, futures."[59] This conception obliterates the notion that there are other alternatives for human futures. It naturalizes globalization and capitalism in modernity. When the West meets other races, ethnicities, or societies that have not gained the level of control over nature and capital as it has, the perception is that these groups are just behind[60] or—as was made to be believed of "the Negro"—are "incapable of all historical change."[61] This closed conception of human futures, along with the boundary-laden conception of culture as a realm of exclusion, can be used to justify redevelopment triggering displacement through claims of cultural superiority. Superior thinking perpetuates the invisibility of Black culture.

Another way to understand how the hegemonic view can orient us to see people of color as "phenomena on the surface" is through the concept of invisibility. Throughout this text, I will use "invisibility" as a gaze of whiteness that sustains cultural gentrification. In critical rhetoric, "invisibility" has been defined as the transparent, unseen power and position of whiteness because it is the norm on which everything else is compared and explained. However, taking a turn from the whiteness-focused view of invisibility as power, I use a

Black-centered view of invisibility, meaning not to exist or appear in another's perception. The social construction of race in America has rendered Black bodies invisible. Explored by Ellison in *Invisible Man*, invisibility goes beyond the notion of being unseen. To understand its complexity, let's hear it from Ellison. He writes, "I am invisible, understand, simply because people refuse to see me. Like the bodiless heads you see sometimes in circus sideshows, it is as though I have been surrounded by mirrors of hard, distorting glass. When they approach me they see only my surroundings, themselves, or figments of their imagination—indeed, everything and anything except me."[62]

As Ellison describes it, the invisibility of Black people is not simply because they are absent from view. He writes that even when this Black man is available to be seen, he goes unnoticed. Ellison continues, "That invisibility to which I refer occurs because of a peculiar disposition of the eyes of those with whom I come in contact. A matter of the construction of their inner eyes, those eyes with which they look through their physical eye upon reality."[63] He affirms that invisibility is due to how others look at him. In such a sense, invisibility is a function of the eyes that behold the subject, not of the subject itself. If this is the case, invisibility must be defined from the perspective of the onlooker. Thus, to pinpoint invisibility in the geography, we can define it as Craig Barton has, as someone "consciously removing from the public gaze that which is neither intended nor desired to be seen."[64] In this case, the public gaze is the dominant white gaze, and when those eyes look upon Black spaces, they seemingly do not exist. And note that it is not just white people who use the white gaze. The ideological ideas undergirding this perspective have been globalized, making the white gaze common sense and affecting everyone's perception of reality.

This white gaze of invisibility works itself out through two ideologies, or common-sense forms of thinking, in American culture: neoliberalism and racism. Neoliberalism is an ideology that defines how capitalist societies should be run. It directs the dominant contemporary narrative of the West. Neoliberalism, an abstract symbol for the normative order, ideology, and political reasoning, places everything within business logic and economic value, promoting the free market, privatization, deregulation, and reduction of social welfare.[65] Within this order, people are commodified, discussed as statistics and dollars necessary for labor value. Neoliberalism can be easily understood if we think about the two forms of argument used in American political deliberation. In the United States of America, the dominant strategy for winning a debate on a policy issue is to argue that a particular political choice would promote individual progression and competition. This stands in opposition to arguments that support policies for a collective or public interest, which aren't winning in contemporary debate. Instead of representing "the people" as their constituents, government leaders represent the capitalist class, those who own the means of production.[66] By doing so, "the people" cease to exist in a governing system that has a social contract with businesses that outweighs that with individual citizens. And this ideology as common sense inhabits space affecting development plans and policies that choose the economic will of investors over residents. Neoliberalism presents itself in the revitalization and renewal of our cities by making Black culture—or, more likely, a white conception of Black culture—a commodifiable good. As you'll see in the cases throughout the book, Black culture is dispatched and repackaged to attract investors and new residents to Black neighborhoods; meanwhile, Black bodies are moved out. Neoliberal thinking, along with racism, is how "blackness, but not necessarily Black people, can be cool."[67]

Second, invisibility is practiced through racism, the ideology reproducing racial hierarchies, rationalizing that one race is naturally superior to another. Black studies and cultural geography scholars align conclusively on the argument that race is lived through space, and the hegemonic ideology has used spatialization of race to reproduce racism through the unjust enrichment of white Americans and unjust impoverishment of people of color.[68] Rather than perceiving space as an "empty vessel within which social processes are located," these scholars see space as being actively produced and shaped by racist social policies like stop-and-frisk laws, anti-immigration, housing discrimination, and policies that lead to segregated neighborhoods.[69]

As defined by Ellison, "geography" is both the place and its racial social conditions.[70] Similarly, Katherine McKittrick and Clyde Woods theorize that there are Black geographies, arguing that racialized "demographic patterns as shaped by historical precedent" determine human environments' material and physical geographies. They argue that essentialism has set a hegemonic norm that erases and excludes the struggles and concerns of Black communities. Thus, lived citizenship is worked out through space as the hegemonic order maps out permission and exclusion through spatial assignments. The dominate modes of power desire conquest and perceive places as "sites to be dominated, enclosed, commodified, exploited, and segregated." But people from communities that have been displaced have desires to "build new homes in places that have barred their entry." They "reimagine the politics of place," perceiving place as "the location of cooperation, stewardship, and social justice."[71]

To combat racialized space, African Americans have taken the crumbs of unwanted neighborhoods that the dominant white governing bodies have allowed them to have and turned them into locations they can proudly call home. Black communities form in segregated neighborhoods and designate them as cultural havens. Furthermore, using naming conventions, like for street, school, district, and church names, African Americans make the classification of the space as their home known to passersby. In this way, these places, like all places, are defined by the words and symbols used to communicate "this is mine." But it can only indeed be yours if those passersby see it, acknowledge it, and identify it as yours. So, when your space is invisible, passersby looking upon it with a white gaze—a view from the dominant mode of placemaking—will never transition to identifying it as yours.

Black space is faced with a constant threat of painful displacement. The general process of displacement could be said to start with the characterization of Black spaces as "deviant or problematic."[72] Rather than considering the city's disinvestment in Black neighborhoods for decades as a systemic issue often leading to the problems poverty and high density produce, this dystopic characterization of Black space is used to justify the revitalization of Black neighborhoods at any given time that white people want the land. While displacement can undoubtedly occur through violent force, more ominously, the threat to Black space comes from gentrification. Eddie Murphy likens gentrification to a "disappearance" because that's how it feels. Take Charlotte, North Carolina's Second Ward, 125th Street of Harlem, New York, and U-Street in Washington, DC, for instance. Known as Brooklyn Charlotte, Charlotte's Second Ward was home to a thriving Black community from 1900 to 1968. Still, in the 1950s, Black neighborhoods were targeted for demolition. With its high level of blight and proximity to the city, Brooklyn Charlotte was completely leveled by 1968, becoming a parking lot and displacing 1,007 families.[73] Harlem's 125th Street is best known for its cultural landmarks, including the Apollo Theater and Cotton Club. But new developments on the street, including prominent business chains like H&M, Victoria's Secret, Bath & Body Works, and Whole Foods, gentrified the cultural aesthetic and, with rising housing prices, led to the displacement of long-time Black residents.[74] Then there is U-Street in Washington, DC, nicknamed the Black Broadway as it was home to famous African American jazz clubs and theaters. But the 1968 race riots after Martin Luther King Jr.'s death destroyed the city, leading to a blighted, dangerous, and drug-infested community. By 2018, U-Street was home to high levels of luxury housing with home values at over $450,000. Urban redevelopment in this neighborhood so severely increased the cost of living that long-time residents had to move out.[75] The Black heritage of the area, including the content of the self-guided tour City within a City: Greater U Street Heritage Trail, was romanticized, making the contentious politics respectable for would-be investors and gentrifiers.[76]

In all these cities, former residents have been displaced, but there is another element of loss that is not always quantifiable—it is the loss of common language, traditions, and collective connection to a home, a displacement of culture. These examples reflect the nature of gentrification as a form of a "disappearance" of a culture that was once identifiable by a place and identified by that place. While space, place, and gentrification scholarship has aligned with the theory that neoliberalism leads to displacement of low-income, indigenous, long-term residents and residents of color, what has not been thoroughly explored is the connection of the neoliberalization of space to the concept of cultural gentrification, which I argue is white people's response to fears of powerlessness and of the loss of property and morality—the same concerns that brought the settlers to the "New World" and led them to make people of color their subordinates. That history left its ghosts. Cultural gentrification, moving and removing the spirits, is the process of avoiding the ghosts without reckoning with them. The term "cultural gentrification" signals the moment when a cultural group's visibly distinct language, traditions, and practices in a space are displaced, subsumed, or appropriated by the dominant ideology. This doesn't occur via a fixed set of rules. Instead, as you'll see throughout the book, it involves specific rhetorical strategies ranging from outright erasure to narrative appropriation and romanticization that works to preserve the racial order at the cost of diverse historical narratives in space.

I use "cultural gentrification" rather than "gentrification" throughout the text to get at the experience of gentrification's outcome of an ethnic or racial group's disappearance more specifically. This disappearance results in African Americans feeling "unwelcome and uncomfortable in areas where they have lived and roamed for years,"[77] marking what it means to be both present and absent simultaneously. Cultural gentrification is a process of transformation that leads to the displacement of the collective identities and cultures that once made up a space. The process starts when a marginalized group forges a home in white space. White people leave that space. The area is marginalized and devalued in the market, making it an "invisible" space. They are not invisible because of a magical invisibility cloak, like Harry Potter's, or a holographic projection, like Wakanda uses to stay in hiding. Instead, they are invisible because when "the gentry" set their eyes on a marginalized group's space, they do not see them. When they look for a new place to move to, they look directly at the Black space and seemingly say, "there is nothing here." Or, maybe recognizing their vision issue, they say "this is such an eyesore." Either way, they do not see the family dinners, barbecues, or band rehearsals but rather a blank slate of old homes that they are determined to bring "culture and community back to." Through a systematic process, the gentry carry their contemporary symbols of home—yoga studios, craft-beer breweries, and cafés—and slowly, the diverse culture is turned back to that mythic American narrative of homogenously white space.

Cultural gentrification is an exemplary instance, somewhat like a disappearance, in which "the boundaries of rational and irrational, fact and fiction, subjectivity and objectivity, person and system, force and effect, conscious and unconscious, knowing and not knowing," private and public, and laws and spirit become unsettled.[78] Throughout the development of this research, I've attended grassroots meetings of organizations seeking to stave off cultural gentrification, hearing how the people most affected by urban development are grasping and resisting the experience. I've also frequented Atlanta BeltLine Inc. (ABI) meetings to understand better what goes into revitalizing a city on such a large scale. These experiences have given me an appetite for ruminating on the complexities of cultural gentrification and its unstable tensions. The lines between the rational and irrational are unsettled because, while improvements to neighborhoods are expected and often welcome, people still want some things to remain the same. Mostly, they want both their cultures and their bodies to exist in the space. Once people are displaced, what fights to endure are the stories, often turning to myths and legends, bordering on reality and imaginative nostalgia for what once was and grasping for a writer, a speaker, a soul to take them out of the shadows. Scholars, journalists, philanthropists, bloggers, tour guides, and the curious latch on to a piece of the ghost. Some try to understand the effects of gentrification by interviewing people, quantifying the home costs, or accessing city and state policies. Others require a critical interpretation of the unique phenomenon of each neighborhood and home and the powers that engulfed them.

We find both the objective and subjective are necessary to know the causes and the solutions. Researching gentrification can be difficult because, as persons are both displaced and replaced, the systems of racial conditioning are refashioned, more ominously at this juncture, but they still survive. They find ways to romanticize Black experiences in the space, making it digestible for investors, garnering a semblance of racial neutrality for the leaders of urban redevelopment. The covert existence of racialized systems disguises what is changing in our neighborhoods. It becomes a part of our unconscious, common-sense habits and actions. So even those with the best intentions find it hard to truly know what the new revitalization plans are up to in the residents' private homes. But Black residents know. Long-term Black residents' private interests become public interests, upending the difference between what is mine and ours or, more commonly, what belongs to a Black person and what the dominant group wants to recoup.[79] Black people learn from experience that the city is not only constructed by the laws of the town that they thought protected their property, land, and residential status. More readily active is a spirit pervading this American nation space, one imbued with an evolving white supremacy. And the way the "spiritual quality of our American principles" plays out in revitalizing neighborhoods leaves behind ghosts.[80]

CULTURAL GENTRIFICATION IN ATLANTA

Today, the racial conflict over space in Atlanta can be studied and uncovered by critically observing the known cultural displacement that is occurring with the construction of the Atlanta BeltLine. The BeltLine and additional renewal activities it influences add to the revolving loop of temporary placement and continuous displacement of African American collective identities. Gravel proposed the idea for the BeltLine in his master's thesis, written while he was a student at the Georgia Institute of Technology. Gravel considered Atlanta to be the symbol of the modern city. But he was troubled that Atlanta had placed the automobile and the interstates and other roads on which it traversed as the method of expansion. Like the railroad, highways—not public interest, according to Gravel—determined Atlanta's city design.[81] Interstate and transit development was used to reestablish the racial hierarchy in the city. In the 1920s, transit availability and discriminatory FHA (Federal Housing Administration) loans allowed white residents of the central city to disperse to the suburbs, creating the sprawl we know today as metropolitan Atlanta and leaving the central city to the urban poor and African Americans through processes of racism and redlining. In the 1940s, Interstates 75 and 85 were purposefully designed around Eastside Atlanta to separate the white business district from Black neighborhoods.[82] The interstate system and the 1967 federal project Model Cities inevitably led to the deterioration of the Black business district on Auburn Avenue.[83] Based on Larry Keating's research, it's possible that 68,000 people, representing 19,000 to 22,000 households, were displaced from the center city, with nineteen out of every twenty people displaced being Black.[84] So while Black people continued to shape culture, network, and make their place within the city, they struggled to progress economically due to the concentration of poverty, disinvestment, and systemic oppression plaguing their communities. After spending a semester in Paris, Gravel imagined a new design of Atlanta's infrastructure to relieve the issues that racism and transit design had created. His goal was also to reinforce downtown Atlanta as the city center by layering transit around it. He reimagined the unused rail lines as a walkable path and a streetcar path that could unite the neighborhoods. At its inception, it was touted as an ambitious project and has continued to win awards nationwide.

The Atlanta BeltLine is yet another transit system that will determine the city's racial hierarchy. It is set at odds with the communities it seeks to revive as Gravel's initial goals to protect historically Black neighborhoods in Atlanta from gentrification have been subverted. When those "profound physical spaces" between the forty-five neighborhoods were made known to the public,[85] investors came in droves, purchasing properties and building homes and businesses—all in anticipation of the capital the BeltLine would bring. Gravel has since stepped down from leading the project. But the futurist visions continue to draw more power away from those marginalized communities as it draws investors into them. Despite original promises of affordable housing and alleviation of displacement risks, the project has contributed to Atlanta's affordable-rental-housing crisis.[86]

A study by the *Atlanta Journal-Constitution* in conjunction with students from Georgia News Lab found that on the east side of Atlanta, where the BeltLine first opened up, average rents increased by 59 percent between 2005 and 2017.[87] Further, a study by Dan Immergluck and Tharunya Balan on the property value changes from 2011 to 2015 reveals that homes within a half mile of the BeltLine had a valuation increase between 17.9 and 26.6 percent more than homes further away from it. Of course, these rising valuations benefit some property owners and prospective owners and improve the city's tax revenue. But for those low-income residents, the fast-paced value increase adds to the taxable value and cost of living. The percentage increase in property taxes for initially lower-valued homes will become higher over time. Based on an example from Immergluck and Balan, if a home value increases 50 percent over four years, they could see their property taxes tripled.[88] Homes that started with a higher valuation would have a lower percentage increase. As the housing researchers attest, "the shock of the property tax increase will fall heaviest on those with lower-valued homes."[89] In addition, rent prices will increase as property owners pass the burden of increased taxes onto the renters. While an Affordable Housing Trust Fund had been established to keep Black and low- to middle-income residents from displacement, the money allocated for affordable housing was not spent, and the funding from the city for low-income residents was not processed. There were initially 5,600 affordable homes and apartments within the BeltLine tax allocation district allotted for availability by 2030.[90] However, that number of units isn't enough to house the rent-burdened residents. Scholars and activists continued voicing housing-affordability issues, engaging Atlanta city leaders to implement new policies beyond the affordable-housing missions of

ABI. Former mayor Keisha Lance Bottoms released a citywide plan in 2019 to develop or sustain twenty thousand affordable housing units by 2026 with an investment of $1 billion (half coming from city-controlled public sources and half from private and philanthropic investors).

As the city works to put these measures in place, many of Atlanta's low- to middle-income residents are already being displaced. Atlanta's population has shown significant growth since 2010. The new residents are one reason the housing supply is shifting; less rental housing is available, and the cost of rentals and housing is increasing. Atlanta added more than 21,000 new families between 2010 and 2018, the bulk earning more than $45,000 per year. Households earning less than $45,000 yearly make up a smaller percentage of the city's population. About four out of every ten households earn less than $45,000 annually. Considering affordable housing as housing for which the resident pays no more than 30 percent of their gross income for rent or mortgage and their utilities,[91] those making less than $45,000 a year would "need housing options that cost $1000/month or less."[92] However, the market trend for housing is steadily moving upward. From 2010 to 2018, Atlanta "lost 5,400 units priced under $800 per month."[93] At the same time, the city produced 14,212 new units priced above $1000 per month.[94] Based on the 2018 assessment of equitable housing needs in Atlanta, with the drop in affordable housing, "the housing gap is likely to more than double to over 35,800 units by 2030."[95] Ultimately, during the two decades from 2010 to 2030, the city will bleed out many existing and long-term residents that have been a part of the culture and aesthetic that feed into Atlanta's position as a Black Mecca. As Immergluck attests of the BeltLine, "Instead of focusing on acquiring property for affordable housing while land values were low, and putting in place measures that would protect existing residents from rising property taxes and rents, the focus was on building trails and parks that would enhance land values. . . . The fact that the beneficiaries of these trails and parks would increasingly become white and affluent seemed to be of little concern."[96]

Despite gentrification, the city has remained the Black Mecca. Cultural gentrification has not yet completed its work in the city, meaning it is still a space that could teach "a nation how to live," allowing for diverse races to prosper economically and politically while maintaining their distinct historical trajectories within the spatial narrative of the city. The Atlanta BeltLine and gentrification processes across the United States make it clear that spaces of African American collective identity, like the Black Mecca, are not safe from encroachment and disruption when hegemony, capital, wealth, and race are constituted spatially. Notwithstanding efforts to service marginalized groups, neoliberal goals for economic progress inevitably propagate the racialization of spaces.

Because of its designation, Atlanta is integral to African American existence. If you're concerned by the amount of emphasis that I put on place as regards a group's existence, consider the following: Abraham Harold Maslow's hierarchy of basic human needs considers the physiological needs (food, water, and shelter) and safety needs (security, health, and property) as necessities that must be met before a person can ever reach a point of achievement and purpose.[97] In the United States, the Federal Housing Act of 1949 decreed that having a "decent home and a suitable living environment" was a right of all Americans, thereby giving generations upward mobility.[98] This human right to a home is further supported in Abrahamic religions as God blessed Abraham and His people with a land of their own, recognizing that a collective home was an initial requirement for God's chosen people to become what they must. The assumed permanence of having a place provides the comforting image of continuity for the individual, her heirs, and collective identity.[99] The cultural attributions the group applies to a space, representing their values and morals, guarantee that the culture will continue. This is what Atlanta has been for African Americans in an anti-Black society. This book explores how African American historical narratives can be lost or maintained within current urban-redesign projects and the more significant issue of narrating an American identity inclusive of all Americans.

A BRIEF NOTE ON METHODOLOGY

Some of my favorite doings in the city now are walking the Atlanta BeltLine, biking the Atlanta BeltLine, watching the construction of the Atlanta BeltLine, and, as you'll see in this book, tragicomically condemning the Atlanta BeltLine for all its losses and praising it for all its pleasures. The currently finished portions of the BeltLine have provided me great escapes to Ponce City Market and an old Sears building turned cafeteria and shopping center, quiet walks on the Westside Trail of the BeltLine past new craft-beer locations, and short walks off course to Slutty Vegan, a Black-woman-owned restaurant. In all the newness, you can't help but peek at the changing neighborhoods as developers have come into Black South Atlanta neighborhoods, flipping homes, building new white enclaves in the middle of Black spaces, and strategically buying, rebuilding, and readjusting the culture of the city. I see the signs of Black residents pushing back as they put posts in front of their homes that read, "Home not for sale" and "Stop gentrification." As the BeltLine development continues, the diverse spaces are slowly coming to look a lot alike, reflecting how a place with visible signs of America's various cultural trajectories can transition to represent the homogenously white space of America and make Black people but ghosts.

The method I use here focuses on how our spaces communicate, influencing our collective identity and acting as created interpretations of our collective identity. This reflects the goals of the spatial turn in communication scholarship, which calls for scholars to "interrogate the spatiality of power."[100] The United States defines itself legally, economically, and constitutionally under the premise of whiteness, turning words into actions that, at the outset, hinder diverse groups in America, making them *in* it and not *of* it. This inevitably threatens the entire national institution. A nation, like any organization, exists in language. Language, including narrations that express our values and precepts, determines the nation's being. For example, the Declaration of Independence, the Constitution, and the Bill of Rights are just a few of the significant discursive projects that wrote America into existence. They are more than abstract ideals; the words affect and influence our societal structure and the welfare of those that live in it. Rightfully, activists have focused on the failures of primary and secondary education to represent American history and identity accurately. Yet we cannot forgo our landscapes. We may spend fifteen years in public education. Still, our entire lives will traverse this geography, making the buildings, names, brands, street corners, parks, advertising, and art everlasting educators about our identity. Aesthetic practices, such as music, poetry, speech, architecture, and names in local neighborhoods, define the nation as much as Pennsylvania Avenue, the Smithsonian National Museum, the Statue of Liberty, and Mount Rushmore. These aesthetic locations in the landscape communicate our identity to visitors, influence who we think we are, and define who we are not. For residents, if the narratives in their lived spaces don't reflect that they belong, exist, or ever existed, they become shadows in areas they were never intended to be. However, the authors of our nation's landscapes (the politicians, developers, architects, historians, passersby, public artists, residents, migrants, and you and I) have a choice to represent America with a veil that leaves Black lives as invisible shadows or lift the veil, humanizing Black bodies and reflecting the reality of our presence in the landscape.[101] To save the nation, the United States needs an aesthetic facelift, reinterpreting itself in terms of a culturally diverse identity to align with what I believe is its substantial truth and destiny. America is to be, as Ellison defines it, a "nation of nations," a "culture of cultures."[102] The impulse of *Ghosts of Atlanta* is toward this identity wholeness.

Thus, as stated previously, I follow the ghosts in this work, considering them as Morrison does—as presences that can move texts. The texts, in our case, are the physical, urban spaces and places in the city of Atlanta.

The study of cultural gentrification relies on understanding the geography of memory, which "locates history and its representations in space and landscape,"[103] and the narration of collective identity within that space. The historical trajectory is the culture's narrative as it moves through time. A trajectory's spatial position regarding other trajectories affects its evolution, movement, and makeup. Using spatial narratives, David J. Bodenhamer helps us conceive of historical trajectories as discursive. Rather than stories having settings, histories are inscribed in space and spatially situated. Tracking the narrative of people and their ghosts as they unfold in space and bump into, converge, and interconnect with other spatial narratives allows scholars to assess the effects of power on cultural narratives.[104] In this book, I use what Annette Kuhn describes as an "unselfconscious methodological bricolage" that produces an innovative means for tracing the history and extrapolating narratives from the critical objects of study.[105] My integrative approach to methodology brings together narrative criticism, oral history interviews, archival studies, and narrative mapping. Part of my argument is that extracting the spatial narratives of underrepresented voices will provide critical evidence for urban planners, policymakers, and community leaders to reimagine American spaces and what makes a place home.

African American spatial narratives can be found in material sites of meaning, such as monuments, museums, art exhibitions, place-names, and the built environment. They can also be found in the everyday vernacular as residents communicate their connection to a space. In this research, I assess place naming, an open-air history museum, and sites of memory in the built environment. Worthy as histories of place, these narratives can also be used to analyze the dynamics of power, voice, and mobility in neighborhoods affected by various stages of gentrification. As Kent A. Ono and John M. Sloop state, a critique of vernacular symbols makes power relations visible and can move scholarship from challenging to transforming power relationships.[106]

I come from a critical rhetoric studies background. Embracing that training in this work, I will assess these three cases of cultural gentrification in Atlanta with a critical race lens inspired by Morrison and Ellison. The critical race epistemological lens directs my stance that race and racism are fundamental problems in the workings of our world and a part of the "common, everyday experience of most people of color" in the United States of America.[107] Racism is a part of the social structure. Racism, like race, is socially constructed from our relationships, and these relationships are built through the exchange of language, broadly defined as symbols of communication. While traditional and contemporary rhetorical scholarship may turn to Kenneth Burke and his theory of identification to assess how communication symbols produce and are produced by identity, I turn to Ellison as he is more helpful in providing an African American standpoint, which improves Burke's theory of identification for a racialized world. Ellison's position outside the dominant society gives him information that Burke does not have. Ellison watches and experiences both the ills and the possibilities of America, thereby providing a new and more complete interpretation of symbolic action and identification. Using Ellison's work as poetry and theory, as well as inspiration for my own poetic approach, I will articulate how applying rhetorical genres of the blues, songs of freedom, and trap music as psychic and sensual human representations of Atlanta's gentrifying spaces gives us access to lifting the veil.[108]

The method used here is primarily sense making: using all my senses and my emotions to discern how spaces create an identity and how we identify home. Thus, I argue that rhetorical criticism is not an emotionless, desensitized practice, but rather it requires the coming together of deep feeling and critical thinking—the spiritual and the political. Rhetoric, in this way, is rooted in what Audre Lorde defines as the erotic, a resource "firmly rooted in the power of our unexpressed or unrecognized feeling."[109] Following a devised, replicable, and generalizable procedure for criticism can suppress erotic inclinations. It leads to conclusions that overly determine the good and success in terms of capital and profit rather than meeting human needs. Or these procedural types of research define the human condition as devoid of the psychic and the emotional, focusing only on necessities. In contrast, an erotic rhetoric considers how our external environments meet human needs rather than attempting to define humanity around alien structures. Though this work could be replicated and generalized, replicability and generalizability are not the goals. The goal is to personify love to reclaim "our history," our spaces, "our language," and our home.[110] As Lorde reflects, when we become in touch with the internal elements of self, we will become wholly dissatisfied with oppression.

Let's be clear: *Ghosts of Atlanta* doesn't offer brand new ideas that have never been conjured. As Lorde states, "there are no new ideas. There are only new ways of making them felt."[111] So in this text, I take ideas from Ralph Ellison, Toni Morrison, Avery F. Gordon, W. E. B. Du Bois, Frantz Fanon, Audre Lorde, and artists like the various freedom song singers of the civil rights movement, including Bessie Smith, 2 Chainz, and T.I. I create new combinations and applications, relating these ideas to the way we build community and place because I have a "renewed courage to try them out."[112] I attempt to make the possibilities of these writers and artists real. In the end, *Ghosts of Atlanta* reveals, through Atlanta as a representative case, that though gentrification racializes America's geography as a place only for whites, our cityscapes can be used as a canvas for lifting the veil, bringing diverse, marginalized, oppressed, and intentionally erased narratives out of the shadows. Such an act would be a strategic rhetorical reconstruction of America as a "nation of nations," a "culture of cultures," using public space to witness the continuing stories of diverse groups coming together in a singular place.

CHAPTER BREAKDOWN

In this text, I will take you through the hauntings that found me as I roamed the city between 2016 and 2019. *Ghosts of Atlanta* decenters the neoliberal spatial narrative to uncover African Americans' coexisting spatial histories. It critically evaluates how, if, and to what extent cultural gentrification produces more ghosts and through what aesthetic practices those ghosts may be humanized by Black culture. In the following chapters, I use a nonlinear, narrative approach to rhetorical criticism of these historical narratives by charting them against the current spaces they inhabit. Chapter 1 furthers the context by exploring the characteristics of Atlanta as a Black Mecca worth being saved. In chapter 2, I search for the ghosts in Blandtown, one of the first Black enclaves developed after the Civil War. It has now been completely gentrified. With its name left as the headstone reminding us of its Black past, I identify place naming as an act of permitting some and erasing others and the blues genre as the sound of the ghost calling out for "something-to-be-done" about it. In chapter 3, I walk along the completed portions of the Atlanta BeltLine, viewing an outdoor pictorial history exhibit, *Images of America: Atlanta and the Civil Rights Movement*, that can be used to both witness the past and romanticize the ghosts for would-be investors. Here, I call on freedom songs to bring soul to the phantoms. In chapter 4, I center our discussion on the Lee + White development in the West End area, dubbed Malt Disney, as it provides a legible text for unveiling how cultural gentrification is dependent upon and intertwined with the racism of the past and American individualism. I consider the new craft-brewing subculture that has become synonymous with gentrification and the phantoms of the Atlanta 1906 race riots. Yet Atlanta's trap music may harbor the rhetorical ingredients for lifting the veil between the white present and the Black past, bringing skin and bones to the invisible. In chapter 5, I conclude by revealing the broader contributions of this research and looking forward to the continuation of its ambitious goals through its readers.

In this research, I seek to readjust our gaze to view Atlanta not as transit crossings, interstates, highways, railways, or physical land of conquest. I also challenge our disunited binary view of the city as Black or white to instead conceive of the space as "one and yet many." We will look directly at kinships—that is, the areas created through social connectivity of bodies upon bodies and people within space—as well as methods of communication and aesthetic renderings of identification, which comprise the collective identities of some of the disparate neighborhoods of the Black Mecca.

CHAPTER 1

"BACK TO WHERE THEY COME FROM, OF COURSE—ATLANTA"

On October 25, 1912, a crowd gathered at a hillside in Forsyth County (an Atlanta metropolitan county, forty miles from the city center) to witness the public lynching of Black teenagers Ernest Knox and Oscar Daniel. It wasn't supposed to be easy for crowds to form. The judge ordered the execution to occur discretely, concealed behind a wooden fence near the county courthouse in Cumming, Georgia. But a few hours before the events, a mob tore down the fence, making the gallows visible for more than five thousand fathers, mothers, and children to watch the Black boys' lynching. This sea of appeased white faces would be Knox and Daniel's last sight before they took their final breath. The two would be the second and third capital punishments administered to avenge the September 9 assault, rape, and death of Mae Crow, an eighteen-year-old white girl. The first execution was of Rob Edwards, who, just after being arrested, was dragged by vigilantes from his jail cell into the Forsyth County town square to be hanged in front of a mob and thousands of white spectators. Though it is now largely agreed upon that the men were innocent of any crimes against Crow, the events of 1912 marked a turning point for Black people in Forsyth County. Family by family, the 1,098 Black residents who lived and worked in the rural farming area were tormented with dynamite and arson by the northern Georgia mountaineers, threatened by screaming mobs of "rock-throwing whites," and expelled from the county, leaving Forsyth the only known Georgia county "without a Negro in it"[1] until 1990. The expulsion of Black people from the county and the subsequent tales of haunting that predominate popular culture about this place are reminders of the horrific results of white desires to dominate the world and the importance of a Black Mecca to Black collective interests and equitable survival in the United States.

The characterization of Forsyth as having not a single Negro was not an embellishment. Between 1913 and about 1990, white residents worked outside constitutional law to keep Black people from stepping foot on the land, whether as passersby, drivers for white people, servers or cleaners to white homeowners, or tourists. Black people were not allowed. So much so that in 1980, when Black couple Miguel Marcelli and Shirley Webb took a trip from Atlanta city proper to Forsyth County for a work gathering at Lake Sidney Lanier, Marcelli was shot in the head by Bob Davis. Davis had pursued Marcelli with Melvin Crowe, a relative of Mae Crow. They saw themselves as defending "the 'whites only' rule that had been in effect for nearly seventy years."[2] Today, the African American population of Forsyth has increased to approximately 11,500 people (4.4 percent of county residents)[3]—a rise that only occurred after civil rights activist Hosea Williams led Coretta Scott King, John Lewis, Jesse Jackson, and twenty thousand others in a protest to Cumming Courthouse in an event named the Brotherhood March of 1987. They raised national awareness of Forsyth's whites-only dictate. But the county's history of lynching, murder, and expulsion has been perpetually silenced over the decades. As new transplants from around the nation move to the Atlanta metropolitan area, the collective memory of that past is forgotten, keeping it all but erased. Yet there is one thing about Forsyth County that newbies will learn through the grapevine: Lake Sydney Lanier is haunted.

Named for Confederate army veteran and poet Sydney Lanier, Lake Lanier was formed in 1956 when then Atlanta mayor William B. Hartsfield got his wish to construct Buford Dam on the Chattahoochee River's crossing of Hall and Forsyth Counties, forming a 38,000-acre reservoir over the previous agricultural land. The Chattahoochee flows southwest from the north Georgia Appalachian Mountains into Atlanta before it continues between Alabama and Georgia through the Florida Panhandle to empty into the Gulf of Mexico. River development had been necessary for Georgia to control the water levels and provide hydroelectric power and downstream navigation. As Atlanta industrialized after World War II, it attracted Ford and General Motors plants, the Center for Disease Control and Prevention, and Delta Airlines to the city. Because of this, the river's water resources became increasingly important for the ever-growing city.[4] According to Hartsfield, the Buford Dam was crucial for its formation of a new reservoir to supply Atlanta's water—a reservoir that was argued to enhance recreation as well. The dam's creation required the removal of about 528 farms and the local businesses and schools around them.[5] Though there were debates surrounding the "fair compensation" of land and business owners,[6] affected residents of Forsyth and Hall Counties sold off their land to the government and were relocated. When the dam gates closed and the lake began to fill, the water covered areas where Black families had once lived and where some of their burial grounds remain.

The majority of the haunted lake discourse has proliferated from the frequent deaths that have occurred there. More than five hundred people have died at the lake since it was formed. When R&B singer Usher's stepson, Kile Glover, died from injuries in a jet ski accident in 2012, Black people became even more suspicious of the lake's phantoms. The rational worldview would blame much of the deaths on the debris and rubble from the city that lies underneath the waters. But after Patrick Phillips published *Blood at the Root: A Racial Cleansing in America* in 2016, unveiling the silenced story of the 1912 lynching and expulsion of Black residents in the county, many African Americans pondered whether these deaths were tied to the ghosts of Forsyth County's hundred-year-old past.

The first victims of Europeans' savage seizure of Georgia lands were the Cherokee and Muskogee Creek nations, whom the white "pioneers" imprisoned in "removal forts" and then expelled them "like a herd of livestock" from their homeland in the 1830s.[7] As pioneers settled, they brought their enslaved with them. According to Phillips, in Forsyth County, there were 890 enslaved and about two hundred slave-owning families before emancipation.[8] After emancipation, the Freedman's Bureau was set up in the area, formerly enslaved people were empowered to work (though for menial wages) for their old masters, and some purchased their own lands. But during the 1912 white terror against Black residents, these families ran from their homes, leaving behind all they had, including farmland. The terrorists, again finding "empty" pastures, took over these properties without legal recourse. As Phillips attests, "in 1912, the expulsion of Forsyth's Black population had made news all over the country, but the thefts that followed were given a legal stamp of approval by the state, and they went unnoticed by anyone but the expelled Black property owners themselves."[9]

In 2007, journalist Elliot Jaspin surveyed the land transactions available in the basement of Forsyth County Courthouse. There, he found twenty-four African American landowners and seven churches had sold their property, some selling for less than a third of the land value. Yet there is no record of land sales for thirty-four other known Black landowners in the area. It's presumed they just walked away, possibly thinking they'd be able to return when the racial unrest subsided. But between 1912 and 1915, "two-thirds of the black-owned farmland that had not been sold was appropriated" by white people paying taxes on the lands they did not own.[10] Phillips explains that these acts were considered legal under the "common-law principle known as adverse possession," or squatters rights.[11] If the original owner didn't take steps to regain possession of the property within seven years, the land would be considered abandoned. Even though the common-law principle required, among other things, that the new claim to the land must not be fraudulent and must be peaceable, the court turned a blind eye and allowed the grounds to be appropriated. The displaced Black residents moved to other cities in Georgia or migrated to the North during the Great Migration. There is "no record of a single warrant or arrest for any of the crimes committed against the property and people of black Forsyth in 1912."[12] After Lake Lanier came to fruition, the same lots that once housed the farms of Black landowners became home to a "600-mile lakeshore lined with multi-million-dollar homes and boat docks."[13] In 1972, Lake Lanier evolved into a full-service public resort, including beaches, hotels, and camping sites along the shore. In 1987, when Williams's coalition called for reparations to be made to the known descendants of these Black landowners, then governor Joe Frank Harris never acted.

The white residents of Forsyth closed their doors to any racial mixing. They were pressing the city dwellers in Atlanta to keep their Black people with them. Just forty miles away, Atlanta steeped in Jim Crow laws, segregation, and racism was being considered "the polar opposite of Forsyth."[14] For Black folks, it was really just a choice between the lesser of two evils: one area guaranteeing immediate death and the other holding the possibility of a slow malaise. The base distinction was that, unlike Forsyth, in Atlanta in the 1920s, Black people, white Americans, Jews, and immigrants from Russia, China, Turkey, and Italy could be found living in proximity to each other, under a system of class-based zoning ordinances.[15] However, Forsyth threatened immediate death for Black Atlantans crossing their border. When Charles Blackburn, a white man and the originator of the Brotherhood March of 1987, started making plans to protest Forsyth's racial isolation, he received harassing calls and threats.

> The mildest was a caller who said, "I just don't think it's a good idea for you to try to get the n-----s to come up here. . . . That's why we live in Forsyth County—to get away from them" . . . and added an overt threat: "You can't change it, no matter how bad or how hard you try," she said. "You're going to have to end up leaving this county. Or leave in a box."[16]

Due to these threats, Blackburn dropped the plans, so Williams and Blackburn's friend Dean Carter took the lead. Forsyth residents did not want anything resembling the racial mixture found in Atlanta. Phillips, a white man, recalls a Forsyth man spitting at his father during Williams's protest, saying, "Go back to Atlanta with the rest of them. Back to N-----town, you white n-----s!"[17]

Since the publishing of Phillips's book, the feeling of a haunt that Black people have often attested to now has historical reasoning behind it. It has become popularized in eerie depictions in television shows like Donald Glover's *Atlanta* (season 3) and vehemently debated on Black Twitter. The phantoms of Lake Lanier are what is left after a culture and its people are driven out. Let's be clear: what happened in Forsyth between 1912 and 1990 was not gentrification but rather forced expulsion. This deliberate terrorist act was meant to exclude Black people from American lands and dispossess them of all ownership and citizenship. The result was that for nearly seventy years, Forsyth County remained an actual homogenously white space. And even today, while Forsyth has a slightly more racially diverse population, through the forgetting of history, it has maintained a mythic narrative of homogenously white identity. The veil still exists for the 11,500 African Americans (4.4 percent of the population), 25,200 Latinx (9.7 percent), and 40,300 Asians (15.5 percent) who live close to Lake Lanier.[18] No, this wasn't gentrification, but gentrification (slowly and steadily) offers the same results (as we'll see in chapter 2) of white domination over space.

But Atlanta! Eddie Murphy says Atlanta is where we go when we've been displaced everywhere else, and indeed, those exiled from Forsyth found a thin semblance of safety and belonging in Atlanta. Atlanta, according to that old *Ebony Magazine* profile, can teach the nation how to live. Atlanta, according to Black Panther enthusiasts, is our Wakanda. Yet with all that we know of this nation and the region's fraught and complex relationship with African Americans, I find the Black collective these days asking, Who is this city really for? And what and who will it be for if gentrification gets the final say?

This chapter takes the nation and the city's history of displacing Native Americans and Black folk into account while explaining the characteristics of the city that led it to be known as the capital city of Black America. Here, I first explore how we conceive of America as a binary nation space to illustrate how European settlers made meaning of themselves in relation to the people they enslaved and subordinated. Then, I turn to the city of Atlanta as the hope of redemption for the Confederate South and the descendants of the enslaved while examining the intersections of racism and neoliberalism within the context of Black and white migration patterns between the city center and the suburban ring of metro Atlanta. Finally, I connect these events to the more extensive discussion of cultural gentrification and hauntings and their complexities to make way for witnessing some of the ghosts in Atlanta's gentrifying areas in the coming chapters.

AMERICA'S HAUNTING

Like any nation space, the American nation space describes the self-identity produced by the people forming the nation under a shared common language or historical experience. The evolution of America as a nation is one of the most important and world-changing formations of the modern era. Initially, European immigrants seeking refuge from poverty and monarchy fled to the "New World" in the fifteenth and sixteenth centuries, imagining the possibility of an idealized utopia that could distinguish itself by being different from Europe. This was the start of the binary attitude, or what historian David W. Noble calls the "two worlds" conception of space; the New World—the place and its white settlers—was positioned as "an island of virtue in a global sea of corruption."[19] Morrison also suggests that "young America" had a binary impression of its universe, differentiating itself by "pressing toward a future of freedom, a kind of human dignity believed unprecedented in the world."[20] This is evident in the Declaration of Independence, in which Thomas Jefferson declares that the king of Britain had established a system of "absolute Tyranny" over the colonies. Therefore, the people had the right to sever ties with the Crown. Our founding fathers were transitioning from a place of inequality and constraint to one of equality and freedom based on the most enduring principle of our time—"that all men are created equal, that their Creator endows them with certain unalienable Rights, that among these are Life, Liberty and the pursuit of Happiness." But amid reidentifying themselves in a space they deemed the New World, they replaced their former oppression with the oppression of others, committing genocide and making other humans their property in order to feel the great promise of freedom for themselves. No one is a more appropriate example of this than Jefferson himself, who, while writing the declaration, also had an established property of land and people at Monticello in Virginia. During his lifetime, he enslaved more than six hundred people. It is difficult to reconcile the dissonance between the words of the founders and some of their actions. Morrison argues that the love of power took over the young Americans: "Power—control of one's own destiny—would replace the powerlessness felt before the gates of class, caste, and cunning persecution. One could move from discipline and punishment to disciplining and punishing; from social ostracism to social rank. One could be released from a useless, binding, repulsive past into a kind of history-lessness, a blank page waiting to be inscribed."[21] Accordingly, the fear of loss of property and power and the desire for land provoked the young Americans to oppress others. These historical experiences and pivotal choices contributed to the formation of America as a nation space. It distinguishes the early and continued expression of white American identity. From the outset, the United States of America we know today was developed for white supremacy, an American identity of unrelenting power amassed from the "wholly available and serviceable lives of Africanist others."[22] As Morrison proports in *Playing in the Dark*, "American" has historically been defined by whiteness, and this whiteness is dependent upon othering Blackness with inferiority. Whiteness is empowered by making Blackness its unequal and opposite. Though the "two-worlds" conception of young America was based on differentiating the nation of freedom and possibility from an outside world characterized as immoral and oppressive, the fledgling nation created an internal binary that separated Black people from white people. As George Lipsitz writes, "people from communities of color could not access the metaphor of two worlds because it required their subordination, humiliation, exclusion, sometimes even their annihilation."[23] This placed a veil between Black lifeworlds and white lifeworlds, and it forged Black lifeworlds as a shadow supporting white lives.

These conditions reflect an internal contradiction in America, which decrees "all men are created equal" and wanders internationally to save the rest of the world from crimes against humanity while continuing to support a racial caste system within its own borders. As a result of this internal contradiction, our spaces are troubled and haunted by Black lifeworlds, which live in the consequences of this hypocrisy. As Frederick Douglass powerfully stated in 1852,

> What to the American slave is your Fourth of July? I answer, a day that reveals to him more than all other days of the year, the gross injustice and cruelty to which he is the constant victim. To him, your celebration is a sham; your boasted liberty, an unholy license; your national greatness, swelling vanity; your sounds of rejoicing are empty and heartless; your denunciation of tyrants, brass fronted impudence; your shouts of liberty and equality, hollow mockery; your prayers and hymns, your sermons and thanksgivings, with all your religious parade and solemnity, are to him mere bombast, fraud, deception, impiety and hypocrisy—a thin veil to cover up crimes which would disgrace a nation of savages.[24]

The Ladies Anti-Slavery Society of Rochester had invited Douglass to give an Independence Day oration. They may not have expected him to blast the nation with reproach in his fiery speech. His words summarily define why African Americans are the ghosts haunting America. In the Black body, when made fully visible, white America sees its hypocrisy.

This is more fully established in another oration. In Ralph Ellison's commencement speech at the College of William and Mary in 1972, he symbolized himself as the representative ghost. He said he was present to evoke a certain feeling of fear brought on by the interconnections of his identity as a writer, an American, and a Black man and the college's linkage to the founding of the United States of America. He started by referencing the African tradition of wearing ritual masks at initiation ceremonies. The African ritual mask, with its "frightening features," reminded the initiates that "the spirits, the ghosts of the honored dead, are present on the scene. And in the presence of such terrifying images, as are symbolized by the mask, the initiate is tested as to his ability to endure pain and his suitability for fulfilling the new role which he is about to assume."[25] Ellison likened the commencement ceremony to the African initiation. The commencement admits newly minted graduates to the world beyond their homes. But in this particular commencement initiation, Ellison didn't need to wear a mask because he served the mask's function. Ellison identified himself as having the role of "inflicting pain" and fear for the new graduates. He was the ghost. Due to the college's associations with the American ideal and its glaring contradictions, it was a prime location for a haunting from the ghost before them. William and Mary was chartered by the king and queen of England in 1693, becoming the nation's second college. Presidents Thomas Jefferson and James Monroe studied there. And George Washington was its chancellor after his presidency. Accordingly, Ellison saw the connection of William and Mary to the founding ideals of democracy and freedom, universal education, and uniform language. He argued that the university contributed to assimilating various accents, different spellings of English words, and the diverse cultures of African slaves into a uniform or common tongue to unify the new nation. He continued, saying that while building America, the founders created a rift, a contradiction in who could be free and how it would be applied. And even while attempting to use a single language to form an empire for whiteness, they had a "war of words" over the "distribution of authority and power," which erupted into the Civil War. And the Civil War, Ellison argued, "cast a shadow upon the lives of millions yet unborn." Through the Civil War, the "future was formed." Mistakenly, after the war, the nation developed a "technique of avoidance" as it moved into the industrial age. And this technique was a means for them to evade their ghosts. Thus, "Americans are known as people without memory." But the spirits "accuse the nation and insist upon a rectification."[26] In this case, Ellison being invited to speak at William and Mary was another thin veil to cover up America's hypocrisy.

Like Ellison and Douglass, the ghosts inform the audience that "the over and done with 'extremity' of a domestic and international slavery has not entirely gone away, even if it seems to have passed into the register of history and symbol."[27] And these ghosts, who are also haunted by that traumatic past, require a "something-to-be-done." The question that lingers is, "What is to be done?"[28] After assessing the ghost in Morrison's novel *Beloved*, Gordon argues that the ghosts "will have to be evicted" and "the trauma of the Middle Passage" must be confronted.[29] By "Middle Passage," she is referring to the transition of African humans to dehumanized property on the journey between the coast of Africa and the New World. However, America has yet to reckon with the Middle Passage and its aftermath. Instead, the nation avoids the ghosts by maintaining the veil.

This book exists because the United States has not reckoned with the ghosts born from its internal contradictions. Instead, the "many white US Americans looked outward, seeking in the global marketplace the perfect harmony and happiness they had failed to produce in the national landscape."[30] And domestically, the nation keeps itself busy, attempting to use the land to form and reform an imagined utopian space. It initially occurred with the move westward to reimagine the frontier. But it continued in urban areas, with the development of white enclaves, neighborhood sanctuaries, and exclusionary spaces, like Forsyth County. Contemporary times show that renovation and renewal efforts across America's central cities is just a continuation of the pursuit of the utopia.

Atlanta is a bit of a crucible for this active pursuit of creating an idealized space, and it started just after the Civil War. In *The Souls of Black Folk*, W. E. B. Du Bois argues that the Civil War left white southerners to "live haunted by the ghost of an untrue dream."[31] For the daughters and sons of the Confederacy, the dream was an empire where cotton was king and Black people were subdued under the language of white authority. Ultimately, the cotton empire could not exist without the brutal abuse of Black bodies to furnish the labor for the capital system. The dissolution of slavery revealed the abusive system of contradictions between modern capitalism and democracy. But rather than settle the haunting honestly or sit in mourning, Atlanta, of all the southern states, removed itself from "sulking, brooding, and listless waiting" and, as Du Bois puts it, "turned toward the future; and that future held aloft vistas of purple and gold:—Atlanta, Queen of the cotton kingdom; Atlanta, Gateway to the Land of the Sun; Atlanta, the new Lachesis, spinner of web and woof of the world."[32] After the Civil War, Atlanta set forth, during Reconstruction and post-Reconstruction, to rebuild and transform its economy from agricultural to industrial, with Black men and women still serving racism's handiwork in the convict-leasing systems, chain gangs, or for small pay. Over the twentieth century, the city rebuilt itself, led by the business elite. The process of building and rebuilding had become so repetitive that by the mid-twentieth century, Atlanta's Chamber of Commerce branded Atlanta the "city too busy to hate." And with its continuous tearing down, upending, and reconstructing in order to get to some form of idealized urban utopia, many of Atlanta's earliest buildings lost the fight for preservation. They were torn down or left in disrepair as Atlantans moved on to something new. Thus, Atlanta also became a city without memory.

In Du Bois's description of Atlanta, which he wrote in the halls of Atlanta University (today's Clark Atlanta University) in the first decade of the 1900s, he calls Atlanta the "new Lachesis," associating the city with the Greek daughter of Zeus and Themis. She was responsible for deciding the length of each living being's life and determining each person's destiny. Atlanta's haunting drove the city to "do something." If Du Bois's metaphor is correct, what has been done, is being done, and will be done will together determine Black and white destinies. In this chapter, I consider more explicitly what makes Atlanta a Black Mecca and a Black cultural bastion worthy of protection.

ATLANTA, THE BLACK MECCA

I want to add to the previous discussion of an American haunting a more nuanced connection to the city of Atlanta as a haunted space and the role of cultural gentrification as a contemporary iteration of Americans avoiding their ghosts. This is my concern and focus: What would happen to our ghosts if we reckoned with them? How might that change our already unsettled boundaries and restructure our binaries? Instead of considering spaces for Black people or white people, what if America's geography represented it as a culture of cultures? What does that take? Focusing on the anti-Black racial matters that compose America's identity, *Ghosts of Atlanta* takes up these ambitious questions, utilizing the city of Atlanta, or what it could be, as a space that represents the identity of America as "one, and yet many." "Atlanta might well turn out to be the town that taught a nation how to live."[33]

For the geography to be used to reckon with the ghosts, our landscapes must include that which has originally been excluded. Metaphorical origins like the Black Mecca are significantly crucial to African American collective identity as they (1) harbor the remembrance of collective trauma, which is necessary for African American collective identity; (2) provide an origination story for an African American homeland post–Civil War, which is a necessary anchor for dispersed people; and (3) provoke "something-to-be-done," motivating the group toward a world of possibilities, or a utopian vision of the future. In this section, I intend to review the original discourse that led to Atlanta's label as the Black Mecca and elements of its history that support this connection. This is not intended to be a review of Atlanta's history. Instead, throughout the book, in a nonlinear fashion, I bring to the fore ways Atlanta's Black spaces have been created and threatened over time. The history of Atlanta and the narratives that support it as a Black Mecca work dually in self-defense of Black life and for the moral repair of America's identity. While cultural diversity is hard to chew for many people, Atlanta could have the symbolic ingredients to mediate America's greatest conflict—race.

Collective identities are socially constructed and formed through collective remembrance that people across a nation or across the world have, even if they don't know one another.[34] Identity is constituted through communication with a group whose unity and uniqueness are based on a "common image of their past."[35] The collective identity of African Americans is based on the peculiar institution of modern slavery. While the articulation of a separate African American identity didn't occur until post–Civil War, the makings of the identity were formed by the unique experience of American slavery and the trauma of that experience. Slavery had the effect of alienating Africans from their homeland and African consciousness. Turning humans into commodities dehumanized African Americans, causing them to lose their subjecthood. Through the memory of this trauma, a person defines herself as African American. According to Ron Eyerman, African American identity requires continuous remembrance of the trauma to sustain itself. Sustained remembrance links the past to the present and reproduces collective identity for future generations. A remembrance process is an act that mediates the trauma to identity caused by modern slavery. African Americans renarrate and reinterpret the past to address the tear and build continuity with their future existence.[36]

Because of its location in the southern United States, Atlanta harbors the spatial narrative of the trauma and is also within a region where its remembrance is continuously reenacted and rearticulated for the purposes of mediation. Public articulation of Atlanta as the Black Mecca began with the August 1971 edition of *Ebony Magazine*, which was dedicated to the South. In his publisher's statement, John H. Johnson recollects the South drawing upon its long history, starting with New England settlers' hopes for the southern colonies, the exceptional ability of African labor, and slavery in the South on to the Civil War and Black northern migration in the early twentieth century. Johnson argues that though African Americans moved north before and after the Civil War, fleeing slavery and the "semi-slavery of the post–Civil War years," during the civil rights movement, Black people drew their eyes back toward the South as their "point of entry" to America.[37] While Black people migrated north, they didn't lose recognition of their collective consciousness and identification with the South. The South became a necessary anchor and origin for African Americans as they dispersed across the nation and internationally.

According to Maurice Halbwachs, groups do not have to be connected by proximity to have a collective identity; they just need a shared spatial image.[38] By remembering their old home, groups stay united even after they have been dispersed from their physical location. Spatial images and, I would argue, spatial narratives are essential to collective identity as they are necessary for remembering home. The past is preserved in the physical surroundings. As Black communities disperse, either by choice or displacement, the creation of imagined places to ensure the continuation of the collective identity becomes a necessity. According to Akhil Gupta and James Ferguson, "Remembered places have often served as symbolic anchors of community for dispersed people."[39] Remembered places are the "homeland" necessary for unifying people who are displaced to different locations. Because of the erosion of traditional territories, spaces are imagined "but not imaginary."[40] The Black Mecca is an imagined homeland, "a symbolic anchor" of community for dispersed African Americans. A metaphorical space is an imagined space within a nonimaginary physical space. While groups do not need to be in the same physical area to have a collective identity, a social group does need to develop unity and strength to lead a particular region.[41] An already-fortified collective identity improved the probability of Atlanta becoming an African American cultural stronghold, even though African Americans didn't have economic dominance.

Further, as a bedrock of postbellum African American intellectual thought and identity creation, Atlanta provides an essential origination story for an African American homeland. In Atlanta, Du Bois wrote *The Souls of Black Folk*, articulating the double consciousness of the African American identity. He theorized the "New Negro," an African American part of the "talented tenth." While Du Bois was a progenitor of the civil rights movement, Martin Luther King Jr., born and raised in Atlanta, Georgia, has the legacy as the prophetic leader of the movement. In the 1960s, as more laws were passed providing greater protections for Black people in the South, those second generations in the North looked "backward to the land of their birth," wondering "what the South is really like today." In describing the South as the "point of entry" and the "land of their birth," Johnson, founding editor of *Ebony Magazine*, along with other Black people, identified the South as the "origin" for African Americans.[42] He was not alone. Julian Bond, Georgia state representative, called northern Black folks back to the state, saying, "Black people, come home. We need you. . . . Your roots, like ours, are here." Bond declared a new Black South, saying, "black soil here—actually and spiritually—is rich."[43] And then, vice mayor of Atlanta Maynard Jackson proclaimed, "there is a growing movement toward Atlanta as the 'Mecca' of Black America."[44] The promotions must have worked; from 1995 to 2000, the Great Migration north seemed to have reversed, with Atlanta being the "top destination for Black migrants."[45]

But the city deemed as a Black "origin" was fraught with trauma. In the same edition of *Ebony Magazine*, staff writer Lerone Bennett Jr. wrote about the South that "it is here that we first served our apprenticeship to horror."[46] The southern coast carries the pain as the place where Black people met the completion of their transition from human to property, the alienation of their identity, and the separation from their actual origins in Africa. However, the South serves a second purpose as the origin of a new people—African Americans. The struggle with Atlanta, Garland concedes in her article, was that the city tried to make it seem as though that struggle—the African American struggle—was over.[47] People like Maynard Jackson perpetuated that appearance, saying, "I consider Georgia most advanced in race relations. That is primarily, though clearly not exclusively, attributable to the presence of Atlanta in the state of Georgia. Atlanta is the best city for black people in America."[48] This utopian vision of racial existence is also a necessity for Black collective identity. Atlanta's Black leaders created what Benedict Anderson calls an "imagined community." According to Black studies scholar Clyde Woods, imagined communities command "emotional legitimacy" and are "bound by deep horizontal networks of kinship, fraternity, sorority, and obligation."[49] These bonds are forged by their relation to some heritage that connects to the people's past, present, and future.

Metaphorical origins provide a continuation of the collective identity's historical trajectory. African American existence is disempowered when subjected to living only in the past. The continuous repetition of displacement from locations identified as places of "origin" causes new tears in the social fabric that must continuously be mediated. The level of connection a collective identity has to a particular space is often recognizable by the amount of resistance the people have when it is encroached upon.[50] Encroachment by gentrification-led displacement continues when there is a proliferation of dystopic-future narratives because information about the future determines capital valuation and investment. Dystopic futures about a place demoralize the people, making space safe for corporations and industries to stake a claim.[51] Afrofuturist theorist Kodwo Eshun argues that counterfutures that predict a utopia focus the oppressed group's attention on its potentialities by mediating the traumatic tear and responding to the structural and psychological alienation of Black identities.

Atlanta was particularly appropriate as a space for this utopian future because of the increased political and economic power of middle-class Black people in the city. In 1971, Atlanta University—now Clark Atlanta University—had the only Black graduate business school.[52] As a sign of the economic prosperity of African Americans, the richest Black American, Norris B. Herndon, resided in Atlanta. He had amassed a nearly $18 million private fortune and was president of Atlanta Life Insurance Company.[53] Atlanta was also the home of one of the largest Black banking institutions, Citizens Trust Company of Atlanta, which owned a twelve-story office building downtown.[54] Atlanta had several Black people moving up in political positions. Three years after the *Ebony Magazine* publication, Maynard Jackson was elected mayor. Beyond the economic and political growth of Black people, what made Atlanta an apt space for the Black Mecca metaphor was the seeming way middle-class Black people had created harmonious relations with white people. While most major cities with large Black populations had race riots in 1968 after King's death, Atlanta did not. Black restaurants, like Paschal's, were determined to never turn away whites during segregation, which helped it grow. And before Jackson's mayoral run, he served as vice mayor on the staff of Jewish mayor Sam Massell. Sam Massell had also hired Black attorney Emma I. Darnell for his team.[55] While imperfect, the city was promoted to the Black Mecca, given its close appearance to a future Black utopia.

While this branding strategy was successful in deeming Atlanta as the Black Mecca, if we go beneath the surface, look around in the breaks, and follow the ghosts, we will find that Atlanta's ethos—characterized by practices of renewing urban areas that utilize neoliberal ideology and racist logics to homogenize the narrative of the city—poses a threat to this identity. Historical research on the spatial landscape and segregation in Atlanta reveals racism and neoliberalism at play in the city's construction, leaving ghosts throughout the geography and thus a "something-to-be-done." The story of Atlanta's haunting starts before the Civil War and even before European claims to the New World. Under the bonds of kinship, the confederation of tribes that came to be known as the Muskogee Creek and Chickasaw native tribes settled the land where today's Kennesaw Mountain and Stone Mountain take root. The tribes located themselves in a collective identity. To be a member of the tribe was to share a common way of life, communication symbols, and networks.[56] Social commonality, rather than territorial boundaries, determined tribal space. But in the sixteenth century, the English colonies forcefully removed the tribes from the region and enforced territorial lines. Native tribes were expelled.

By the nineteenth century, just before modern industrialization, a Western community emerged at the terminus point where the United States Western

Railroad and Atlantic Railroad crossed, marking the central area that became Atlanta. The colonizers equated their "sense of place" to the fixed coordinates of the rail connection. Terminus, as the city was named back then, was the "end of the line"—a depot station. It was a locale for people *on* the move. Construction continued on the railroad, extending it from the Zero Milepost into southeastern and internal Georgia. With this growth, the depot station evolved from being a place of transit and movement to becoming a destination for some and an origin for others. After the remaining Native Americans were expelled from the state of Georgia in the nineteenth century, the city—governed by railroad men—continued to grow.

By 1850, it had metastasized to a population of 2,058 white people and 511 Black people, with 493 of them enslaved.[57] Many of Atlanta's historically Black neighborhoods originated from two major events: the post–Civil War Reconstruction period, during which African Americans were constrained to designated areas for Black living quarters, and the era between and after the World Wars, when out-migration of white Atlantans to the north of the city isolated African Americans in the southern portions of the municipality. During the Civil War, Atlanta (as it was renamed in 1847) became an important manufacturing, distribution, and transportation hub for the Confederate army. On September 2, 1864, the city lost the final battle with Union forces. The railroad depots, homes, and businesses were demolished when Union army general William Tecumseh Sherman had buildings and homes burned down.[58] There was a need to rebuild, and newly freed Black folks flocked to Atlanta, where Union troops offered protection from whites. They took up homes in areas along the railroad tracks that were unwanted by whites. These areas, known as "the bottoms," had horrible conditions as they subsumed the environmental hazards of buildings and industries of the Reconstruction era. Further, African Americans were often policed and convicted for petty crimes and placed in the convict-leasing system, where they would find themselves toiling in deplorable conditions to help literally build the budding city brick by brick and rail by rail.[59] Still, freed Black people set stakes and built up their communities around the railroads and the newly founded Black educational hubs, Atlanta University (founded 1865) and Morehouse College (opened in Atlanta in 1867). Railroad jobs in working-class neighborhoods, like Pittsburgh, Mechanicsville, Blandtown, Oakland City, and Edgewood, and domestic jobs in otherwise white areas, like Johnsontown, gave African Americans the income to become property owners. By 1920, the Black population grew to 67,796 and the white population grew to 137,785.[60] While whites and Black people in the area were largely poor and uneducated, the Black communities continued to grow and form a communal identity.

White supremacy was the hegemonic order arising with the overturn of Radical Reconstruction.[61] Racist ideology and the New South's advocacy of industrial development heightened the oppressive spatial environment for newly freed Black people in Atlanta. Jim Crow laws and vigilante white terrorism of the early twentieth century decreased Black mobility by constraining them to designated neighborhoods.[62] Redlining—the practice of refusing home loans to specific racial groups—throughout the nation kept African Americans out of homeownership and maintained segregation. White Americans gained new prosperity and economic relief after the Great Depression through President Franklin D. Roosevelt's New Deal policies, including the establishment of the Federal Housing Authority, which made homeownership affordable to the majority of white America. White flight in the 1950s and 1960s—due to the development of suburbs and interstate highways, as well as the GI Bill and subsidized home loans—contributed to the suburban sprawl that created the Atlanta metropolitan region. The fear of Black people being their neighbors led whites to flee urban areas for suburban rings, helping preserve a segregated status quo.[63]

Although isolated to the urban core and southwestern portions of the city, African Americans continued to mark Atlanta's spaces as their own. The creation of the Atlanta University Center (AUC) in 1929 forged a consortium among the former Atlanta University, Spelman College, Morehouse College, and, later, Clark College (joined in 1957), Morris Brown College (joined in 1957), Interdenominational Theological Center (joined in 1959), and Morehouse School of Medicine (joined in 1983).[64] Located on the west side, these institutions contributed to the education of African Americans across the nation and the growth of a professional class of Black people in neighborhoods like West End and Westview. On the east side of town, Black life grew in areas like Old Fourth Ward and the prominent business district on Sweet Auburn Avenue, which a 1956 *Fortune* magazine article called "the richest Negro-street in the world."[65] Auburn Avenue is the home of Atlanta Life Insurance Company, founded by a formerly enslaved person and one of the first Black millionaires, Alonzo Herndon, and many churches, including Ebenezer Baptist Church, where Martin Luther King Sr. and Martin Luther King Jr. were copastors. While "Sweet Auburn's" economic and social strength for the Black community diminished in the mid-twentieth century due, in large part, to the construction of I-20, which divided the area, it as well as the many Black enclaves growing in the 1900s attributed to the wide consideration of Atlanta as a Black Mecca. African Americans also gained political power after the civil rights movement and the Voting Rights Acts of 1964 and 1965. Though Atlanta elected two Black mayors in the twentieth century, Maynard Jackson (1974–1982; 1990–1994) and Andrew Young (1982–1990), both demonstrated neoliberal common sense in their economic practices. Specifically, according to Maurice J. Hobson, Young used a neoliberal style of government that contributed to the standard neoliberal model of urban development and gentrification in Atlanta.[66]

For example, consider the story of Atlanta's public housing. In 1936, Atlanta became the first city in the country to build a public-housing project for whites only, known as Techwood Homes. And in 2011, Atlanta became the first city to demolish all its public housing. To build Techwood Homes, the federal government's Public Works Administration, established under the New Deal, cleared a low-income neighborhood of 1,600 Black and white families. More than five hundred Black families were evicted from the area known as the Flats to establish the white-only, 604-unit project. Many Black families had to combine with each other to afford rents elsewhere, which caused high density in Black neighborhoods, turning them into slums.[67] In 1938, an African American project named University Homes opened near Atlanta University Center. But many of the African Americans displaced from the Flats "were never rehoused."[68] Because of income qualifications, some were even too poor to be eligible for public housing. Techwood Homes was integrated in 1968, and white people quickly moved out. Just six years later, the housing project was 50 percent Black. Coca-Cola Company executives with headquarters nearby wanted to demolish the complex in the 1970s because of the rise in Black residents.[69] Further, while the homes were in need of repair, local, state, and federal funding decreased when the resident population shifted to majority Black. Still, tenants organized to advocate and retain funding for public-housing improvements.[70] During his tenure, Mayor Jackson used federal funds to improve the building. Then, in the 1980s, the drug epidemic came to Atlanta in full force and significantly harmed public-housing communities.[71]

Many national and local debates contributed to the demise of public housing nationwide, but one event made Atlanta the first to let them go—the 1996 Olympic Games. In the 1980s, Mayor Young made a deliberate bid for Atlanta as the site of the Olympic Games as part of his move to improve the city's economy by focusing on the needs of international investors and businesses. In 1990, Mayor Jackson, elected to his third nonconsecutive term as mayor, received the exciting news that the International Olympic Committee had selected Atlanta to host the games.[72] In the rousing excitement, Atlanta would have much work to do to prepare the city in less than six years. The designated location for the Olympic Village was already occupied by two public-housing projects—Techwood and Clark Howell Homes, high-poverty and drug-affected areas. Considering the poor as a blight on

Olympic plans, within the year leading up to the games, the city arrested nine thousand homeless people, choosing "criminalization, demonization, and disenfranchisement of the city's black poor and homeless" to support economic progress.[73] Backing rose to demolish the two projects and make way for the Olympic Village and housing Olympians. The plan supported by Mayor Jackson was to replace the projects with mixed-income units to deconcentrate poverty in the central city. However, the white business elite overpowered those plans. After the Olympics, the University of Georgia, which funded Olympic housing, took over the redevelopments for Georgia Tech University and Georgia State University student housing.[74] Combined with federal HOPE VI funding,[75] Atlanta continued flattening the public-housing projects throughout the city until there were no more. There was no one-to-one replacement of units, so of the approximately fifty thousand public-housing residents that were relocated, only about 17 percent were placed in mixed-income redevelopments, and the vast majority were given voucher subsidies to find units in the private market.[76] In this way, the public mechanism of housing residents was outsourced to the private market, further representing the neoliberal ideology of the city and the nation.

Since that time, Atlanta's Black spaces have been compressed due to the migration patterns of white people. Contemporary gentrification of urban areas is primarily spurred by the reverse of white flight, the in-migration of whites to central cities. Migration patterns have shifted since the era of white flight in the 1950s, '60s, and '70s. Now, white and nonwhite migrants are favoring noncoastal areas, like Atlanta, Phoenix, and Las Vegas, due to lower living costs, new amenities, and growing industries. For Atlanta's central core, this in-migration is essentially of young transplants cashing in on devalued homes in historically Black neighborhoods. From 1990 to 2010, Atlanta had the second-largest growth in white migrants.[77] Within the city, the Black population has remained almost constant over the last thirty years, hovering between 185,000 non-Hispanic, Black adults. From 2000 to 2010, the Black population decreased by about eleven thousand, rebounding back to 185,000 by 2020. Meanwhile, the non-Hispanic white adult population's rate of increase has doubled since 2000. From 1990 to 2000, the white population increased by less than one thousand people per year. From 2000 to 2010, the rate of increase was about 1,800 people per year. From 2010 to 2020, the adult white population had a net increase of approximately 32,000 individuals, a rate of about 3,200 per year.[78] While white flight in the 1950s and '60s was blamed for creating segregated cities, today, reverse white flight is considerably responsible for the gentrification of Black spaces in the urban core. Younger Americans are flocking to inner-city communities, bringing investors with them. These Black neighborhoods were historically devalued due to the race of the occupants, also termed the "segregation tax" or "drag," which occurs when race is a factor in housing choices.[79] While these "hood" homes had deflated values when Black people lived in them, they became excellent investment properties for white migrants looking to cash in on new developments in the city. As low-income communities become more desirable, low-income families are displaced. Gentrification in Atlanta, sped up by the Atlanta BeltLine project, can also lead to the compression of Black culture in the city as the dominant population transforms neighborhoods that contribute to Atlanta's identity as the capital city of Black America.

So is Atlanta a Black Mecca? Thus far, I've presented the highs and lows of the city, contributing to the complex nature of naming any place a Mecca. Compared to exclusionary white spaces like Forsyth County, Atlanta is a treasure for Black lives. Though, for many who live here, including me, we know that underneath the excitement is an aggressive buzz of retaliation from white angst that gets louder and louder daily. Take, for instance, the New York transplant Bill White, who—after Georgia greatly influenced the 2020 election loss of former president Donald Trump and Republican senators David Perdue and Kelly Loeffler— reinvigorated a push to separate Buckhead, a wealthy white neighborhood in Atlanta, from the city. The Buckhead City movement, as the political drive was named, used rhetoric of rising crime rates to convince residents that Buckhead needed to separate itself from Atlanta. Yet the move has largely been a form of white rage,[80] a retaliation against the political progress of Black residents. It's a way for white residents to run away from their Black neighbors, if not physically, at least rhetorically and for public perception. If Buckhead City were to form, it would become another symbol of homogenously white identity, deeming who is included and excluded from a space.

Reverse white flight, the Buckhead City movement, and the haunts of Lake Lanier comprise another layer in the complexities of cultural gentrification—a term that collects the intrinsic connections between the landscape's physical and migratory changes, methods of making meaning out of space, and the practices of ghosts. Cultural gentrification entwines these systems. Reading space with the process of cultural gentrification in mind requires us to find the ghosts, make sense of cultural symbols, and register shifting spatial dynamics. Criticizing cultural gentrification allows us to theorize the relationship between physical spaces and the diverse historical narratives they embody. I insist that these narratives must be recovered for a moral reckoning to occur. The events chronicled in this chapter are a part of the reason for the question of who this city is really for. These incidents reflect the violent, political, physical, economic, and symbolic terrorizing actions that are all mastered to subordinate African Americans and restrict their experience of full citizenship in these united states. At the same time, the white race is uplifted at the expense of those who are othered. When we run from our ghosts, we inhibit a moral reckoning and romanticize the space.

A brief example that harkens back to Forsyth County and the haunts at Lake Lanier reviewed in the opening of this chapter demonstrates my point. This example comes from the FX series *Atlanta* created by and starring Donald Glover. In the season 3 opener, titled "Three Slaps," the main characters from the show are not featured. Instead, beginning with what Glover calls a "black fairytale,"[81] the episode details the popularized version of Lake Lanier's haunt and a fictional reenactment of the Hart family murder-suicide that occurred in Mendocino County, California, in 2018. In the tragic murder, white couple Jennifer Hart and Sarah Hart drove their vehicle off a cliff, killing themselves and their six adopted Black children. Devonte, a six-year-old adopted child of the pair, gained national attention before his murder due to a famous photo of him hugging a police officer during a Black Lives Matter protest in Portland. The plot-twist portrayal of the Hart murders and opening dialogue about the haunt at Lake Lanier are included in the season premiere to illustrate the moral blindness caused by whiteness's relationship to Blackness in America.

The first scene starts with White, a white man, and Black, a Black man, fishing in a boat. The story they proceed to discuss follows the popularized conception of Lake Lanier and Forsyth County. Black starts by saying he wants to get out of the water, attesting, "this place always gave me the heebie-jeebies." He recalls that he almost drowned in the water. Then, White proceeds to explain why Black almost drowned. Though the narrative White tells doesn't exactly keep with the historical timeline, White divulges that the lake is haunted because of the Black town underneath. "State government built a dam and flooded the place," he says. "People who didn't leave drowned. Town was Black too. Self-governed Black town." He continues, saying the Black people chose not to leave because they thought they were safe and "almost white." He argues that "almost" being white is possible because white is a social construct. "With enough blood and money, anyone can be white," he says.

> Thing about being white is, it blinds you. It's easy to see the Black man is cursed because you've separated yourself from him, but you don't know you're enslaved just like him—cold whiteness. You're hypothermic. You lose logic. You see the blood, and you think someone else is bleeding. Everyone is screaming at you to turn the machine off, but

> you can't hear them. You can't even hear yourself saying we're cursed too. We're cursed too.

At his last words, White turns to Black, his face ghostly and without eyes. Then dark arms surround Black and drag him into the water. The haunting monologue divulges a definition of whiteness and the resulting blindness from white positionality. White argues that while white people may think Black people are cursed and injured, white people are hurting themselves by subordinating Black people, blind to their self-inflicted wounds.

The rest of the episode can be read as a series of events in which white people think they are saving a Black person from a curse but fail to see their own moral battles. This is illustrated to viewers through young Black student Loquareeous who finds himself in a living nightmare where white people think they are saving him but reveal their own moral dilemmas and sentence him to death. Early on in the episode, his teachers send him to the principal's office, where a counselor deems him remedial because he disrupted class. His mother protests the accusation. After seeing Loquareeous's mother's unconventional disciplinary actions and her forceful warning to him that "if you don't start using your common sense and acting right, these white people gonna kill you," the white counselor calls a social worker to his home. He is taken to a foster family, where his new white foster mothers feed him microwave-cooked fried chicken, among other oddities. While out with his foster family, Loquareeous runs to a white police officer to save him from his foster parents. But once the officer sees the foster parents are white women, he deems the boy safe. Each of these events resonates for Loquareeous as a confirmation that his mother was right when she told him that if he didn't get his behavior together, these white people would kill him. It isn't until after these "three slaps" (the counselor, the foster mothers, and the police officer) that Loquareeous shows signs that he may now understand what his mother tried to teach him about living in an anti-Black world. Loquareeous becomes suspicious of his white foster mothers. When they pack him and their three other Black foster children into a minivan and claim they are going to the Grand Canyon, Loquareeous looks at the other kids and says with his eyes, "these white women are gonna kill us." He devises a plan for them to escape. Somehow, he gets the other kids out of the vehicle and then jumps out of the car himself before the foster mothers drive off a cliff into what is inferred to be Lake Lanier. The mothers crash into the lake haunted by the Black bodies of those young Black men who were lynched there (Daniel, Knox, and Edwards), never to be saved from anti-Black racism. The moment symbolically reflects the meeting up of ghosts. In the narrative, the white mothers embody whiteness and its freedoms of space, movement, and property, while Lake Lanier, which has already revealed itself as a landscape deep with historical significance, represents the Black victims created for whiteness to have its freedoms.

After saving himself from drowning in the lake, Loquareeous runs home—not to school and not back to the foster home but to the home with his Black mother and grandfather. He isn't welcomed by any hugs or kisses or a look of a desperately thankful mother. Instead, he unceremoniously finds the key under the front door mat and lets himself in. His mother, unsurprised when she sees him, says, "so you finally decided to come home," and confirms that there is spaghetti in the refrigerator. For Loquareeous, a home is a place where he knows where the key is and where he'll have permission to open the door. Home is the place where he can find kin who will do all they can to protect his Black body and teach him how to protect himself. It doesn't look like the warm, nurturing embrace his white school counselors or foster mothers expected, but it's what he needs to feel hope for survival in an anti-Black world. This, too, is the role of Black Meccas in Black lifeworlds.

In this eerie story, we find the purpose of the Black Mecca as a "home" complete with "kin" who strive to protect each other from anti-Black racism. It's a place where, whether real or mythological, Black people find a key that permits them entrance. This narrative also echoes the significance of a haunting. In White's assessment of whiteness from Lake Lanier's haunting context, the audience sees the character, a white man, admit to his blindness. The scene offers hope that by excavating the story of the ghosts of Lake Lanier, we may also meet a moral reckoning. Following the efforts of Atlanta neighborhood activists and organizers like Alison Johnson and Tanya Washington of the Housing Justice League, a primary goal of *Ghosts of Atlanta* is to encourage Black people to protect our homeplace in Atlanta while revealing the stories of the ghosts left behind by cultural gentrification so that, just maybe, a moral reckoning can come forth in our shared spaces.

CHAPTER 2

"POOF! ALL THE BLACK PEOPLE ARE GONE," OR AN AMERICAN HAUNTING

Black Atlantans often use the terms Old Atlanta and New Atlanta to differentiate those Atlantans born and raised in the city before the 1996 Olympics and those that migrated after. Sometimes, when you say "belt line" to someone from Old Atlanta, it is not the "BeltLine," Gravel's twenty-two-mile loop of trails and streetcars, that they assume you are referencing but rather the original "belt lines," the four railroad lines arranged in a rough circle outside of the center city. The railroads are what they remember first because they worked them, laid the tracks, kept them maintained, and cut the grass around them.

The belt line elucidates as much about Atlanta's formation as the BeltLine explains its future. As mentioned in chapter 1, the city was founded in expectancy of the railroad junction between the Western and Atlantic Railroads in 1837, connecting trade routes into the southern United States. Toward the Civil War's end, on September 1, 1864, Union general William Tecumseh Sherman followed the Western and Atlantic Railroads south, fighting along the way until he captured Atlanta for President Abraham Lincoln. Before heading to Savannah, he burned the city and destroyed the railroads. Atlanta's rail networks were rebuilt during Reconstruction, and the economy expanded. New line systems linked at the junction amounted to congestion and backups along the train routes for passengers and freight to Atlanta. To relieve the traffic along the commute, four companies built four railroads that would become the belt line; they were the Seaboard Air Line Belt Railway, Louisville and Nashville Belt Railroad, Southern Railway Decatur Street Belt, and Atlanta and West Point Belt Line. We start this chapter here: at a Black neighborhood that formed after the Civil War at the Seaboard Air Line Belt Railway.

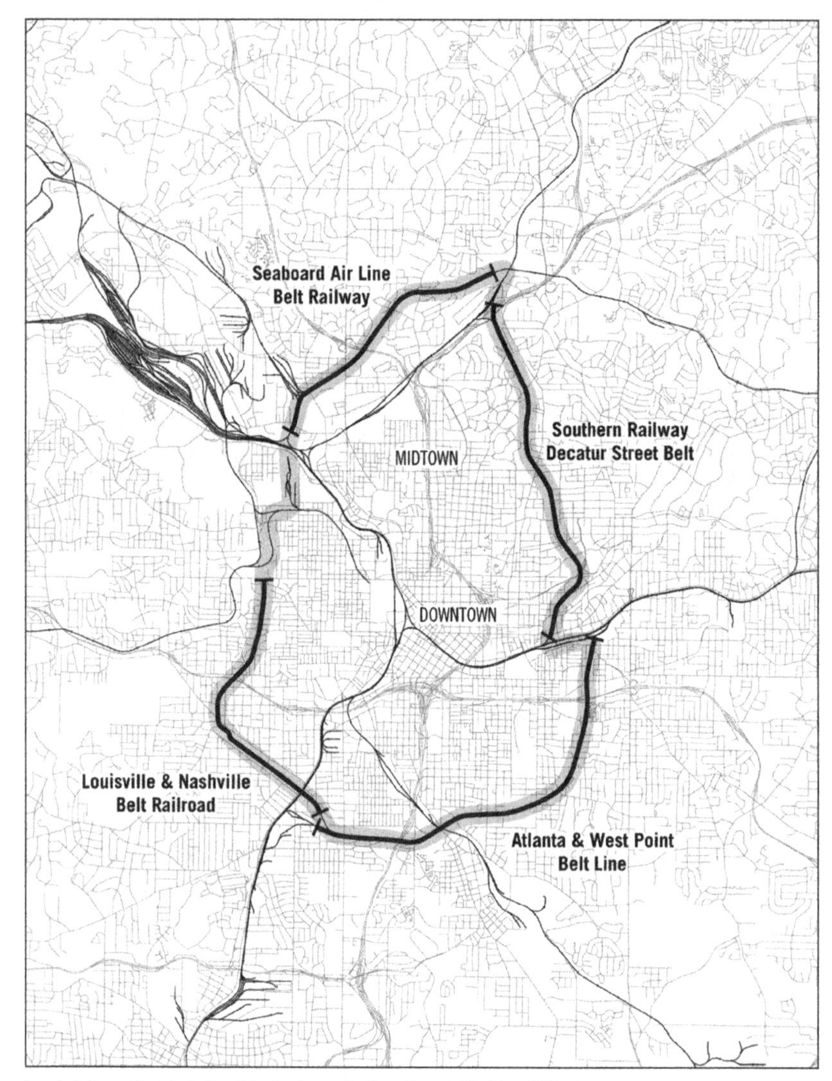

Four belt line railroads circling Atlanta. Image by Ryan Gravel / Perkins+Will, 2015.

HOW WE MEET GHOSTS

In 2014, artist Gregor Turk, commissioned by Art on the Atlanta BeltLine, developed public art along the future space of the Northside BeltLine that would cross through the neighborhood Blandtown, which is adjacent to the Seaboard Air Line Belt Railway tracks. Using billboards, Turk lined the future trail with images of General Sherman's eyes, making a statement that intersected public memory of the Civil War battle that won Georgia from the Confederacy with the current conception of Atlanta's present and future outlook. Once the temporary art installation was over, Turk was inspired to reuse one of the billboards, this time to engage another portion of our memory—one of neighborhood identity. At this time, gentrifiers started buying property around Turk's studio, a repurposed cinder-block house built in the 1940s. They started referring to the area as West Midtown, leading him to create a signpost for his front yard. He covered the remaining billboard with an image of an Indian-head test pattern, a symbol he remembered from the 1970s, used by television stations to note that they were off the air. Across the signal-test image, he inscribed the words "Welcome to the heart of Blandtown." The gridded horizontal and vertical lines that make up the Indian-head test pattern are formed using the repetition of the name Felix Bland.

At the time of its original installation, Turk's billboard represented the ambiguity of the neighborhood's name. Luxury condominiums, apartments, single-family homes, and retail spaces built in Blandtown in the early twenty-first century use the term West Midtown in their signage and public documentation, erasing the vestures of the working-class Black neighborhood Blandtown that formed around the belt line. The repetition of the name Felix Bland was a call back to the neighborhood's Black namesake. For Turk, the billboard begs the question—as gentrifiers without a connection to Blandtown's past move in and developers continue tearing down and building up—Is Blandtown going "off-the-air"? And like when waiting for television networks to sign back on air in the morning, one wonders, What will it be when it comes back?

I met Turk in 2017 after the name Blandtown drew me into a mystery I could not shake. That summer, I was feeling a bit annoyed with myself. I hadn't updated my profile picture on Facebook in a few months and hadn't taken any social-media-ready, professional pictures in at least six years, which meant I'd been living in Georgia for four years without an image that properly reflected the new "Georgianness" of my identity. So in the true fashion of a millennial, daughter of the digital age, and New Atlanta transplant, I called a favorite photographer from Fort Lauderdale to take some pictures of me in the city. She proposed a location—the Goat Farm Arts Center. Having been the site for scenes in *The Walking Dead* and *The Hunger Games* and because of its unique construction, the Goat Farm had become a popular location for artists and photographers. The building was erected in the late 1880s as a cotton-gin factory. During World War II, the space was used to manufacture artillery. Then, in the 1970s, industrial engineer Robert Haywood used it to produce sheet metal and invited artists to use some of the open rooms for their work. It became known as the Goat Farm when Haywood brought goats to eat the growing kudzu around the complex.[1]

After my photographer suggested it as an ideal location, I started looking up pictures of the Goat Farm. The images of the old, red brick building with broken windows, train tracks, and machinery left seemingly precisely where it was last used in the 1940s insighted my curiosity.[2] It is rare to find such an antique structure in the city. It was more perplexing that this gem was hidden in the middle of what I knew to be West Midtown, a quickly developing hot spot of luxury apartments, boutiques, and restaurants attracting New Atlantans. Confused by the Goat Farm's existence, I wanted to know more and headed to Wikipedia for a quick primer. At that time, Wikipedia noted that the Goat Farm was in a neighborhood called Blandtown. My next thought was, What in the world is Blandtown? Isn't this West Midtown? I followed the next breadcrumb to see what Wikipedia and the referenced sources could tell me about Blandtown. I continued to newspaper accounts in the *Atlanta Journal-Constitution* and academic books on the city. Together, the authorities reiterated the same story—always terse but still intriguing. To summarize, as rumor has it, after the war over union and slavery, former slave Felix Bland came to own land in today's northwestern Atlanta. He'd been owned by a woman named Viney Bland. And when slavery ended, she deeded her property to Felix and paid for his education at Tuskegee Institute in Alabama. But having not paid his property taxes, Felix lost the property in the 1870s. Soon after, Bob Booth obtained property and developed it into a residential subdivision on the outskirts of Atlanta.[3] It is said that today's Blandtown neighborhood is named for its one-time Black owner, Felix Bland.

The funny thing about rumors is that though they suggest uncertainty, there is a drop of warrant in them that allows them to ring true for an audience. For a Black audience, maybe the credibility came from a spark of pride to find a town named for a formerly enslaved person. For a white audience, perhaps it was a release of guilt from the story of the kind enslaver. But I've been Black long enough to have doubts that Felix so unceremoniously lost the land to unpaid taxes. The issue with rumors is that the suggested uncertainty, the tinge of doubt, is the space where the ghosts live. And these ghosts require an investigation. So I followed them. And in that doubt, I found the Bland family and the reality: the rumor is not valid. Viney and Felix existed but not in the social caste or experiences here described. The short version of historical fact is Viney Bland was a Black woman, and Felix Bland was her son. In 1870, Viney's Black husband, Samuel Bland, purchased four acres in the area in question and soon after willed the land to his wife, who later willed it to her children, leaving Felix with significant ownership into the second decade of the twentieth century. There were no records found confirming that Felix ever attended Tuskegee Institute. During the Blands' residence in

Blandtown and into the 1970s, Blandtown had grown into an unincorporated, small, Black, mostly self-sufficient enclave of formerly enslaved people and transplants from neighboring states attracted by the available jobs constructing Atlanta's railroads. When I started this research, you could drive straight through the neighborhood, stop at a new restaurant, visit a friend in a luxury apartment, or move into your newly constructed single-family home without finding a single sign that marked the neighborhood name of Blandtown. I located the first one, for years the only one, in front of Turk's art studio that summer. Soon, I would tell him the real story of Blandtown I'd researched, and he would share the power of visual art to reclaim lost histories. We were connected because we had followed the same ghosts.

Turk and I met because the shadows of Blandtown called out to us both, and they did it through a neighborhood name unknown to most. The name led Turk to an impactful art exhibition and brought me to my research on gentrification. Our actions in response to the name Blandtown provide insight into the power of place-names to draw witness to collective identities and the domination of other names (i.e., West Midtown) to gentrify culture. The power of names as more than just signifiers of a place has become an area of interest in multiple fields of scholarship, including geography, anthropology, psychology, and communications. Star Medzerian Vanguri, editor of the volume *Rhetorics of Names and Naming*, attests that commemorative place-names circulate cultural narratives that are rhetorically influential in linking the past to the present.[4] Current research in rhetorical onomastics and place has focused on street naming. Derek H. Alderman's extensive research on Martin Luther King Jr. street names reveals how the power over naming reflects social injustices, giving some the "right to participate" and others the "right to appropriate."[5] In another example, Derek Handley reveals how, in the 1960s and '70s, naming a Pittsburgh street corner Freedom Corner in connection to its historical significance, using the corner for protest, and adding visual symbols helped Black residents reclaim ownership of the space in a counterhegemonic move of resistance to urban renewal.[6] But beyond understanding who has the power to name and how they use this power, it is a necessity to reflect on what makes cultural domination possible, how the narratives associated with a name are altered to make Black racial subordination and neoliberalism common sense, and what forces continue the establishment of a racist social order.

That the rumor about Viney and Felix's identity was produced and redistributed unquestioned over the past 150 years leads me to interrogate the ways that white dominance over public memory asks us to deny reality and forgo our connections to a homeplace. How do we reconcile the current cultural and biological demography of West Midtown with the fact that somewhere within the space and time of its establishment are the Black Bland family and other Black families that called it home? If displacing Black bodies depended on starting a rumor that would discredit Felix Bland and, in turn, Black property ownership while justifying white claims to the land, how might the lived experiences of the now ghosts be another story by which to recognize the identity of the place? What are the differences in how these stories may narrate who is permitted and who is excluded? In this chapter, I rethink gentrified West Midtown through the eyes of the ghosts of Blandtown as a way to pull back the veil, permitting Blackness into the space. I excavate Blandtown as a former Black homeplace that has been wholly displaced. As our first case study, this chapter is centered chronologically after the Civil War. It continues to the present day, generating at least one story of what can occur when cultural gentrification runs its course. The rumored story of Blandtown's past exemplifies how cultural gentrification in local narratives turns Black lives into shadows to buttress white power. Blandtown, the place-name, is a community asset that reminds us of what is here—ghosts—and what is missing—the previous Black community and culture. The ghosts it creates keep the records of the long-standing urban-development strategy under a racialized neoliberal capitalism driven by white desires for domination.

MODERN AMERICAN STREAMS OF THINKING

W. E. B. Du Bois argues that there are three streams of thinking in the modern age—an age that began when the first enslaved Africans arrived in what was the "New World" to Europeans. The first mode of thinking is that developing "culture-land," or land for their cultures, which an increasing amount of people want, calls for cooperation and human unity that pulls differing races into one nation. Yet the idea of cooperation across races is accompanied by the temptation to use force and domination to retrieve the desired culture-land. The second stream of thought is the belief that Black people are inferior by creation. The accompanying afterthought is that some Black people may turn out to be "men," but for the preservation of the dominant race, white men cannot let them. And the third way of thinking comes from Black people themselves, who have a personal belief in and yearning for freedom, liberty, and opportunity. They are also accompanied by the fear that the second way of thinking is correct and that they might prove to be inferior. The three modes of thinking complicated by thought and afterthought co-occur within individuals, communities, and governments. Our cities have been formed with these entangled thoughts, yet I argue that the temptation for force and domination and the notion of Black inferiority prevail. And as far as these modes of thinking succeed, so does cultural gentrification. At the outset of European exploration of the Americas as a new world, the colonizers assessed the continents as a frontier, with ample land supply for white families to forge a sense of place. By defining Native Americans as "savages," and thus less than human, Europeans justified their acts of force and genocide. This continues today. Now that most of the useable land has been settled, the United States faces a low supply of frontier scape, as well as a high demand for a sense of local place, or culture-lands. By the subtle yet deliberate use of narratives to support Black inferiority, the dominant ideology justifies acts of spatial domination and cultural gentrification, thus continually confirming Du Bois's three streams of thought of the modern age. I'll use these streams of thought to explicate the nature and uses of the rumored Blandtown narrative.

It is unclear where the rumor got its first conception. But it materialized in extant texts of writers at the beginning of the new millennium. By the time I discovered the error, the story had already become a part of the landscape. Current and former residents of the area couldn't recollect where the neighborhood name Blandtown had come from, so the rumor became sufficient. With the name attached to the landscape and the rumor attached to the name, this fictive story narrates the space and becomes a determining factor in defining who is permitted and who is excluded. What this rumor is utilized for and how it operates in cultural gentrification are relevant since a detailed examination of Felix Bland's character in the rumor reveals the nature of white domination. By assessing it, we gain a clearer understanding of the role of white dominance in creating the Black Mecca.

The characters described in the rumor are personas of the unknown author's (or authors') making. And by assessing the personas, we may better come to understand the author(s), their desires, and their fears. As Morrison writes of literature, "The fabrication of an Africanist persona is reflexive; an extraordinary meditation on the self; a powerful exploration of the fears and desires that reside in the writerly conscious. It is an astonishing revelation of longing, of terror, of perplexity, of shame, of magnanimity."[7] And these ways make themselves transparent and self-evident when we review the stories and consider the streams of thought that govern the modern age.

Blandtown is named for Felix Bland; Felix Bland was a Black man—these are the starting points of the rumor, and based on the accurate historical record, these are the only statements and inferences gleaned from the various renditions of the rumor that can be corroborated. The other reports, carrying themselves as fact, seem to encircle these two.

Regardless of how the other statements were chosen, they seem to have been put to care for the fact that what is now approximately five hundred acres of land surrounded by clearly defined white space was named for a Black man. As Du Bois assesses, when it comes to dealing with Black people, the modern line of thought follows the second stream of thought:

> The sincere and passionate belief that somewhere between men and cattle, God created a tertium quid, and called it a Negro,—a clownish, simple creature, at times even lovable within its limitations but straitly foreordained to walk within the Veil. To be sure, behind the thought lurks the afterthought,—some of them with favoring chance might become men, but in sheer self-defence, we dare not let them.[8]

In keeping with this argument, the story must address how an un-man came to own land. This was navigated by fabricating a white protagonist in Viney Bland and ensuring her moral superiority through comparison to the inferiority of Felix. Felix is personified as her slave. And Viney is the allegorical representation of a white savior and kind master who supported her freed property after the war. But the formerly enslaved person cannot be more remarkable than the enslaver. Therefore, he loses the land by not paying taxes. The claim supports the premise that the Black man is a "simple creature" and maintains the order that validates the veil. Like unpaid rent, the failure to pay taxes is unforgivable and untied to systemic and historical racism and capitalism.[9]

The other portions of the short rumor corroborate the first stream of modern thought. Du Bois writes, "the multiplying of human wants in culture-lands calls for the world-wide cooperation of men in satisfying them. Hence arises a new human unity, pulling the ends of earth nearer, and all men, black, yellow, and white. . . . To be sure, behind this thought lurks the afterthought of force and dominion,—the making of brown men to delve when the temptation of beads and red calico cloys."[10] It is a common aspect of humanity to want a land of their own, and it is by choice that human beings decide to unite with other collectives or dominate other collectives. Supported by the claims of Black and brown inferiority, domination has been white men's modern choice. This mode of thought frames the rumored story as it states that a white woman first owned the land. And after Felix lost the land for not paying taxes, the property went to the hands of a presumed white man, Bob Booth. (While the name Bob Booth has not been found in records, English real-estate agent Samson Booth lived and sold property in Blandtown and may be the intended reference.)[11] Human beings want property for their communities, and the rumor of Blandtown conditions this territory as originally and continuously being white cultural land unless white property owners choose to give it away to someone else.

The third mode of thought, which focuses on the Black perspective, cannot be extrapolated from the rumor because the rumor doesn't give Felix human will or agentive power, which is identifiable by choice and action. The rumor does give Viney and Bob this agency. Viney owned and Viney gave. Bob purchased. While other characters are identified by action, Felix is identified by his inaction. He was given something, and he lost it. Felix is never shown as doing anything. In fact, he loses the land for *not* paying taxes. The rumor puts his life in the will of others, removing his perspective and personal determination.

Through the first and second modes of thinking, the rumor is written in the language of white dominance, and when it was grafted to the landscape, it supplanted all other narratives. It worked to culturally gentrify public memory and make Felix a ghost in the narrative of his neighborhood. My original suspicions with the rumor stemmed from the appearance that the story was about Felix, but it was really about slaveowner Viney. The lack of attention to the Black person for which a neighborhood was named caused the rumor to lose its coherence. Further, in this version, the fictive slaveowner Viney's moral identity was concretized by the shadow of Felix. Morrison notes that in the literature of white authors, what became transparent to her "were the self-evident ways that [white] Americans chose to talk about themselves through and within a sometimes allegorical, sometimes metaphorical, but always choked representation of an Africanist presence."[12] The gist of it is that Black people are the defining other for America. Similarly, Felix is made into a persona developed to maintain white superiority and claims to Blandtown. Felix is an accomplice to his so-called white enslaver; he's an accomplice that empowers her identity, releases her of guilt, and whitewashes the stain of slavery from Atlanta's history. The rumor supports the concept that white people have tried to help Black people but are inherently better at economic progress and land development. Through this rumor, Blandtown becomes the "unconsulted, appropriated ground" of white inquisition buttressed by a story that supports the "reckless unabated power" of a white person through the suppression of a Black family's lifeworld.[13] When others have the power to fabricate your history, you become a creation of their making, losing your agency in the process.

Despite the rumor, Blandtown left a cultural asset, an epitaph that speaks out from the graveyard of lost, stolen, disappeared, and replaced place-names. The name is the last available asset since the displacement of the former Black community. As Black-owned-museum curator Anyka Barber argues about the city of Oakland, while others may focus on mapping the withering Black population, it is necessary to consider the cultural asset of this community so that we can remember what's here and start to fight for what's here.[14] The neighborhood name remains bonded to the place. It is a metonymy, standing in for the whole of what it meant to the past inhabitants.[15] The name "stand[s] in for what remains but can no longer be restored to presence."[16] It allows that which has died to surpass death into a new form of survival as an intangible cultural resource linked to a historical trajectory and narrative part of defining of the Black Mecca. In the next section of this chapter, I attempt to move Felix out of the shadows by following the ghost in the remaining cultural asset—the neighborhood name Blandtown. I complete a "historical diagnostic" of the neighborhood,[17] uncovering hidden histories that hint at alternative futures and recovery. As Frantz Fanon attests, "without a black past, without a black future, it was impossible for me to live my blackness."[18] The aim is that by uncovering this history, the Black people affected by it may come closer to living out an identity defined by their own experiences.

CULTURAL GENTRIFICATION OF THE BLACK NEIGHBORHOOD

Unlike other Atlanta neighborhoods we will discuss in this book, the cultural gentrification of Blandtown is already complete. Though the process started decades before the Atlanta BeltLine was ideated, the investment-driven project sealed its fate. Blandtown, located roughly between Huff Road, Marietta Boulevard, Chattahoochee Avenue, and Howell Mill Road on the west side of Atlanta, was one of the northernmost Black suburbs in the city until the population progressively decreased between the 1960s and '90s. The neighborhood represents common placemaking strategies of newly freed African Americans. Unlike some of the southwestern Black suburbs in Atlanta that have garnered attention from historians interested in the Black business, education, and financial districts, Blandtown has been left unexcavated. What is known is that the neighborhood was once a growing and thriving lower-class Black area, whose residents found employment with the belt line railway, reflecting Black agency and placemaking. Yet they were displaced because of white desires for land and property, instigated by the neoliberal and racist ideology of politicians and developers. Space is actively produced and shaped by racist social policies.[19] Blandtown exemplifies Black geography, a racialized demographic pattern "shaped by historical precedent" in Atlanta.[20] The racial pattern forming Blandtown has been produced by separatist ideology, which forges distinct Black spaces and white spaces.

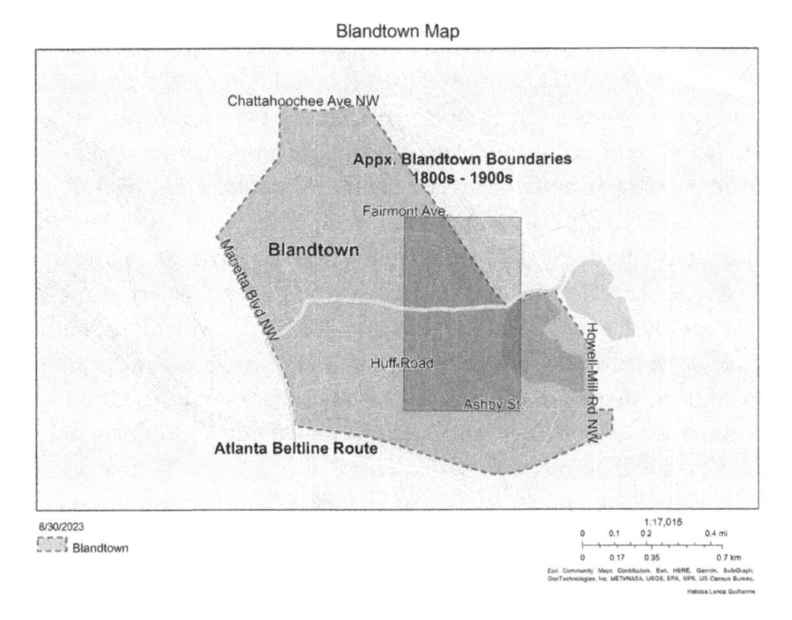

Map of Blandtown boundaries by Heloisa Lanca Guilherme. The dashed lines represent the official bounds of Blandtown as they stand today. The solid gray box is an approximate representation of the connotation of Blandtown's bounds as a Black settlement in the late nineteenth century. The solid line running more or less through the center shows the projected future location of a BeltLine trail segment. Copyright © 2023 Esri and its data contributors. All rights reserved.

THE TRUTH OF BLANDTOWN'S ORIGINS

Today, Blandtown is the area between Marietta Boulevard (to the west), Howell Mill Road (to the east), and Huff Road (to the south). However, when spoken of in late 1800s and 1900s news articles, maps, and real-estate sales, the Blandtown area is sometimes referenced as the smaller "Negro settlement" roughly between Fairmont (to the west), Ashby (to the east), Morris Avenue (to the north), and just beyond Huff Road (to the south) by the Seaboard Air Line Railroad lines.

After the Civil War, Blandtown became a place for Black people because it was an unwanted portion of unincorporated land. Nine years after the Emancipation Proclamation, on October 2, 1872, freeman and plasterer Samuel Bland (born perhaps in 1821—though unconfirmed), a "mulatto" according to 1880s census data,[21] purchased four acres of land for $200 from Rev. Francis A. Kimball. The latter owned twenty-six acres in that area.[22] In 1873, Samuel willed the acreage to his "mulatto" wife, Lavinia "Viney" Bland (1821–1914).[23] The small plot of lower-level land sat between the property of white owners A. K. Seago and the aforementioned Kimball. It is written that the Bland family was thought of highly by their white neighbors, and "Aunt Viney" was the midwife for many of the white children's births in Cook District, as it was known at the time.[24] Viney retained the complete four acres until 1892. Other freed men and women bought properties around hers.

In 1891, Viney invested in twelve Southern Mutual Building and Loan Association (SMBLA) stocks. She requested an advance on her shares before their maturity, thus losing a portion of the land for payment on the stock-backed loan the following year. In 1892, she sold another part of the land for $800 to the Georgia Northern Railway Company,[25] which the Southern Railroad Company later bought in 1966. Viney's son Felix bought another one eighth of an acre of adjacent land from a Black landowner.[26] In 1901, Felix purchased a portion of the land from his mother for ninety dollars, and Viney willed the rest of the land to her children, Felix, Richard, Cherry, and Charlie.[27] Felix sold his portion to Mr. and Mrs. R. A. Sims in 1916.[28] By 1923, Felix was the last living of his siblings. Before her death, Cherry sold some of her land to James Irwin, who served on the Board of Trustees of the Blandtown Christian Church, and R. A. Sims.[29] In 1923, Cherry's two children, heirs to the rest of her land, sold the remaining parcel to the church for $500.[30] The Blandtown Christian Church may have also gone by the name of Rocky Mountain Christian Church, formed by Irwin in 1901 and possibly led by Felix for a time.[31] What is clear is Cherry and Felix intended the land to be used for church purposes as a continuing legacy.

Having been retained by the Blands for at least fifty years, the area became known as Blandtown, and the street they lived on, Bland Street.[32] The neighborhood was home to an elementary school for Black students, three or four churches,[33] approximately 194 nonwhite-occupied housing units, and a nonwhite population of roughly 855 people by 1960.[34] Before 1921, the Black children traveled more than a mile over dangerous railroad tracks to get to Rockdale Park School. However, after St. Peter's Baptist Church trustees offered space in their building, the Fulton County Commission provided equipment and teachers for a school in Blandtown in 1921.[35] Proving how Black people were financing, in whole or in part, their own education,[36] in 1924, parents and businesses put their money together to purchase a lot and build a two-room school. In 1934, they added one and a half rooms to the building. By 1956, the enrollment was 138 and there were five teachers.[37] Former residents were proud as they referenced the community's work to establish a home in this environmentally inhospitable portion of Fulton County.

An early resident, Johnny Lee Green, who first moved to Blandtown with his parents from Virginia in the 1920s and found their home in a small plot of land, recounts, "We weren't there because it was the best place to be. We were there because it was the only place Black people were allowed to be."[38] Indicating geographic and social inequity, the neighborhood had no running water, no inside toilet, and no electricity. It was a plot of unwanted ground surrounded by heavy industry, railroad lines, and white residents in neighboring areas. This was common practice in the region. While white and Black communities were often in close proximity to one another, the Black communities were often relegated to "property lacking water and sewer service."[39] These conditions proved to be hazardous. A fire struck Blandtown on March 13, 1938, "destroying 15 houses, a church, and two restaurants."[40] A local newspaper stated that the blaze started in a neighbor's home and was easily spread by the wind because the "negro settlement" was on rolling ground with no buildings or trees to break the gust. Such information reflects the continued environmental danger that Black residents have faced there.

The space for Black folks was made even more distinctive as real-estate agents designated surrounding properties as white only. An advertisement for an auction sale of lots bordering the Black area of Blandtown on April 22, 1911, reads, "The property is restricted to Whites and no negroes can ever own this property, thus insuring its character and worth."[41] While Blandtown was left as an industrial designation on the 1938 Home Owners Loan Corporation residential security map (largely recognized as the map used for redlining),[42] city government maps of Atlanta employed for city-planning sessions of the 1950s designate it as a "Negro Residential Area."[43]

In newspapers from the first decade of the 1900s, Blandtown residents were described as "vagrant" and living "profligate existences" at the "negro settlement."[44] Such characterizations continued into the mid-part of the century as patrolmen stalked residents of Blandtown, taking them to jail on Sunday if they were found not attending church services. There was a report that two county patrolmen told a group of Blandtown youth "to go to church or to jail." When the youth didn't go to church, at least one was threatened by the officers and taken to jail, where he stayed for eleven days.[45]

Socially, neighboring white areas attempted to distance themselves from the stigmas of poverty and crime that characterized Blandtown, even though these stigmas were brought on by the apartheid-style development strategies that limited the mobility of Black people by relegating their livelihood to sites with unhealthy conditions.[46] After a murder in Blandtown in 1914, the *Atlanta Constitution* reported that neighboring "citizens" on Howell Mill Road "want it understood that Blandtown . . . is not located on the Howell Mill road." The writer quoted a Howell Mill resident saying, "our people are not the sort who do such a thing."[47] Distinguishing the assumed white "citizen" on Howell Mill

Road from Blandtown's "negro settlement," the writers in these papers from the first decade of the twentieth century rhetorically marked the difference between white space and Black space. The spatial assignment was also used to characterize white people as "citizens" and Black people as inhabitants of the area. Throughout these newspaper articles, we see white residents' efforts to make Blandtown a phantom. Due to the neighborhood's proximity to white lifeworlds, it could substantiate the argument of white superiority. The writer defined Howell Mill Road by what it is not, thereby collecting the white citizen's community identity from the negation of the Black community identity. Blandtown, like Ellison's invisible man, is a "personification of the Negative" and "the most perfect achievement" of the Howell Mill residents' dreams.[48] By being the Negative, the white populace nearby can conveniently distinguish themselves as having the "quintessential American identity."[49]

Even today, in a more affluent and gentrified Blandtown, if we look at it from the scope of greater Atlanta, it becomes a centering point for Atlanta's segregated geography and intentions to exclude Black Atlanta from northern Atlanta's white enclaves. Current resident of Blandtown and former neighborhood association president Renee Wright describes the moment she noticed the separation between Black and white space in Atlanta and the significance of Blandtown to this spatially. The Atlanta Police Department breaks Atlanta into six defined zones used to distribute officer assignments and manage response times. Each of these zones has public safety meetings with residents in the area. As of March 2019, the Blandtown zone was realigned to Zone 1, northwestern Atlanta.[50] Before that time, Blandtown was part of Zone 2, encompassing the majority white and affluent neighborhoods to the north, including Buckhead. Having the opportunity to go to both Zone 1 and Zone 2 meetings before the change, Blandtown's neighborhood association president was given a distinct view of the two zones between which Blandtown lies. Wright remembers walking into the Zone 2 meeting and immediately noticing that she was the youngest person in the room of retired white men and women. She recalls, "I'm not saying they were assholes. But there was no diversity around that table. It was an old white man talking to a bunch of old white people. And I was one of them [laughs]. But I'm the only one that seemed to notice this. I walked in . . . I was like . . . Is this the city of Atlanta? Or am I finding myself transported to East Cobb somehow? It was bizarre."[51]

At the Zone 2 safety meeting populated by the white men, the safety discussion revolved around decreasing car break-ins. But in March, Blandtown was moved to Zone 1, primarily encompassing areas southwest of Zone 2, with a majority Black (at least 80 percent of the population) and a greater population of lower-income families (averaging less than $46,789 yearly).[52]

When Wright walked into her first Zone 1 meeting, she was now representing one of the more affluent areas in her zone, and she and a friend were the only white people around the table. She also recognized that there was a different set of problems. "As a community, they were getting together, talking about how do we get people to actually call 9-1-1." She recalls, "And just as I sat at that first meeting and went, 'holy shit, this is two Atlantas right here.' I just went from one Atlanta to the second Atlanta, and Blandtown is a crucible for that. Blandtown is like one little piece that reflects that dichotomy."[53]

Blandtown sits in the middle of white, affluent Atlanta to the north and Black, less affluent Atlanta to the southeast. While Blandtown started as a "negro settlement," remnants of that past are far gone because of cultural gentrification. According to census tract data, the annual growth rate was 5.8 percent from 2012 to 2017. Approximately 70 percent of housing units in the area were built after the year 2000, which reflects the amount of new development in Blandtown and indicates higher income levels. The largest race in the area is white (non-Hispanic), accounting for 59.8 percent of the population. Most units are renter occupied, with 75.4 percent of renters spending $1,000–$1,499 monthly. The average household income is between $60,539 and $76,163. Comparatively, to the southwest of Blandtown, the average income is less than $46,786. And neighborhoods directly north of Blandtown have higher income averages, upwards of $102,392.[54] The change in racial diversity and income there can largely be explained by cultural gentrification.

CULTURAL GENTRIFICATION OF BLANDTOWN: PHASE ONE

Blandtown's past and present history have a common conflict that goes beyond race: it's the tension between industry and residents. However, the disparate results of that conflict, when white residents face an industrial threat versus when Black residents face the same competition, reveal the racial social order in geography determining our pleasant or painful fate. The story of Blandtown's cultural gentrification exemplifies the detriment of invisibility on Black posterity.

After reconstruction, Blandtown became an industrial hotbed. The 1895 Cotton States and International Exposition held at today's Piedmont Park in Atlanta promoted the entire city and the southeastern United States to businesses and investors worldwide over the one hundred days it was open. At the exposition, Booker T. Washington made his famed "Atlanta Compromise" speech, assuaging white fears of the Black race and encouraging African Americans to join agricultural and mechanical fields. This exposition led the way for industry growth in Blandtown and provided a frame for understanding the economic plan that still drives Atlanta.

It was during the final decade of the nineteenth century that Blandtown would become an industrial area. In the 1890s, Seaboard Air Line Railroad Company built several secondary tracks west of Blandtown. Other industries—including stockyards, a mill, and a fertilizer factory—came into the area.[55] These businesses made it inhospitable to residents, but African Americans moving from other southern states, like the Carolinas and Virginia, could find jobs at the railroads. A part of the original Old Atlanta, the neighborhood and community were developed by these Black workers. Residents that lived in the area from the 1920s to the 1960s recall the awful smells from the fertilizer plant and slaughterhouse. They were aware that they lived in unhealthy conditions.

Until 1952, Blandtown had been unincorporated, but a need to dilute the growing Black vote led Mayor William B. Hartsfield (for whom Hartsfield-Jackson International Airport is named) to expand the city. In the mid-twentieth century, the city of Atlanta was experiencing large amounts of white flight, with the white population moving to northern unincorporated suburbs and thereby decreasing Hartsfield's political power. To weaken Black voting strength, Hartsfield initiated Atlanta's northern expansion. Reporting to the white residents of unincorporated Buckhead, Hartsfield wrote,

> But the most important thing to remember, cannot be publicized in the press or made the subject of public speeches. Our negro population is growing by leaps and bounds. They stay right in the city limits and grow by taking more white territory inside Atlanta. Our migration is good, white, home owning citizens. With the Federal government insisting on political recognition of negroes in local affairs, the time is not far distant when they will become a potent political force in Atlanta if our white citizens are going to just move out and give it to them. This is not intended to stir race prejudice, because we all want to deal fairly with them, but do you want to hand them political control of Atlanta?[56]

Here, Mayor Hartsfield identifies a potential issue: the loss of white political power in Atlanta to Black people. In doing so, he executes the first and second streams of thought and afterthoughts espoused by Du Bois. As a reminder, the first is the desire for culture-lands through conquest and domination, and the second is "the inferiority of black men, even if forced by fraud."[57] In a desire to maintain the absolute power of white people over the state's capital city, Hartsfield pleads to the white residents of Buckhead to join the city and its voting populace. By establishing that Black residents have taken white territory, he determines that Atlanta's spaces have a previously established, permanent owner specific to race. Therefore, it is up to white people to retrieve their space. Further, by calling Black residents the "negro population" and white residents "citizens," Hartsfield makes a clear distinction that rhetorically removes Black citizens' rights to property, leaving them unprotected populaces. He establishes that the Black populace must stay behind the veil. They are but shadows left out of full citizenship and political influence. Through this, he summarily commences the process of cultural gentrification of Blandtown, and other Black neighborhoods across Atlanta, and the future events of Blandtown reveal this ideology's material effects.

In 1952, Hartsfield got his wish by annexing unincorporated territories to the north. Blandtown, one of the most northern Black neighborhoods, was incorporated into Atlanta along with the majority white Buckhead and its neighbors. New maps of the expanded city were drawn, designating all the Black residential areas.[58] In it, Blandtown is noted as a "Negro Residential Area." Despite the residents' wants, in keeping with processes that would reduce the Black population, zoning decisions in 1954 revealed the city's plan to rezone the area to industrial, making it a part of the Northwest Industrial Corridor.[59] A 1953 Atlanta Urban League (AUL) report of the neighborhood notes that people who worked in the community but lived outside of it had contacted recorder Jesse A. Gibson to suggest the neighborhood be dissolved. However, the AUL recorder recommended a professional agency provide assistance for the community since residents within the neighborhood were organizing, showing signs that they sought improvement and care for the neighborhood, which was more than sixty years old at this point.[60] Still, in 1956, Blandtown zoning was switched from small single-family residential (R-4) to heavy industrial (I-2). The main streets going through Blandtown were classified as truck routes by the Georgia Department of Transportation. The industrial zoning stipulated that those residents could not repair their homes if the damage to them was above 50 percent of the property value. In addition, any new residential construction was prohibited. Because of these restrictions, from 1960 to 1990, the community population declined by 71.9 percent.[61]

Issues between the remaining residents and businesses persisted. As of 1989, an estimated sixty-five companies were identified as having hazardous chemicals in Blandtown's zip code area, 30318. Outspoken neighborhood president Azalee Wharton invited officials to hear about the toxic chemical issues in her town. Residents complained about the smell as warehouses, chemical companies, and salvage yards took over the area. One person was hospitalized for three days after exposure to chemicals from a Nottingham Chemical Company spill in the area.[62] The persistent geographic inequity reflects the unfortunately common suffering of communities of color in sites with noxious facilities, exposing the residents to more significant health risks than white, more affluent neighbors.[63]

The residents fought to get the zoning back to residential, but politicians favored the industry's voice over Black citizens. Despite several reported issues between business practices and resident needs, the businesses argued that the law was in their favor. Speaking on behalf of the companies that operated in and around Blandtown, Dan Little of Nottingham Chemical Company and Allan Venzer, who owned a warehouse, argued that the area was never zoned residential. In addition, they didn't honor a tentative agreement made in 1991 that they would settle for I-1 (light-industrial) zoning,[64] which would shift business from being material oriented to business and end-user oriented and help with some of the chemical pollutants. City councilwoman Clair Mueller was able to get Blandtown coded as low-density residential in the 1991 Comprehensive Development Plan (CDP). Still, the zoning review board, listening to the attorneys for Nottingham Chemical Company, did not approve the rezoning. Thus, while a map in the 1991 CDP designated the area as low-density residential, the change wasn't executed.[65]

Much of this occurred because business needs were placed before Black residents. Nottingham Chemical Company formed a neighborhood association and represented itself to the city as "the neighborhood." Regarding the Nottingham Chemical Company, Larry Keating recounts,

> They tried, sometimes successfully, to intimidate the residents by telling them that their property would decline in value if residential zoning were obtained. They hired lawyers and planning consultants to attack and try to discredit the residents' positions. And finally, in their most cynical move, they created a nonfunctioning charitable foundation, supposedly designed to aid residents in need. This foundation existed only on paper and never dispensed any money to anyone.[66]

By 1993, the new community-development plan designated Blandtown as industrial again. The city council voted to maintain the plan in 1994, citing that the houses were too dilapidated to remain residential. According to the *Atlanta Voice*, only one council member voted against it.[67] These events are detrimental yet unsurprising considering that Mayor Hartsfield voiced what many politicians were thinking: Black property is not protected when a white person wants it. It is much easier to "unsee" Black residents by removing their existence from local maps and disfranchising their voice in political deliberation. These acts are not unique to Blandtown but are a familiar pattern. Rezoning is a covert way for local governments to uphold discriminatory practices against Black neighborhoods. Such behaviors decrease the value of homeowners' properties, hasten physical degradation, and encourage community disinvestment, allowing the space to be freed up for white resettling.[68]

Even though the neighborhood has been completely gentrified, conflicts between residents and industry persist, yet the new, whiter, wealthier voices are seen and heard in the arena of democratic deliberation. For instance, recently, the neighborhood association was reinvigorated by a proposal made by the Smyrna Ready Mix concrete-mixing facility at the end of 2018, which would bring the concrete plant to Blandtown. The part of Blandtown that the property would sit on is zoned as heavy industrial but is also less than a mile from the future BeltLine Northwest Trail and newly developed residences. Along with its environmental consequences of sulfur dioxide, nitrogen oxide, and carbon monoxide emissions, the plant would hinder the already-traffic-constrained roads in the area, with approximately sixty truck trips per day through their major streets.[69] Outcries from residents led the City of Atlanta Zoning Review Board to deny Smyrna Ready Mix's land use permit in March 2019. However, the residents aren't out of the woods yet, as the company can still apply for another special-use permit.[70] What continued conflicts between residents and industry reveal is that the neoliberalization of space affects not only low-income communities but also newly gentrified ones. It is also essential to recognize that when it mainly affected low-income Black residents, businesses' attempts to maintain control of the space were unjustly accepted, while those same attempts to majority white and economically more vital residents have been more effectively quelled. Yet the differences in how the groups of residents have been treated "cannot be explained by class factors alone."[71] As environmental justice scholar Robert D. Bullard argues, because of limited options for housing and mobility, Black people "do not have the same opportunities to 'vote with their feet' and escape undesirable physical environments" as white people do.[72] And the state has failed to protect Black residents from "the ravages of industrial pollution and nonresidential activities."[73] Such considerations amplify the claim that neoliberalism more readily persists as a form of systemic racism, instigating the impoverishment of African Americans for the profit of white hegemony.

CULTURAL GENTRIFICATION OF BLANDTOWN: PHASE TWO

The actions of Mayor Hartsfield and the Nottingham Chemical Company set in motion the cultural gentrification of Blandtown, but they did not complete it. It would be new developers looking upon Blandtown as an undiscovered residential territory that would close the coffin on Black Blandtown. In 1996, developer James F. Jacoby set his sights upon a hundred-year-old steel mill just east of Blandtown. He had the idea to raze the building and use the 138 acres of space to build a commercial, residential, and retail center in Midtown Atlanta, now known as Atlantic Station.[74] Though others had been leery because of the risks of redeveloping an environmentally hazardous landscape, Jacoby's moves inspired developers to look west of Midtown, where they found but didn't "see" the remaining relics of Black Blandtown.

Between 2006 and 2018, various parcels in Blandtown had their zoning changed from heavy industrial to mixed residential/commercial or multi-family residential. Interestingly, noted in one such developer's appeal for a zone change, the city required details on the new development's impacts on affordable housing. The developer sought to construct seventy new town-homes valued at $375–$440k. The known effect was that "the sales price exceed[ed] the affordable home price" for household incomes below 80 percent of the average median income (AMI) of the Atlanta metropolitan statistical area, which is used to assess housing affordability.[75] Therefore, the zoning approval also consented for housing that would only be affordable to those making above 80 percent of Atlanta's AMI.

Cultural gentrification requires erasing the people of the past—in this case, the African Americans and the racial tensions that formed the neighborhood. It depends on the manipulation of language to rhetorically identify who is permitted and who is excluded. Newspaper articles, public articulations of the region from the Atlanta Convention and Visitors Bureau and the Atlanta BeltLine, in addition to changing the unofficial naming standard for the neighborhood have all been a part of the systemic erasure and covering up of the Black past, leaving the Bland family and the neighborhood's history as shadows employed for the collective fulfillment of white lifeworlds.

First, as discussed at the beginning of this chapter, the counterfeit narrative about Blandtown has been spread through newspapers. As journalists caught on to the rush of developers coming to the west side of Midtown at the turn of the century, the fictional story was brought to broader public attention as others utilized unverified secondary research. In one version of the history, David Pendered writes about a development site: "[The] site is at the western tip of a historic black community called Blandtown. Bequeathed to a former slave who quickly lost it for not paying taxes, Blandtown grew after the Civil War as a housing development for blacks working in the freight yards and related industries."[76] In another article, journalist Diane Glassi reminisces on the industrial enclave's past "country feel" in a neighborhood formed initially for mill and railroad workers. She begins the spatial history before the Civil War, appropriately marking the location as originally home to Cherokee and Creek Indians. Then, she continues the rumored history of Blandtown: "Around 1890, the Seaboard railway supported a small community of homeowners in the area now known as Blandtown. Author Sarah Huff credits its name to an African-American named Felix Bland, who took his surname from the white family who supported his education and deeded him land."[77] This white-savior narrative reinstates white supremacy. David Pendered's remarks claim that people "have been accepting" these development changes, yet Black residents attempted to resist this through the political system that left them voiceless. In addition, the false stories of white benevolence to formerly enslaved people erase the history and double down on the act of forgetting rather than witnessing the racism that brought Blandtown into being.

Furthering erasure, some twenty-first-century journalists removed original Black residents and the antagonistic business owners from the story altogether. Instead, they personified the industries and buildings as the agent actors in the neighborhood's history. This action reflects a neoliberal framing in narration that gives businesses the power to act and prioritizes the business voice at the expense of silencing human actors or placing responsibility on inanimate objects rather than holding those responsible accountable.

At the turn of the century, the *Atlanta Constitution* dedicated at least two articles to changes occurring on the northwestern side of Atlanta. Positioning the focus on the new housing market in zip code 30318, journalist John McCosh briefly writes about the area's past:

> The northwest side of Atlanta is home to the R. M. Clayton sewage treatment plant, an aging, smelly behemoth known for its spills into the Chattahoochee River. For decades the industrial area at the northern end of ZIP code 30318 was infamous for its drug-plagued apartments and public housing. But now a caravan of people buying in to the first new neighborhoods built there since World War II are bringing rapid change.[78]

Using the terms "drug-plagued apartments" and "public housing," the author erases the human element, deciding to talk about buildings as actors and problems instead. In fact, in this article, people do not enter the spatial narrative until the "caravan" of new (presumably white) people arrives. The writing gives a negative connotation to the sewage treatment plant and other industries but references the businesses, not the people operating them. In the early 2000s, Blandtown was depopulated but still an inhabited neighborhood. A depopulated area isn't the same as an empty one.[79] Yet the depiction of Blandtown in this article describes it as an urban wilderness. Like the wilderness narratives that the original European settlers used to displace Native Americans, these urban-wilderness descriptions legitimate development and displacement. They are like frontier narratives, which characterize a space as "empty" and waiting for inhabitants, justifying development and displacement.[80]

In the above caricature of the neighborhood, buildings where the poor live (noted as apartments and public housing) are used to represent human life. Coded language like "drug-plagued apartments" and "public housing" stand in for "African Americans" and the "poor." In this way, the author diagrams the area as needing "rehabilitation not only of the physical space but also of symbolic codes of blackness."[81] McCosh reinstates white supremacy, suggesting that before the new arrivals, not only was the neighborhood undesirable, but the people were too.

Personifying buildings and industries is a practice that takes place in other public narrations of the space. For instance, as of 2023, the Atlanta Convention and Visitors Bureau did not mention Blandtown, instead articulating the neighborhood name colloquially as West Midtown and discussing the space in terms of a change just in building use rather than a change of people. Inviting visitors to the area, the text reads,

> Atlanta's West Midtown is reinventing itself. Once largely industrial, this area of town is now home to a lively selection of urban lofts, art galleries, live music venues, retail shops, restaurants and modern office space. Spanning from the southern tip of Howell Mill Road to 17th Street—and located minutes from downtown, Buckhead and all of Atlanta's major highways and interstates—much of West Midtown retains its loft-style industrial identity as most of the new developments in the area have restored the once-neglected factories and warehouses that date back to the 1880s.[82]

In this articulation, human actors are entirely removed, and the place holds all the agency. The "new developments" take on the animate action of "restoring" the "neglected factories and warehouses." Giving the building the agency reflects a neoliberal framing that thinks and speaks in terms of economic factors. Images of lofts and art galleries reflect a higher income. The writer does take note that the factories and warehouses were "once neglected" and draws the neglect back to the 1880s, implying that before the present moment, the space was uncared for, erasing the perception that it was ever home to anyone else. Similar to Brandi Thompson Summer's analysis of DC's H Street Corridor as a place "reimagined to attract individuals with cosmopolitan tastes who value diversity,"[83] I bring to the forefront the language choices made here to alter the neighborhood's narrative from a space of urban blight to something attractive to an affluent populace.

Other descriptions of the space erase Blandtown's past by starting the past at the turn of the century, absenting everything that came before. This strategy was notably used in the BeltLine master plan for the area, which articulates the planned build-out of trails, parks, and public transportation. Pronouncing the future of this region under the BeltLine-development plan, ABI writes, "The character of the Huff Road area has dramatically changed in the past ten years. What was historically a small railroad community (Blandtown) surrounded by rail lines and industrial development, is now a growing mixed-use neighborhood."[84] In this short description of the area, which is supposed to be used as the anchoring point for future design ideas, the plan writers focus only on the "past ten years," as though history starts there. The "small railroad community" is not described here, and the critical elements of Blandtown's historical past as one of the first Black neighborhoods in the city are lost. This inhibits planners and readers from connecting the future BeltLine trail to Blandtown's past.

All these actions of symbolic erasure require us to remember that history is written memory. Those who write history write memory and have the power to decimate memory for future generations. The final ploy in the decimation of Black Blandtown's memory has been the deliberate strategy to rename the area West Midtown, which has been successful based on the fact that it is the name most Atlantans know it by. Even I called it West Midtown when I first researched the Goat Farm. Based on interviews, the colloquial use of the term "west" as a descriptor for the area roughly began in the 1990s. It was also referred to as the "industrial corridor" or "industrial enclaves." Distinguishing the area as Midtown separates it rhetorically from the nonwhite majority in downtown and southwestern Atlanta. It also segments the site from the older, wealthier neighborhoods of northern Atlanta, or Buckhead, positioning West Midtown for a certain kind of gentrifier with economic-growth potential, such as working professionals and young, college-educated families. The dominant narrative, reinstated by the name West Midtown, sets the "long ago" era of drug-infested, dilapidated homes in contrast to the new luxury standard, intentionally using the past to define the present as progressive and superior.

In interviews, some current residents involved in the neighborhood association use semblances of the metaphor of whitewashing to describe the meaning attached to West Midtown. To whitewash something is to cover it up, and in the case of Blandtown, the metaphor specifically references the cultural whitening of the neighborhood by changing the name. One current resident that wished to remain anonymous expresses angst over some businesses seeking to rebrand the area as West Midtown or West Buckhead. Some companies supported hanging up signs with those names. Speaking of West Midtown, the interviewee says, "I think it has to do with them wanting to erase the history of the name and create the new whiter version of the neighborhood." He continues, "West Midtown is a way of further erasing the history."[85]

Wright, former president of Blandtown Neighborhood Association, attests that reclaiming history is a way to keep from "whitewashing it." When asked about the name West Town, which one of the largest developers in the area used for his residential subdivision, she states, "Honestly, it pisses me off every single time." She continues, "West Town seemed so contrived. And so unnatural and so clearly a marketing device that had no connection to the community at all."[86] The name new developers and business owners seek to use is considered a form of "branding" or "marketing," concludes these residents, gentrifiers of Blandtown themselves. Reflecting on the naming device in this way raises a key point about place-naming as strategic and whitewashing as a rhetorical device for claiming the space for the dominant culture.

Former residents of Black Blandtown have a slightly different take on the name West Midtown, reflecting their concern for the loss of memory and history. One displaced resident who was born and raised in Blandtown in the mid-twentieth century responds at length about how the new name affected him, saying, in part,

> So now people want to do away with that whole existence of what was and replace it with what is now, and that's what you call "renovation." And you know, sometimes, you just can't renovate things. Sometimes, you can only desecrate, and so that's what Blandtown is to me now. It's a desecration of memories that, in my mind, were so important to my life until the only way that I can go out there now and be comfortable is to start in my mind flicking pictures—snapshots. I got my camera on automatic, and I'm not taking pictures; I'm putting pictures in place of what's there now.[87]

After his family moved from Blandtown in the 1970s and he came home from the Vietnam War, he longed to return to the place he remembered as home.

He visits the neighborhood now and sees what city planners and developers call "renovation." But to "renovate" is to repair, restore, or refurbish. The term "renovate" is most accurately used when we fix or clean up things that have been damaged by age. But he describes a fundamental struggle with the use of "renovation" in the case of Blandtown and other areas experiencing redevelopment. He argues this is not "renovation" but "desecration" because no elements of the past remain after they are done.[88] The name West Midtown reflects this desecration because it removes the last relic of Blandtown's past—its name.

Take for another example a previous resident of Black Blandtown who, when asked what West Midtown means, stated matter-of-factly, "It means that they left something out." Expressing the importance of connecting to history, he says,

> Whoever Felix Bland was or whatever, people ask questions. Somebody oughta be able to tell them. You know, it's like when we dealt with schools. First lesson you're gonna have regardless of subject is who your school is named after and why was it important. Why was he important enough for them to build a school in his memory, honor, or whatever you want to call it? So when you say "I'm a proud graduate of Booker T. Washington, Henry MacNeil Turner, David T. Howard," who is this man? "George Washington Carver." But see, the average Black kid didn't know anything about Black leaders but Booker T. Washington and George Washington Carver. So after those two, they say, "Who is David T. Howard?" over there on the east side in Fourth Ward. I say, "You don't know?" Well, that way, when you speak up, you can look 'em in the eye and tell 'em who David T. Howard was—the impact he had on Atlanta. Just like you talk about Martin Luther King. You can say it with pride and conviction. That made you feel good, and it makes you feel more confident when you know why you're doing what you're doing.[89]

Using key examples of how names are used on school buildings, he gives the impression that by leaving out the name Blandtown, people who visit it miss out on the pride and confidence that come with being connected to history. He also distinguishes how names function rhetorically to commemorate the past by providing the impetus for passersby to ask questions. This way, the name metaphorically "speaks" and continues to "live." But the name West Midtown erases all of that. Attempts to remove the bindings of name, place, and people are a part of "systemic efforts to exploit the powerful linkages between language and culture."[90] As Sara Safransky attests of early colonization efforts, changing a name is about "taking possession and creating a new world in which the colonizer belonged."[91] Similarly, West Midtown dispossesses Black language and culture from connection to the place to reinforce white space. I must emphasize that this isn't new. Throughout the world, Black "customs and the agencies to which they refer, were abolished because they were in contradiction with a new civilization that imposed its own."[92]

BLANDTOWN'S BLUES IS AN AMERICAN HAUNTING

West Midtown, its design, and the public narratives used to describe it reflect the mythic American identity of a homogenously white society. The popular descriptions of the area are historically neutral, providing little to grasp about the past that would support the preservation of the name Blandtown or the culture and Black agency that comes with it. In a city known for its middle-class Black demography and culture, such narration neutralizes racial tension by resolving white guilt or Black distrust with stories of white saviorhood. It thereby allows the assumption that current changes will benefit the diverse populace and support neoliberal development. But similar to Summers declaration that "race is always already present despite efforts to produce race-neutral policy and results,"[93] I attest that our racial history—managed by the first, second, and third streams of thought explicated by Du Bois—is always present despite efforts to erase and displace it. Though that presence may be a ghost, phantom, or shadow, it brings us closer to a moral reckoning when it's made visible.

Earlier in the chapter, I elucidated Du Bois's claims of three streams of thought in the modern age. I argued that the first and second streams were most assertive in our shared spaces, lending to the use of force and domination against people of color for want of culture-land. I also described that the first stream of thinking includes an afterthought: though the wish for culture-land can be granted by force, it can also be established through human unity and cooperative use of limited land and resources. In addition, I introduced the third stream of thought, the drive of African Americans toward "Liberty, Freedom, and Opportunity."[94] Furthering our understanding of this drive, the liberty, freedom, and opportunity being sought by Black people do not constitute an acknowledgment "that the black man is equal to the white man," but rather, as Fanon reiterates, "what we are striving for is to liberate the black man from the arsenal of complexes that germinated in a colonial situation" or, correspondingly, the situation of slavery.[95] It is to make African Americans human, saved from the dehumanizing experience of bondage. Humanity "is a 'yes' resonating from cosmic harmonies"; humanity is "what brings society into being."[96] The rumored story of Blandtown and dominant recollections of the Black neighborhood rhetorize the first and second streams of thought, justifying the exclusion of Black culture from the space. But what if thoughts of cooperation and Black people's agentive drive toward their own humanization were prominent in the place? What do we stand to gain by maintaining Black culture? This final section is aimed at these questions.

Until recently, Blandtown's Black history has been traced as a mere phenomenon, like a natural disaster or disturbance that occurred in the environment before developers rediscovered it and made it habitable. It's as though when Rene Descartes extolled "I think, therefore I am" in all human thinking, he lost the ability to feel concrete reality, making much of the world invisible. What was Blandtown has become, for the new gentrified suburb, a defining other, a shadow employed to demonstrate American progress. This progress is defined by domination over the land and the inferiority of Black people. As long as Black lifeworlds remain invisible, this form of development will continue unchecked. Yet I view American society as something becoming rather than something settled. And as Fanon attests, "It's no longer a question of knowing the world, but of transforming it."[97] Toward those ends, unlike Descartes, I'm encouraged by Audre Lorde and Ralph Ellison to think and feel, combining the theoretical and the poetic to uncover the ghosts and realities of America for that moral reckoning. A theory is a system of hunches about the way things work. Poetry is the act of revealing and distilling experiences. Brought together, we can apply emotional insight to the principles of community. I've found that while the name West Midtown encourages white domination, incorporating Blandtown's Black history enables us to witness the realities of our society and retain an alternative placemaking strategy through the blues. I'll explain.

Despite actions to change it, Blandtown is still the official name. And as long as that's so, the Bland family ghost will haunt us, showing up where they are no longer wanted and requiring us to "do something." Those gentrifiers who recognize the name of West Midtown as whitewashing reflect the power of Blandtown not just as a place-name but also as an epitaph over the graves of the past neighborhood, calling out to passersby and new residents. Epitaphs address visitors to a graveyard, becoming the deceased's voice and warning the living of their mortality. In the same way, as the last remaining relic of the body, the name Blandtown warns of the mortality of our homes, emphasizing, from the grave, that there was "something-undone."[98] In its best efforts, the name brings the desire to the visitor and the gentrifier to "make something meaningful of them in the present."[99] It is a countergrammar that breaks away from white possession, illuminating the presence of the displaced others.

And through this, we learn the power of a haunting to, if not change the past, call it forward amid cultural gentrification. When a haunting occurs, it opens blind eyes. It forces the haunted to look at themselves in the mirror as if wondering if they've just seen an aberration or gone mad. They look back at the conditions of their current state, the place they are in, and search around feverishly for the vestige of the living soul or the circumstances that made the ghost appear. What they will find, if their eyes are fully open, is the realities of the space. In the case of cultural gentrification, an interceding haunting will bring us closer to envisioning the presence of diverse narrative trajectories in our spaces. And so this is what has occurred in Blandtown. Maybe because of its unique name, likened to that which is regular, dull, or boring, the neighborhood seems to capture attention. Some of Blandtown's gentrifiers are actively working to reclaim the name of Blandtown, repeating a story of Blandtown's blues to visitors and passing their guilt onto the conscience of America.

The blues genre, according to Ellison, is the vernacular of Black communities that brings together the terrible and the marvelous, the tragic and the comic, in a form that not only allows Black people to narrate their own experiences but also rebuilds spaces where Blackness can live and influence members of the dominant group toward a different way of living. This is how it works: in a tragedy, the scapegoats are villains that must be destroyed; in a comedy, the fool is meant to be forgiven not in a funny way but by revealing the incongruity between human ideals and behavior; however, the blues is a Black form of symbolic action through a story that "represents the past, the present and future" as both "near-tragic" and "near-comic."[100] In the blues, both pain and pleasure are experienced together. In the end, the storyteller blames themselves for painful experiences but not in the sense of self-extinction as in mortification. Instead, the storyteller places a mirror on themself to force a self-evaluation of their experiences, to wake up and see their conditions, and to throw the findings of their evaluation "unashamedly into the guilty conscience of America."[101] Plainly, the blues work doubly for Black people to (1) see the world for what it is and develop counterspaces to live in their full humanity and (2) indict the social and environmental inequities of racism in America. This is evident in songs like Bessie Smith's "Poor Man's Blues" (1928), in which she implores "Mister Rich Man," representative of the dominant powers in the United States, to open up his heart to the "poor man" because the poor man has fought in the war on behalf of America. She repeats, "All man fought all the battles / All man would fight again today / He would do anything you ask him in the name of the U.S.A." She urges the Rich Man to see the irony of living as poor veterans, having given your life for the existence of a country that does not provide equal opportunities to all its veterans. She continues, "Now the war is over, all man [*sic*] must live the same as you / If it wasn't for the poor man, Mister Rich Man, what would you do?"[102] This final question in the song requires the Rich Man to reflect on the ways they have benefitted from the poor man's sacrifice. By doing so, the Rich Man would have to formally accuse himself of contributing to the inequality.

Clyde Woods argues that the blues as an epistemology tap the perspective of working-class Black communities, offering an alternative to white possessive forms of spatial development. Woods notes that new options for producing American spaces are conceived out of the blues because it "is an encyclopedia of the multiple forms of traps experienced by African Americans . . . and of how they challenged these practices." In this way, the blues can be a community asset, a discourse of power that drives movement building and Black placemaking. The truth of Blandtown provides one more blues story to America's conscience as Blandtown is representative of a blues bloc,[103] a working-class African American community whose worldview provided a sense of collective self for residents and cultural formation opposing racist characterizations that dehumanize Black people.

By the 1980s, much of Blandtown's humble Black neighborhood and its families had moved, and many headed to southwestern Atlanta, where they could invest in better residential properties for the future of their families. Then, in 2003, artist Gregor Turk spotted a run-down, concrete, masonry-unit home in Blandtown that he thought would be a good space for his art studio. The house had been built by hand by Johnny Lee Green in 1943 for his wife and children. After the zoning change of Blandtown to heavy industrial, Green, along with other neighbors, was looking to move out. They sold their property to Wallace Bibbs. Bibbs, a Black Blandtown native, grew up there before its demise and purchased several homes from Black residents seeking to move quickly and cheaply after the zone change. When Turk showed up, Bibbs had been renting out the property but hadn't visited it for nearly ten years. When Turk moved his studio in, his neighbors approximately included only two home-owning residents. The rest of the neglected properties were home to renters, squatters, and drug dealers. Between 2003 and 2014, Turk watched the neighborhood change, and already interested in city mapping and places, he'd done some research of his own, finding the now-debunked narrative of Blandtown's origins. Like myself, Turk, too, became intrigued by Blandtown's past. Visits from the original builder of his art studio, Johnny Lee Green, and Green's son would inevitably add to his understanding that Blandtown was once a significant home to someone else.

New developer Brock Built Homes razed the neglected properties, replacing them with three-story single-family homes in the small development he named West Town. Thinking Turk's concrete studio was the sales office for the new development, prospective buyers knocked on his door asking about West Town. Turk, exacerbated, responded that this was not West Town: "it's Blandtown." These frustrating references to the area led him to post the "Welcome to the heart of Blandtown" billboard (discussed earlier in this chapter) outside his studio. Turk's symbolic actions and those of other neighborhood members have led to a continued struggle to reclaim the name Blandtown in popular vernacular. While West Midtown signs dominate the space, at the time of this writing, more Blandtown ones are being erected, disrupting the fraudulent identity. The first sign was Turk's billboard marking the "heart of Blandtown" on English Street. The city dedicated a second Blandtown marker at the intersection of Elsworth Industrial Boulevard and Chattahoochee Avenue in 2019 after a five-year struggle by the neighborhood association to get city grant funding and fundraiser support to purchase it.[104] As this research about Blandtown has gained more publicity, some developers in the area have begun erecting their own Blandtown signs and supporting naming new streets in the area after former Black residents.

As Turk has learned the corrected history of the area's origins, he sings the Blandtown blues back to any visitor, passerby, or new resident who is interested. He hosts an annual history tour, for which he used to invite Johnny Lee, who passed away as this research proceeded. Turk has also created an art exhibition that attempts to transcend the painful loss of Blandtown by reclaiming it in the present. In explaining to me why the area was significant, he says,

> To me, it crystallizes a lot about how racial property issues and neighborhood issues manifest themselves and how what may appear to be organic is not necessarily organic. . . . Every neighborhood is different, and every story is different, but this one, this one's unique, but it's still the same story. . . . The unfortunate same story of how poor communities are pushed around despite how strong that community is.

And while explaining the near-tragic change, Turk continues with the near-comic: "I also got a real appreciation for the tenacity of residents here that, no matter how unpleasant the environment was, . . . despite all that, you had a very developed neighborhood." Blandtown, he says, "is a personal story, rather than an abstract story of racial relations. And even non-racial. Home is important to everybody. And when a home is forcibly removed or removed through economic pressure through zoning . . . that has an impact."[105]

We find in Turk's words the effects of a successful haunting. When the ghosts have had their way of it, they expose the cracks in the system, and the blues are recited back to transcend the pain and make the immoral clear. With his ghosts, Turk has chosen spatial-evaluation. And this criticism caused him to look back at the geography. He took a full stare at the place and its racial conditions. His art and his words were thrown back into America's conscience.

In an interview, an anonymous former resident also narrates Blandtown's blues. He was born to Blandtown. His father built a Blandtown home brick by brick for his mother and four other siblings, taking each of the concrete cinders from the rail yard where he worked. The former resident, a Vietnam War veteran, had been spending time reflecting on his past to understand the person he became overseas. In that reflection, he went back to Blandtown in his mind, seeking the memory of his old self, what he considers to be a better self. He says, "and so memory is what keeps me in touch with that person and keeps me in touch with the place that person was brought up in. If it wasn't for that place and it wasn't for that person that I have such a dire need to still have communication and a sense of being with, I don't think I'd be here now." By turning a mirror on himself, the former resident tells us Blandtown's blues, which are easily understood through the many tragicomic events that encompassed his time in Blandtown. His father, focused on providing, was not there to father. Seven people lived in a cramped small home. His sister fell and hurt herself while riding her bike downhill. The smell of slaughtered animals from the local slaughterhouse filled the air. A local juke joint kept the temptation for drugs and alcohol nearby. He saw a boy shot in the street, "laying there with his stomach blowed out" because of a fight over a girl. As he discusses the unpleasant features of his life in Blandtown, he also evokes a longing for that past, bringing us to the near-comic semblancy of these events. If he had the chance, he would go back to Blandtown—not what it is now, but what it was then: his mom giving the love of both a mother and father; when his sister fell, him there picking her up; his father building the small house that brought them closer; his grandad teaching people how to handle hogs and raise them; living in the neighborhood with his three aunts, three uncles, his grandmother, and grandfather nearby, so rather than hitting the juke joint, he could work at the WERD radio-station-broadcasting tower in the neighborhood with his uncles. During this tragicomic reflection on the simpler life of Blandtown, the interviewee identifies something about himself and America, saying that today, people want to possess more and more, and "the more you possess, the less of yourself you possess. Your possessions possess you. So, you are less of who you are."[106]

This interview says something about the psychological state of ghosts. The former narratives about Blandtown would characterize my interviewee as a walking Negative. Such portrayals follow the racial ideology of whiteness as self-consciousness and Blackness as negation. But Fanon argues that "man" is not only defined by "the potential for self-consciousness or negation." Consciousness relates to a spiritual, nonphysical realm, and that realm is "obsessed with the issue of love and understanding."[107] In that realm, we expound feelings. My interviewee expounded on love and understanding—a human consciousness he experienced in Blandtown. During his time there, it was a Black space where he was permitted. In this neighborhood, he and his family built a society. He was human. They maintained their local culture. In Blandtown, he indulged the third stream of thought: "Liberty, Freedom, and Opportunity." Yet once Blandtown underwent cultural gentrification, the interviewee was lunged from one dimension with his fellow Black people to the other with whites. According to Fanon, his culture is made inferior in the white dimension, and for survival, he would endeavor to possess the dominant language, letting go of his own. As the interviewee put it, "your possessions possess you." He may not have consciously been describing the want for the dominant culture or language. Still, when combined with Fanon's psychological explanation of Black men, it can be critically understood that, one way or another, when the interviewee left the Black dimension of Blandtown, he was made to assume a new posture that transposed him from human to invisible man. Stating ghosts are created by experiences of inferiority is an understatement. The feeling of being nonexistent creates the ghost.[108] Black humanization—liberty, freedom, and opportunity—requires their culture, self-determined civilization, and historical past. The interviewee confers that America, too, is losing itself in its possessions. I argue that America is losing self-consciousness. By making Blandtown and the interviewee invisible, America loses the mirror necessary for moral reckoning. The observance and recovery of the culture attached to the name force us to reconcile the romanticized identity of Blandtown with reality.

By hearing Blandtown's blues and excavating the many stories of neighborhoods like it, we can witness history and America's near-wretched, near-splendid identity. I use this example of the effect Blandtown has had on Turk as a gentrifier and my anonymous interviewee as a former resident to reveal two things: (1) how this narrative works to self-defend Black life and (2) the moral necessity for repair. This is what we stand to gain by maintaining Black culture. Blandtown is just a small representative sample of the role of the cultural assets of the Black Mecca in Atlanta for the survival of Black lifeworlds. In this chapter, the ghosts have revealed Black agency in placemaking and the structural inequities affecting Black placemaking through cultural gentrification. In the next chapter, we'll move to Black placemaking during the civil rights movement and the moral reckoning instilled from the blues in freedom songs. In the end, we learn that though white hegemony desires domination of culture-lands, there are counteracting values to white supremacy—"values that can be served only with my [Black people's] sauce."[109]

CHAPTER 3

"THE WHITE PEOPLE CAME, AND CHANGED EVERYTHING," OR A BATTLE FOR A NATION'S SOUL

Death and trauma. As a youth in Florida learning about the civil rights movement, I remembered the images of the four Black girls murdered when white-supremacist terrorists bombed the Sixteenth Street Baptist Church in Birmingham. I recalled the students' impressions at the Greensboro lunch counter sit-in. I memorized pictures of Rosa Parks and groups of Black people walking to work during the Montgomery bus boycott. I could even recollect John Lewis being beaten by state troopers during the march from Selma. But I remembered very little attention given to Atlanta's freedom struggle in the civil rights movement. Because of this, when I first saw images of the KKK and police brutality against direct-action civil rights protestors in Atlanta, I was surprised by how much I didn't know about what had happened in spaces I've walked or driven on many occasions. And it was something about those images published in Karcheik Sims-Alvarado's book *Atlanta and the Civil Rights Movement: 1944–1968* that stopped me in my tracks. For a moment, I breathed in the anger that must've precluded many of Atlanta's activists and Freedom Riders as they drove through the South.

Some sixty-eight years later, why did these images still bring about such emotion in me? It was because seeing seven hundred members of the Ku Klux Klan assembled at Stone Mountain, initiating new supporters beneath a towering burning cross, made me mortified that Christianity was being manipulated for a white supremacy, which Jesus didn't sign up for. Because the Klansmen in that menacing image of Grand Dragon Samuel Green flanked by three children being initiated recapped why this white-supremacist curse continues decades later. Because a picture of hooded men and women walking into a Baptist church in Inman Park pressed me to consider the public spaces I traverse today that are being used for the private deliberation of those who want people who look like me dead. Because the scene of a young Black woman being drug by officers across cement to arrest her during a protest against the KKK resembled the scenes of Black Lives Matter protestors bullied during peaceful assembly too much. Because the photo of the open-casket procession of two Black couples ravaged by sixty bullets from a mob of masked men led me to empathize with those who had been traumatized by seeing their partners die. I was angry because those images exhibiting anti-Black terrorism provoked, again, the need to protect my body and my country. And so my anger, my rage, turned me to passion.

Yet it was not just the photos of death and trauma that enlivened my emotions. If those images previously described provided fuel for my passion, it would be the pictures of others fervently causing "good trouble" that charged the engine on my purpose. An image of six clergymen defying Atlanta's public-transit regulation by riding in the whites-only section made me imagine what would come of my own pastors staging a demonstration and calling the church in. When I saw a picture of four of those ministers in a jail cell, I wondered what they may have talked about inside the cage. A view of seven parents who'd filed a lawsuit against Atlanta Public School District's racial segregation made me remember my mother pleading with principals at "predominantly white upper-ability" schools to admit her "smart children" into their magnet programs in the 1990s.[1] Then, seeing AUC students sit in at a white-only lunch counter pressured me to consider if I'd ever have the courage to do the same. But when I saw 2,500 African Americans rally and assemble at Hurt Park—a park I walked by weekly as a grad student—in downtown Atlanta, I knew that courage was possible. And I must admit, I can get all caught up in the candid photo of Coretta Scott King kissing MLK when he returned to Atlanta after the 381-day bus boycott in Montgomery. I had all the Diana Ross and Billy Dee Williams "feels" of *Mahogany*. They showed me that courage isn't an individual effort but a collective pursuit of American freedom and purpose. As a Black woman reviewing the narrative these photos had to share, I felt that they were speaking both of me and to me, giving me lessons of the past and a means to survive. Sims-Alvarado's artful compilation of these images into a book was done in a fashion akin to the blues genre of Black cultural expression. The blues genre is a form of communication between Black people. It is a narrative structure of the ghosts.

Author Richard Wright first identified this mode of vernacular recourse; Ralph Ellison and Clyde Woods later expanded it, as introduced in the previous chapter. Wright describes the blues genre as follows:

> It was however, in a folklore molded out of rigorous and inhuman conditions of life that the Negro achieved his most indigenous and complete expression. Blues, spirituals, and folk tales recounted from mouth to mouth; the whispered words of a black mother to her black daughter on the ways of men, to confidential wisdom of a black father to his black son; the swapping of sex experiences on street corners from boy to boy in the deepest vernacular; work songs sung under blazing suns—all these formed the channels through which the racial wisdom flowed.[2]

This expression is a "fixed and nourishing form of culture . . . which embodies the memories and hopes of" African Americans' fight for liberty. It emerged from a shared feeling of a "common life and a common fate." And when expressed, it has the power to form a "new culture" inside the confines of the dreaded racial structure. Wright argues that this mode of speech is significant to Black survival because when Black people start to "realize a meaning in their suffering," the civilization that causes the pain is "doomed."[3] He doesn't mean "doomed" to confer that Black people will attempt to rule the world. On the contrary, the ideology espoused by the blues exists for "self-possession and in the consciousness of the interdependence of people in modern society."[4] Its purpose is to abolish racial privilege and support all oppressed people, regardless of race.[5]

In summary, I argue that the blues genre is best translated as a way of knowing that has the potential to serve up an extra "sauce" to the American consciousness, an "insurance for humanity" to keep the nation from losing its "human sustenance."[6] The images in Sims-Alvarado's book represent the attack on Black corporeality (Black being) and Black counterresponse. It reflects the structural deficits imposed on Black lives and Black people's belief that freedom and liberty are possible. In her book, Sims-Alvarado recognizes the ghosts and puts the world they conjured back together. The construction dives right into the heart of the American consciousness.

If the blues genre is a form of Black cultural expression that could bring forth a moral reckoning to America, then cultural gentrification demises both the word "blues" and the reckoning. Cultural gentrification oppresses, in one case, by romanticizing public history and memory such that the blues becomes an inaudible symbol. This was the case when Art on the Atlanta BeltLine contracted a public photo display of images from the civil rights movement along the BeltLine's Eastside and Westside Trails in 2018 and 2019. At first light, public memorials to civil rights may be interpreted as helpful forms of diversification and inclusion, but criticism of these displays within the context of the space and realized history reveals their use to romanticize trauma and attract a new class of investors and residents to "Black spaces." In this chapter, I explore the rhetorical style of the blues and the dominant practice of romanticizing America's traumatic past. I interrogate the cultural gentrification of the blues narrative construction of Atlanta's civil rights movement in public art along the Atlanta BeltLine. The purpose is to both understand the covert ways the blues are lost to attempts to attract white audiences in spaces undergoing urban redevelopment and explore opportunities to redesign our spaces using the moral knowledge supplied by the ghosts' blues song. Ultimately, my goal is to "fight for an oppressed past" and "to make this past come alive as the lever for the work of the present: obliterating the sources and conditions that link the violence of what seems finished with the present, ending this history and setting in place a different future."[7]

ROMANTIC LYRICS OVER A BLUES BEAT

Sims-Alvarado presents Atlanta as the epicenter of the civil rights movement through images collected from the Associated Press and various libraries, universities, and museum archives. Her efforts of "following the scrambled trail the ghost[s]" left behind set down the movement's history from 1944 to 1968 in pictures and captions over ten chapters organized thematically and chronologically.[8] In its entirety, the pictorial narrative is specifically successful at witnessing the scale of activism in Atlanta and the scope of white resistance to social change through the rhetorical style of blues amplification.

Though I've given examples of a few of these captivating images, there is another that I have to attend to. In a photo from the 1960s, two KKK members can be seen walking in downtown Atlanta. They are followed by two young Black men carrying posters that read, "Expose Atlanta's false image" and "Atlanta's image is a fraud."[9] Sims-Alvarado's caption clarifies that members of the KKK often protested in the same public areas as the civil rights activists. Presumably, these young activists were protesting the false public branding of an integrated Atlanta. Yet the photographers framing the peaceful protestors walking toe to heel behind the Klansmen creates an additional message: Atlanta wears a moral mask of racial unification over a white-supremacist face. It also recalls a rhetoric-inspired refrain Ellison expressed: America wears a comic mask over a tragic face, or what I will describe here as "romantic lyrics" over a "blues beat."

While the blues can be a sign from a ghost that something was left unfinished, American romanticism is narrative construction for the white hegemony that clangs over the blues. Romance, according to Morrison, has been the "battle plain on which" Americans "fight, engage, and imagine their demons."[10] Morrison argues against the popular suggestion that romance is a way to evade history. Instead, she attests the opposite. Romance is "the head-on encounter with very real, pressing historical forces and the contradictions inherent in them."[11] Using creativity and imagination, white Americans conquered their fears and deep insecurities by playing with Black lives, justifying their actions by transferring their internal contradictions onto Black bodies. They weren't running away from their history but making their actions ok. She writes, "[White] Americans' fear of being outcast, of failing, of powerlessness; their fear of boundarylessness, of Nature unbridled and crouched for attack; their fear of the absence of so-called civilization; their fear of loneliness, of aggression both external and internal. In short, the terror of human freedom—the thing they coveted most of all" could be articulated through Blackness.[12] During the period of legal enslavement of Black bodies, freedom could be defined as not being a slave. White freedom could be amassed by the subjugation of people of color. And their actions could be justified by rationalizing their treatment of Black people. The "black population is forced to serve as freedom's polar opposite."[13]

Ellison illustrates this point finely in his assessment of American minstrelsy and the use of black masks (regardless of the performer's race) to stylize and modify Blackness so that a white audience could enjoy it. The black mask's role in society was to "veil the humanity of Negroes thus reduced to a sign, and to repress the white audience's awareness of its moral identification with its own acts."[14] While Black people were humiliated by this, white people made a profit and repressed the contradictions between their stated values and their actions. American folklore and entertainment reduced the Negro to a Negative, often worn as a mask over the face of white entertainers. Imagine that: a white man with a black face. The entertainer in the mask would dance, speak, move, and jive in a way that stereotyped Black folks as lazy buffoons. Through this ritual mask of blackface, white people conveyed their dehumanized version of Blackness as a function to moralize their own activities. This stylized image of Black life became a symbol of white American exceptionalism. As Ellison puts it, "down at the deep dark bottom of the melting pot . . . the immoral becomes moral and the moral is anything that makes you feel good (or that one has the power to sustain), the white man's relish is apt to be the black man's gall."[15]

Black people are made to be carriers of the sins of the European slave trade, enslavement, and the resulting structural deficits. Like the scapegoat, the animal used as the symbolic carrier of the sins of a people in Jewish tradition, African Americans have been made to carry the burdens of the sins that formed America. As Fanon reiterates, the white man and the fully assimilated Black man "impulsively chooses" the Black man "to shoulder the burden of original sin." He continues, "the black man is, in every sense of the word, a victim of white civilization."[16] It's not a romantic story at all but rather a tragedy. "Tragedy" directly translates to "goat song" in Greek. In this way, the blues represents "the song of the Goat," and the goats or sacrificial victims of white civilization are Black people. As Fanon puts it, "collective guilt is borne by what is commonly called the scapegoat. However, the scapegoat for white society, which is based on the myths of progress, civilization, liberalism, education, enlightenment, and refinement, will be precisely the force that opposes the expansion and the triumph of these myths. This oppositional brute force is provided by the black man."[17] The romantic lyrics of the dominant American ideology provide a catharsis, averting guilt from the prevailing white hegemony onto the unassuming backs of Black bodies. The romantic lyrics, like the ritual masks in minstrelsy, dehumanize Black people and turn us into phantoms, substantiating the "audience's belief in the 'blackness' of things black" and relieving the audience, "with dreamlike efficiency, of its guilt."[18]

Metro Atlanta is significant because it is home to the largest monument to romanticizing America's relationship with race: Stone Mountain. Stone Mountain, the most intimidating of southern spaces, is a chunk of granite towering 825 feet above ground level and reaching more than five miles in circumference from the base. In November 1915, the KKK gathered there, just eighteen miles from the city center. The day is noted as their symbolic resurgence after federal involvement had caused the group to go dormant during Reconstruction.[19] To reestablish the white-supremacist legacy, the United Daughters of the Confederacy, led by Caroline Helen Jemison Plane, envisioned and garnered federal support and later state funding for the carving of General Robert E. Lee, President Jefferson Davis, and General Stonewall Jackson into the mountain's face.[20] The construction project proceeded intermittently from 1915 to 1972. It made Stone Mountain an ominous Confederate symbol that rhetorically declares white male authority over the southern region. But even more, as a fortified stronghold, Stone Mountain is a reminder of a lost war. Backed by the Lost Cause myth, it maintains a display that romanticizes the Old South and Confederacy as morally righteous. As part of its effort to refute the notion that the Civil War was a war of Southern rebellion, the Lost Cause explanation painted the South as a victim of Northern aggression.[21] By claiming that states' rights, not slavery, caused the Civil War, that the enslaved "liked their status" and were loyal to their master's and the Confederate cause, that African Americans were unprepared for the responsibilities of being freemen, and that Confederate soldiers were "remarkable and saintly creatures, supermen," the myth specifically devalues and discredits Black lives. Black people were dehumanized and demoralized to vindicate the South.[22]

In the foundational fears that incited Lost Cause propaganda, you see the "interdependence of slavery and freedom."[23] White freedom had been defined and understood by its opposite. When slavery was abolished, the Confederates required a renarration of history that would justify the continued subordination of Black bodies. The US Congress's Joint Committee on Reconstruction reported in 1866 that "the Negro is the Mordecai" of the South, a reminder of "their defeat, and of what they call a 'just, but lost cause.'"[24] The lost war brought to reality Southern fears of powerlessness and loss of control. Consequently, the United Confederate Veteran's Association established a six-plank plan for revising the history of the war and Reconstruction. And in that plan, Black people were required as an apparitional presence that was passive, powerless, nameless, nationless, and silenced. In an act of metaphysical condensation, Black identities were collapsed into an illusion of the faithful slave. As Du Bois put it, Southern historians and Northern sympathizers "misinterpreted, distorted, even deliberately ignored any fact that challenged or contradicted" the assumption that the "Negro was admittedly sub-human." Loyalty to the Lost Cause influenced "one of the most stupendous efforts the world ever saw to discredit human beings."[25] This is an act of dehistoricizing—leaving inconvenient details out of the story. Since these historians tried to ignore Black people, we must wonder "why an element apparently so insignificant filled the whole Southern picture at the time."[26] The Black presence in romanticized American history was necessary then, and necessary still, to give meaning to white liberty and white freedom. The goal of the Lost Cause legend "was to hide the Southerners' tragic and self-destructive mistake."[27] And it worked. For those who identify with the Southern interpretation of the war, Stone Mountain is a place that reinvigorates passions to finish what Lee, Davis, and Jackson started. As a result, it acts materially to incite Klan activity and encourage racism.

So, in the mid-twentieth century, ignited to continue the mission of their past leaders, the Klansmen showed up again. After World War II, in 1945, Klansmen lit a three-hundred-foot-wide cross at the top of the mountain. It's said that the cross could be seen sixty miles away, and an attendee announced the visual was necessary "to let the N----- know the war is over and that the

Klan is back."[28] They returned in 1948, commemorating new initiates. And they continued to show up at the civil rights protests countering civil rights activists. More recently, in 2015, white supremacists marched on the mountain again, shouting, "F--- civil rights, this is a Civil War mountain."[29] Then, amid 2020 Black Lives Matter protests, Stone Mountain Park shut down, as white-supremacist groups planned a demonstration there on August 15. Unable to get to their beloved mountain, they rallied in downtown Stone Mountain, facing off in a verbal and physical clash with counterprotesters.[30]

Despite the public face of an integrated Atlanta, the white-supremacist, segregationist ideology empowered by Stone Mountain persists. Throughout my primary, secondary, and undergraduate education, the legacy of the mountain never came across my reading lists. As of this writing, if you visit Stone Mountain Park, you may find that the horrors of the Klansmen's presence are meekly presented in a small inscription in an exhibit gallery at the Historical and Environment Education Center. In inscriptions that reference him, it is not mentioned that the original designer of the mountain's carving, Gutzon Borglum, was an active Klan member (he also designed Mount Rushmore).[31] The story of the carving's completion is disconnected from its history—that while the civil rights movement was occurring, the state of Georgia purchased the mountain and continued with the Confederate carving from 1958 to its completion. Prison labor was used to finish other areas of the park, which were planned to resemble Georgia plantation life before the Civil War.[32] Thus, while the KKK's connection to the mountain is barely a whisper in Stone Mountain exhibits, the symbols of the Confederates make the government-backed plan to maintain white supremacy apparent.

As a result, the racist ideology also continues. I criticize Stone Mountain and the narrative of the Lost Cause in this way to reveal some of the features of American romanticism in Atlanta. When we are not careful, we look at Stone Mountain and Confederate monuments erected before the civil rights movement as practices of the past that are dissolved because King showed the world their immorality. This is an act of foreclosure that is damaging to Black people and Black culture. There are disappearances still happening, and thousands of phantoms are still out there because of "terrible deeds that are systematically occurring and . . . simultaneously denied by every public organ of governance and communication."[33] In American theater, romantic lyrics clang over the low bass of a blues beat.

Romantic lyrics are a veil over the immoral. It turns a tragic incident of white power against Black life into a comedy by placing Black people on trial rather than their white abuser. For example, when George Zimmerman killed Trayvon Martin, an attempt to convict Zimmerman turned into a trial against the deceased Martin.[34] In the court proceedings and practice of public opinion, Zimmerman was narrated as a "fool" for taking the law into his own hands, and Martin was considered a villain for appearing as a thug in a white space. Fools can be forgiven, and villains are punished. In these actions to forgive Zimmerman, Martin loses his humanity and right to exist. As such, the romanticized narrative is a defense against wrongdoing. It represses "the white audience's awareness of its moral identification with its own acts."[35] The mask of modern white society covers up immorality at the expense of Black humanity.

The American myth is that she is the arbiter of moral good in the world, and any glimpse of "wrong" in the United States of America is corrected through our judicial system. Unfortunately, Americans know that they wear masks, but we stand daring someone to uncover our tragic faces. Because of our global economic and military dominance, no one dares, except for us revolutionaries, getting in "good trouble." In my own daring, I disclose how the moral mask maintains itself in our spatial narratives. It publicly rescues whites, creates symbolic closure of any wrongdoing, and leads to a repetition of oppressive action.

The process of forming a moral mask through our landscape is contemporarily illustrated in cultural gentrification. African Americans and diverse allies have attempted to disrupt American romanticism. Within the last one hundred years, the civil rights movement has led the charge globally to use nonviolence to expose violence against Black bodies and to use peaceful protest to reveal inequality. As the movement gained global attention, international distrust of an "unequal" America incited Cold War fears and Communist growth in yellow and brown nations. America was demasked and on the world stage, adding pressure on the United States to change its segregation and voting laws. Yet, as the young protestors addressed in their posters, a lot of "integration" was fraudulent, as evidenced by today's segregation. The movement's goals were left incomplete. The real story of the civil rights movement and its unfinished business is a wholly Black, Atlantan, and American story. But Black urban dislocation is a part of a larger strategy to culturally gentrify the narrative, closing problems that are left undone.

CULTURAL GENTRIFICATION OF THE CIVIL RIGHTS MOVEMENT

As historically Black neighborhoods are displaced, African Americans find themselves in a repetitive cycle of displacement and replacement, always on the move. The repetition should reveal that the same mistake, the same transgression, is reoccurring. When we see things are not changing as "postracial" critics would argue, we must consider that the immorality of the past is present and will continue if it is not reckoned with. The blues beat must drum louder than the romantic lyrics. But unfortunately, what I've found through critical rhetorical investigation of the efforts of urban revitalization in Atlanta is that some representations of history are maintaining American romanticism.

PUBLIC ART IN GENTRIFICATION

A common feature of neighborhoods undergoing urban redevelopment is the public art, monument, mural, performance, or heritage trail. These projects, on their face, are expected to recall the memory of the neighborhood history and the culture of residents who have been displaced. Their initial purpose is to mediate the tensions between "new and old residents by projecting narratives that frame once deviant neighborhoods as historically friendly to a moderately multicultural, upwardly mobile middle class and inscribing them into the landscape."[36] Yet, as Kwame Holmes tells us through his examination of the tour City within a City: Greater U Street Heritage Trail—developed through a gentrifying neighborhood in Washington, DC, in 2001—these forms of public art can more discreetly be used for respectability politics, renarrating the history of Black opposition to align it with the political values of gentrifiers and bring in investors.[37] It's necessary to break out from the rules of the dominant hegemony that are set up to homogenize or silence diverse voices. Yet, like other systems, the museum profession and cultural institutions are often backed by deeply conservative and marginalizing viewpoints that are hard to break from. As a result, some of these public-art projects may further romanticize tragic elements of the past.

In Atlanta, similar heritage projects have been erected. One such display was the *Images of America: Atlanta and the Civil Rights Movement* open-air history museum. This exhibit of images was sourced from Sims-Alvarado's book mentioned at the beginning of this segment. Originally sponsored by Art on the Atlanta BeltLine, from July 7, 2018, to March 1, 2019, the fifty images encompassed about four miles along the completed Eastside and Westside Trails of the BeltLine. And in light of the public nature of the project, Art on the Atlanta BeltLine (AoAB) advised that traumatic images be removed. Miranda Kyle, the program manager for AoAB, notes that in the public realm, there is no liminal space for a person "to confront difficult material," and violent and "potentially triggering" content was flagged. In addition, Kyle worked with Sims-Alvarado, asking "if there was important narrative elements of the photos that corresponded with certain neighborhoods that the BeltLine went through." This way, the storyline was built to "spark memory" and "inspire investigation" for particular audiences using the trail.[38]

A likely unintentional consequence of this process is that the temporary exhibition along the Atlanta BeltLine provided sensation without feeling. A sensation tells the brain that something has happened, whereas a feeling of "something-to-be done" occurs as a result of an emotion-inducing feeling, evidence of a ghost. Witnessing that leads to action occurs when feelings are activated. While the book of archival photographs (discussed in the opening to this chapter) allowed me to witness the death, trauma, courage, and community that imbued the movement, leading me to feelings of purpose and passion, removing the traumatic photos allowed feeling to escape.

We need to rectify this issue of public-art rules. The current language places violence and triumph at odds, forcing curators to choose one. Kyle argues for the necessity of showing images of "joy and triumph" instead of "violence."[39] This binary way of assessing art choices, I will show, forges a narrative that forsakes reality and masks immorality. Feelings of "joy and triumph" come to us through struggle. When struggle disappears in public narration, the emotion-inducing sense is also lost. Rhetorical criticism of the temporary exhibition of civil rights photography reveals that until additional context was added to Sims-Alvarado's public talks, the display romanticized the movement, making the events an additive feature that covered up the oppressive realities of Black people's experience in the geography—another romantic lyric over a blues beat.

AoAB is ABI's public-art program, established in 2010. It was developed to get more people to explore the BeltLine throughout its development process and has experienced continued growth, with new art projects appearing seasonally. Along with the expectation of driving tourism along the BeltLine, the ABI's policy released in 2018 notes a particular cultural interest in maintaining the unique character of the forty-five neighborhoods on its path.[40] Correctly highlighting the effects of displacement and gentrification on neighborhood culture, the policy writers ask, "What makes a place a home?" While they do not answer the question directly, they pose a strategy focused on equitably distributing funding and space utilization to give local institutions the resources they need to provide "place-based public art and culture" to maintain neighborhood character in the wake of displacement.[41]

I invite us to go back to their unanswered question, "What makes a place a home?" and reflect on AoAB's decision to use public space to display the civil rights movement exhibit. Within areas divided on racial lines, like Atlanta, the continued maintenance of Black lifeworlds is done by making moral disorder visible for the purpose of calling people to participate in a moral reordering. King argued that nonviolent protest could construct a tension in the United States that would "help men rise from the dark depths of prejudice and racism to the majestic heights of understanding and brotherhood."[42] It would only be fitting that we'd also share the history of the movement he gave his life for in a way that forms such a tension as this. And this can be done in our use of space. Historical narratives represented in space can either call people to participate in a moral reordering of a tragic situation or leave an audience as entertained viewers of a romance. Ultimately, we must seek to do more than add Black people to public art and instead redefine public art for the sake of summoning people "to participation in a moral universe."[43]

Before we move into this criticism, it's essential to recognize that public art, as a medium, has different constraints than a novel. First, while a book presumably can expand to include a considerable quantity of images and text for the message's rhetorical success, the design, arrangement, and space of the BeltLine regulate the number of images that can successfully be included in a way that is both informative, clear, and aesthetically pleasing. The exhibit consists of a total of fifty signposts. Second, the public is a nearly universal audience of the open exhibition. While the novel is printed for mass communication, its audience is limited by distribution, marketing, and public interest. The novel has a particular audience of people interested in history and politics and is subject to the constraints booksellers impose when they market book categories. Though available to a mass audience, the novel is privately consumed. While it is circulated in print media, it is restricted to those who can pay for it, known more readily to a particular group, and of unique or personal interest.

In contrast, the exhibit is public art, which is best understood as being open to everyone, accessible for free in the public sector, available for common use, popularly known, and in the physical view of its audience.[44] The public for the Atlanta BeltLine includes a diverse group of races, genders, ages, and values, making up a universal audience of multiple particular audiences that the curators want to persuade. This leads to the third constraint: the various persuasive purposes of the curation. The exhibit is sponsored by AoAB, which highlights its goal to provide equity, access, inclusion, interconnection, growth, and leadership in celebrating Atlantan communities' diverse history and culture. But the acts of AoAB are also subject to the goals of ABI, which has the responsibility to raise public and private funding for completing the BeltLine. With the consideration of capital necessity, the AoAB public art also reflects the neoliberal trajectory of the city, promoting a monetary incentive and bringing in affluent interests. To bring in the affluent, heritage projects must align with the political values and sentiments of the gentrifiers.[45]

The selection, removal, and ordering of the photos from the book to the BeltLine caused a romantic makeover of the civil rights movement narrative in three ways: (1) by presenting the goals of the movement as achieved, discounting continuing systemic problems; (2) by containing contested ideas and feelings to show white patriarchal and government cooperation; and (3) by placing blame for ongoing issues onto the victims, thereby portraying any enduring issues as the current failings of the marginalized to help themselves. The understanding that these were unintentional results is a reminder of how any actions to sanitize a traumatic history have far-reaching consequences.

As Karen Cross and Julia Peck attest, photography and its association with mass culture have the power to devastate memory and disengage the audience from the problems that come with capitalism. But at the same time, photographs also can "stand as a witness to the devastation of culture."[46] Even though the memory the photo presents is constructed and produced by the photographer, generally, the camera image is considered to be the eyewitness to the event and, therefore, the carrier of its memory. Images "offer a means to retrieve an experience of the past" from the perspective of the person who captured it, says Marita Sturken.[47] To illustrate the role of photography in memory, I started this segment with an explanation of how the book's images witnessed to me, crossing through places in my own memory and knocking against my future. The goal of historical witnessing is to ignite and activate the moral good in its audience. Witnessing allows us to perceive other alternatives and possibilities than the one that produced the trauma and naturally seeks to restore balance.[48] Making the immoral visible is a form of witnessing that would bring audiences to interrogate past injustices with a motivation to redeem.

Therefore, the narrative construction of history has one of the most fundamental roles in society as it provides the rationale for morality. History is not a list of things that occurred but a story of events that provides a moral evaluation.[49] Assuming that the characters in the story are the same, historical narratives of events and people are differentiated by moral rationale determined by the historian's framing of events. Moral reasoning is comprehended by assessing the values of the characters in the story as framed by the historian. It acts like the theme that we have young readers identify in reading-comprehension questions. The theme gives us the lesson to be learned from history or the moral order that gives history its significance to the present and the future. In other words, the historian's construction of the past can frame an honest reckoning, affecting our understanding of the victim and the victor and the values of good and evil, right and wrong.

To draw witness to African American history and collective memory, the account must be told in such a way that brings a moral reckoning to the oppressive traumas of the past. Sims-Alvarado forges this moral witnessing of the tragic immorality of opponents of the civil rights movement in her book by establishing moral outrage at the white antagonists' violation of human rights. The message of the images and captions is that Atlanta's Black activists and

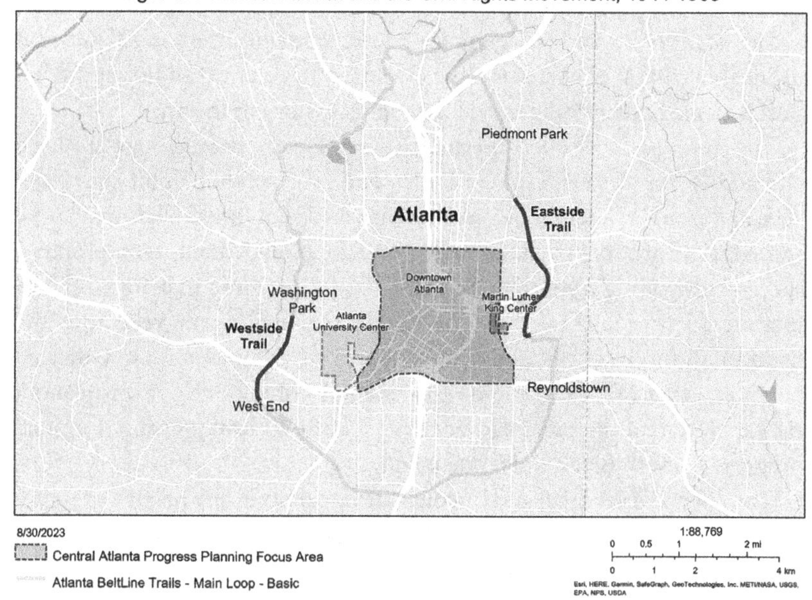

Map of the path of the *Images of America* outdoor exhibition along the Atlanta BeltLine by Heloisa Lanca Guilherme. Dotted lines represent the exhibition route. Solid lines represent the planned paths of the Atlanta BeltLine.

allies fought, as should others, for the values of the United States Constitution and the white adversaries did not. Thus, the audience should choose to follow the activists' trajectory and value that which is more just, more tranquil, safer, securer, and freer for all. Yet the curated exhibit altered the theme.

PRODUCING THE COMIC MASK

At the time of this writing, the Atlanta BeltLine is incomplete. Still, its finished areas during the time of the civil rights movement display covered three miles of Westside Atlanta (with a largely poor to lower-class Black population) and three miles on the east side of Atlanta (with a largely middle- to upper-class white population). Residents and visitors use their imaginations to conceive of the completed Northside and Southside Trails connecting neighborhoods around the city. The *Images of America* exhibit could be found on the two completed walking trails of the partially constructed Atlanta BeltLine. With thirty-two exhibit signs on the west side of the course and eighteen on the east side, the exhibit connects to locations within the city of Atlanta. The civil rights movement images form a spatial narrative along the BeltLine, forging a past at the epicenter of Atlanta's metaphorical stance as the Black Mecca and reflecting the continued segregation in Atlanta that divides the city. We must sense the exhibit in the context of this space. I'll start by shortly describing the demographic history of the area.

The completed Eastside Trail runs between Piedmont Park at its northern end and Reynoldstown at its southern end. The actual exhibit starts and ends at Ponce City Market before it reaches Piedmont Park. Piedmont Park's storied racial history includes Booker T. Washington's "Atlanta Compromise" speech, advocating respectability politics and conceding that "in all things that are purely social we can be as separate as the fingers, yet one as the hand in all things essential to mutual progress."[50] However, as evidenced by the exigence of the civil rights movement, Washington's optimism about the separation of the races had not been fruitful in bringing about mutual progress for both Black and white people.

The effects of separate and unequal are apparent in the history of Reynoldstown, at the Eastside Trail's southernmost tip. A neighborhood on the National Register of Historic Places, Reynoldstown was one of the first developed African American neighborhoods in the city. Formerly enslaved people moved to Reynoldstown after the Civil War, gaining employment at the railroad and manufacturing businesses close by. Named after prominent Black landowner Madison Reynolds, the neighborhood saw demographic changes as the results of industrialization and capitalism brought the trolley system to the neighborhood in the 1880s and, along with it, white middle-class families. After World War II, many of the white residents moved to the suburbs during the period of white flight, leaving the neighborhood majority Black.[51] The demographics of Reynoldstown began to shift again when gentrification started in the 1990s.[52]

Now, the area between Piedmont Park and Reynoldstown is economically prosperous and reflects the racial demographic changes in Reynoldstown as African Americans were displaced. Based on 2010 census data from the *Atlanta BeltLine Westside Impact Neighborhood Analysis*, the neighborhoods along the Eastside Trail had a median household income of $77,350, which was approximately 66 percent higher than Atlanta's AMI at the time. The percentage of poverty in the Eastside Trail neighborhoods was 12 percent compared to the city of Atlanta's 25 percent poverty. From a perspective of racial distribution, the Eastside Trail neighborhoods were 72 percent white, 18 percent Black, 5 percent Hispanic, and 3 percent Latinx or Asian.[53] Such data reflects disparate impacts on race and economic prosperity along this corridor of the BeltLine.

We now turn to the scene of the Westside Trail, which runs between Washington Park at its northern point and Adair Park at its southern point.

The exhibit stops short of Adair Park, ending at a Kroger grocery store in the neighborhood West End. The historic neighborhood Washington Park reflects the history of segregation in Atlanta as the first planned Black Atlanta suburb. Developed for Black folks between 1919 and 1924, the area was home to many influential Black families in the city and neighbors the Atlanta University Center, where Du Bois wrote *The Souls of Black Folk* and opposed the submissive stance of Washington. Washington Park was considered the Black side of town as instituted by a "color line," and white developers left the area.

West End, in contrast, developed a bit differently. It maintained a white population from its beginnings in the 1830s into the 1950s. After the civil rights movement, white flight ramped up as Black people moved into the area and started desegregating the whites-only schools. By the 1980s, West End was predominately Black and middle class as many Black professionals, students, and faculty from the Atlanta University Center began purchasing homes there.[54] Today, the area between Washington Park and West End is seeing a reverse shift with a new influx of white residents in the wake of the Atlanta BeltLine and other developments.

Racial and class-based segregation ordinances, redlining, and white flight were significant factors in the demography of today's Westside Trail.[55] As of 2010, the Westside Trail neighborhoods' racial distribution was 90 percent Black, 5 percent white, 2 percent Hispanic, and 1 percent Asian. This distribution is largely consistent across all the neighborhoods along this corridor. In comparison, as of 2010, Atlanta had an overall Black population of about 54 percent. Furthering the disparities between the Eastside and Westside Trails is the income distribution in the Westside Trail neighborhoods. There, the median household income was $26,035, which is 44 percent below the city's AMI and 66 percent below the median household income of the Eastside Trail neighborhoods. Thirty-seven percent of the population was in poverty, doubling the state's poverty average. And though this side of the BeltLine is home to the Atlanta University Center, it was approximated that only 20 percent of residents had a college degree, which was 27 percent less than the city average. The differences are also represented in housing conditions as 39 percent of homes along the Westside Trail were considered in a fair or poor state compared to just 18 percent of the Eastside Trail homes.[56] Viewing the history of segregation, redlining, the civil rights movement, white flight, and current demographics along the Westside Trail provides a historical and spatial context for understanding the *Images of America* exhibit, which we will discuss next.

The exhibit connects the history of these areas by spatially narrating Atlanta and the civil rights movement through photos. But from the beginning, the exhibit rescues whites by recasting the movement's white antagonists with abstract language, like "status quo."[57] The entrance and exit signs salute African Americans as protagonists in social protest. But rather than setting up an antagonist opposing them, the text rescues whites through personification, placing responsibility on objects and ideas instead of white actors. The exhibition's opening sign reads, "During the first half of the 20th century, a progressive group of black business, civic and religious leaders from Atlanta, Georgia, challenged the *status quo* by employing a method of incremental gradualism to improve the social and political conditions existent within the city." The nonhuman antagonist is the "status quo." Noting the younger generations' shift in social-change methods to direct action, the text then reads,

> A culmination of the death of Emmett Till and the Brown decision fostered this paradigm shift by bringing attention to the safety and education concerns specific to African American youth. Deploying direct-action tactics and invoking the language of civil and human rights, the energy and the zest of this generation of activists pushed the modern civil rights movement into a new chapter where young men and women became the voice of social unrest.

Here an antagonist is not identified for the younger generation. Instead, the focus shifts to the tool of change—direct-action tactics. The phrasing specifically removes the actions of the white antagonist. For instance, using the phrase "culmination of the death of Emmett Till" is a passive construction that eliminates the white agents of Till's murder, never discussing how he was murdered. Phrasing the events of Till's fatality as a "death" rather than a "murder" constrains the audience from the incentive for justice or reparations for the act. By using "death," the message of the exhibit entrance and exit signs are constructed to focus on the tools and methods of change rather than the actors. And that's just the start of it.

Beyond the entrance and exit signs, viewing the exhibit in its entirety within the BeltLine space reveals that the message construction on the Eastside Trail differs from that on the Westside Trail. The images on the BeltLine are primarily ordered based on the book chapters. Still, there are distinct and troubling differences in the chapter order that perpetuates the rescuing of whites, particularly on the Eastside Trail. The Eastside Trail, beginning at Ponce City Market and ending at Reynoldstown, starts in chapter 1 of the book and ends in chapter 6. However, chapter 5 is omitted from this consecutive ordering of the chapters. The Westside Trail, beginning at the West End Kroger and ending at Washington Park, starts in chapter 4 and ends in chapter 10. Here, chapter 6 is omitted and moved to the Eastside Trail, shifting the consecutive order. Chapter 7 is omitted from the exhibit entirely. If the chapters had been perfectly aligned, they may have been constructed with chapters 1–4 on the Eastside Trail and chapters 4–10 on the Westside Trail. Chapter 4 is overlapped on both sides of the trail in the curation. However, the misplacement of chapter 6 and the complete omission of chapter 7 are significant because the deliberate choices reconstruct the retail book's story and eliminate direct criticism of whites, particularly on the Eastside Trail.

Table 3.1. *Images of America* exhibit layout by book chapters of *Atlanta and the Civil Rights Movement*

Eastside Trail	Westside Trail
Chapter 1: Atlanta's Black Voting Power	Chapter 4: Atlanta's Student Movement and SNCC
Chapter 2: And None Shall Make Them Afraid	Chapter 5: Direct Action Tactics
Chapter 3: Destroying Jim Crow and Enforcing the Brown Decision	Chapter 8: SNCC, SCLC, and Selma
Chapter 4: Atlanta's Student Movement and SNCC	Chapter 9: Poor People's Campaign and Opposing the Vietnam War
Chapter 6: The National Campaign for Civil and Human Rights	Chapter 10: Honoring a King and His Legacy
Chapter 7: Atlanta's Response to the Civil Rights Act (omitted)	

On the Eastside Trail, considerable effort seems to be taken to identify King as a loved Atlanta native who was always supported by his city. Chapter 6, the misplaced chapter, is titled "The National Campaign for Civil and Human Rights." The chapter reflects national support for the movement. Along the Eastside Trail, three images from this chapter are used: (1) a 1963 image of Dr. King giving his "I Have a Dream" speech; (2) Dr. King and Mrs. King arriving in Oslo to receive the Nobel Peace Prize; and (3) Dr. King receiving an award from the city of Atlanta as a "Citizen of Atlanta, with Respect and Admiration" in 1963.[58] The third image is fascinating because it directly connects to Atlanta and local government support for the movement King was leading. In the image, Rabbi Jacob Rothschild of the Temple (Hebrew Benevolent Congregation) hands Dr. King a large, crystal Steuben-bowl award. According to the caption, the reception occurred after Dr. King received the Nobel Peace Prize. It was arranged by Mayor Ivan Allen and former and current, respectively, Coca-Cola CEOs Robert Woodruff and J. Paul Austin. The event reflects united support from government and businesses toward racial progress and social change. Together, all three images portray Dr. King as loved and endorsed by the nation, local businesses, and political leaders. These moments of seeming unification did occur. But their designated location on the east side of the BeltLine troubles the narrative reality of the movement, completely disengaging from the hate King received. That inconvenient history was left out of the text, creating what Morrison calls a "dehistoricizing allegory," which forecloses, rather than discloses, the years of a traumatic process—here, that which preceded King's appearance at the ceremony.[59]

This chapter was misplaced from its consecutive ordering, which would have put it on the Westside Trail (primarily Black and lower class). Instead, the images are on the Eastside Trail, with a larger white and middle- to upper-class visiting population. Positioning the images on the Eastside Trail reframes the narrative for this particular audience by focusing on white support for the movement. The audience receives a message that the movement was successful, and government and capitalist entities were a part of that. However, the misplacement of this one chapter is not enough to rescue whites. Other image omissions help it along.

Chapter 2, "And None Shall Make Them Afraid," is the most holistically explicit in documenting white retaliation to direct-action tactics. I discussed a number of the photos from this chapter in my opening, which included images of the KKK presence and resulting violence in Atlanta. Though this chapter, outlining the intensity of trauma and death, is included on the Eastside Trail, the images of white retaliation against Black people, including the prominent Ku Klux Klan images, are excluded from the exhibit. The three images from this chapter that are included are the ones best codified for white racial innocence. The three images used are of (1) the Columbians, an anti-Black and anti-Semitic hate group, entering the Fulton County Jail, (2) a group of white activists that worked to dissolve the Columbians group, and (3) Mayor Hartsfield and Rabbi Jacob Rothchild kneeling in front of the Temple after white supremacists had bombed it.[60] Together, the images focus attention on the real traumatic crimes against Jewish supporters of civil rights and the government's conviction of the white-supremacist group, the Columbians. While the events are real and the stories need to be told, the issue is the inclusion of these images at the exclusion of all the images that focus on retaliation against Black bodies. In addition, focusing on the arrest of the Colombians is a means of creating a "symbolic closure" by ridding the bad apples. The images that created moral indignation for Black people in this book chapter are excluded from the exhibit, diverting attention from the systemic complicity in violence against Black activists.

On the east side of the BeltLine trail, where the incentive for BeltLine investments is the strongest, the civil rights movement is romanticized through the omission of images that would draw witness to moral disorder against African Americans. Furthermore, the Eastside Trail positions a narrative closure for the civil rights movement, providing the message that direct-action tactics were successful, a moral reckoning has occurred in Atlanta because hate groups were convicted, and Dr. King was given his rightful award from local businesses and government. The evidence of this narrative closure becomes more apparent through the criticism of the Westside Trail in comparison.

As noted previously, the consecutive ordering of the chapters places chapters 4–10 on the Westside Trail. However, chapter 7, "Atlanta's Response to the Civil Rights Act," a chapter that emphasizes white retaliation to civil rights, is omitted from the exhibit altogether. Images from this chapter in the book start at President Lyndon B. Johnson's signing of the Civil Rights Act of 1964 and end with a photo showing young white men, self-identified as the Rebels, marching in downtown Atlanta to welcome Governor George Wallace of Alabama, a leading proponent of segregation and white supremacy. While the chapter identifies Mayor Ivan Allen and Georgia governor Carl Sanders as supporters of the act, other images show white protestors against the progressive policy marching in the streets of Atlanta. One photo shows Ku Klux Klan members protesting integrating businesses, carrying signs that read, "DON'T TRADE HERE! Owners of this business surrendered to the RACE MIXERS." The chapter also magnifies businesses that refused to integrate, showing Pickrick Restaurant owner Lester Maddox closing his restaurant after being fined for refusing to integrate. The following image shows Maddox leading protestors through the city, arguing for private rights. But all these images are omitted from the exhibit, eliminating the focus on white anti-Black racism and gentrifying the cultural narrative important to Black lifeworlds.

Instead, the Westside Trail images focus on the memory of direct-action methods on the part of the youth and deemphasize the antagonists' actions. Like on the Eastside Trail, rescuing whites occurs here by omitting images that lead to direct criticism of whites. For example, exhibit sign seventeen on the Eastside Trail shows John Lewis—who was leading two hundred activists in a demonstration in Selma on February 23, 1965—being warned by a police officer that white opposition was high, creating a dangerous situation. This image depicts a seemingly peaceful situation among the white officer, the demonstrators, and the press taking pictures. What is omitted is the successive, magnified image from the book that depicts demonstrators in Selma, led by Lewis and Hosea Williams, on March 7, 1965, being hit with billy clubs and tear-gassed by law enforcement. Another example of such omission is with exhibit sign twenty on the east side. Exhibit sign twenty begins the storyline of Julian Bond's ban from the Georgia House of Representatives "because of his support of SNCC's [Student Nonviolent Coordinating Committee's] anti-war stance on Vietnam." The exhibit includes two images reflecting on this crucial moment in 1966 for a Black politician. The second image, exhibit sign twenty-one, shows Dr. King and Bond casting ballots to get Bond his congressional seat back in the Georgia House. These two images do not accurately tell the traumatic events revolving around the state legislature's decision to ban Bond from his political seat because he refused to disassociate from the SNCC after they issued a statement opposing the war in Vietnam. An image in the book omitted from the exhibit shows white protestors preventing "African American demonstrators from entering the Georgia State Capitol in support of re-seating Julian Bond to the Georgia House of Congress."[61] The exhibit also excludes the images of marchers through Atlanta, rallying support for reseating Bond. The exclusion of these images from Bond's story inhibits the audience's awareness of the scope and scale of retaliation to Black political power and the extent to which Black protestors had to come together to support him. This minimizes the degree of moral disorder and romanticizes the changes these activists were able to make in the contentious environment. Getting Julian Bond his seat was quite difficult. In the 1966 special election and general elections, voters in his district reelected him, but the state legislature prevented him from serving. Bond wasn't officially seated until 1967 after the US Supreme Court declared the exclusion illegal. By making the activists and district voters invisible, the tumultuous road and efforts made to preserve equality are lost.

More disconcerting are some omissions made in the captions and choices made to pair images that reframe the narrative. One such image is exhibit sign sixteen, a picture of King's family, friends, and supporters welcoming him home from an eighty-day prison stay in Reidsville State Penitentiary in Georgia. The first line of the caption under the image reads, "Dr. King was sentenced to four months of hard labor at Reidsville State Penitentiary for violating his probation of an earlier traffic offense." This statement concedes that Dr. King was imprisoned for traffic offenses and is dissociated from a sign featured earlier in the exhibit that notes that Dr. King was arrested in connection to civil rights protests. In contrast, the corresponding event images and captions are different in the book, providing a framing that reflects integration protests as the valid reason for Dr. King's arrest and his traffic offenses as a smokescreen. In the book, the story of the arrest begins with an image of Dr. King protesting to integrate Rich's department store in Atlanta on October 19, 1960. The following image shows Dr. King in the back of a police car. The first line of the caption says, "Dr. Martin Luther King Jr. was arrested along with 52 students on October 19, 1960, for violating Georgia's segregation laws."[62]

The image shows Dr. King walking with police officers on what is assumed to be the day of his release from prison. The first line of the caption reads, "As a result of the arrest at Rich's, Dr. King was sentenced to four months of hard labor at Reidsville State Penitentiary for violating probation for an earlier traffic offense."[63] The fourth image shows Dr. King being welcomed home by family and friends. The storyline in the book has four images that provide a complete explanation of King's arrest and its association with his protests. In comparison, the exhibit displaces the cause and deemphasizes opposition to Black protests. The exhibit distorts the truth.

While there are images on this path that name whites as perpetrators of injustice, the lack of amplification decreases the narrative fullness of the moral disorder of the past and the present and the magnitude of the opposition to the movement. I hope to have revealed here that the omission of white antagonistic actions rescues whites from direct responsibility. It furthers a romantic vision of the civil rights movement for people on the east side and west side of the BeltLine. On the west side of the BeltLine, a primarily Black audience sees the addition of their history to the urban-redevelopment project. However, they do not witness the moral disorder's scope and scale. In addition, within the setting of the BeltLine's Westside Trail, a different ending is portrayed. The civil rights movement narrative begins to conclude as visitors reach Washington Park. The storyline transitions to chapter 10, "Honoring a King and His Legacy." This final chapter reviews King's assassination in Memphis, the outpouring of honor for him at his funeral in Atlanta, and the continuation of the movement with Mrs. King. As the book does, it ends with the movement's continuation and linear progression toward a moral reckoning. On the Westside Trail of the BeltLine, a predominantly Black audience sees the tragedy but is left with an open narrative continuing with Coretta Scott King.

Now, we must view these two different types of endings and the rhetorical messages they give to segregated audiences. On the Eastside Trail, a largely white and affluent audience is provided symbolic closure—there is nothing left to be done here. It's a "postracial" ending that subjects audiences to the belief that racism no longer exists. On the Westside Trail of the BeltLine, a younger, Black audience is left with an open story that reflects their desire for more change. Together, the two narrative storylines romanticize the future for these audiences and deemphasize the glaring obviousness of what is occurring. While Dr. King and civil rights activists fought for integration, Eastside and Westside Atlanta's present reflects that Atlanta is segregated on racial lines. However, romanticizing the narrative hinders audiences on the east side from fully acknowledging that the moral disorder is still present. At the same time, it sends a message to the west side that through their own continued actions, change can still come. In this way, the exhibit perpetuates a cycle; people on the east side are getting the message that there is nothing to do here, and Black residents on the west side are being told to keep trying. As more affluent Eastside residents see the romanticized story, all the reality of racial oppression becomes "invisible" to them. And Black residents continue screaming, "See me." The romantic lyrics perpetuate the veil between Black and white lifeworlds and the continuation of segregation, gentrification, displacement, and violence against Black bodies. The romantic lyrics allow white supremacy to live another day and Black people to die another day.

In sum, the exhibit shifts to emphasize white people who supported racial progress and deemphasize white-supremacist retaliation against racial progress. The *Images of America* exhibit performatively rescues whites because of the order of the chapters, omission of white agency, and institutionalization of segregation within the space. The narrative format of the exhibition is similar to the literature of what Ellison deems the "lost generation" of writers of the twentieth century. He argues that the literary form of writers like Ernest Hemingway rectified personal guilt not by heroically mortifying themselves but by asserting their innocence and casting the sin onto those who have already been defeated.[64] Morrison has similar criticisms of Hemingway, arguing that his work represented American romanticism that excluded inconvenient history. This dehistoricization occurs mainly when the improvement process "becomes indefinite—taking place across an unspecified infinite amount of time." In these cases, "history, as a process of becoming, is excluded from the literary counter."[65] Similarly, the narrative of the civil rights movement is expounded in such a way that it rectifies white guilt by leaving out difficult history, ritually banishing the "bad apple," and emphasizing white allyship. As a result, the issues of the present are placed on the shoulders of the victims. In this form, the audience is conditioned to "accept the less worthy values of society, and it serves to justify and absolve our sins of social irresponsibility. With unconscious irony it advises stoic acceptance of those conditions of life . . . which it pretends to reject." As Ellison argues, the goal of this narrative form may not be so much to "crush the Negro" but to "console the white man."[66] Yet the result of consoling white people is the oppression of Black people. In AoAB's want to focus on triumph over violence, they forgo truth. When it comes to public-art history, rather than choosing between violence and triumph, which considers that choosing one causes you to lose the other, might I propose a third way—a way that accounts for public nature without using romantic lyrics, a method that encourages participation with hope. The civil rights movement left a unique poetry birthed from the blues that structures this rhetorical strategy—the freedom song.

TOWARD A SONG OF FREEDOM IN PUBLIC ART

This unique poetry brought feeling to the exhibit when Jessica Kiger, education manager of the Atlanta Opera, presented the idea of adding music to the outdoor exhibit. On October 27, 2018, soprano opera singers Jayme Alilaw and Mika Wiltz joined Sims-Alvarado in singing spirituals along the trail at an event called Our Walk to Healing. As Sims-Alvarado narrated the history, Alilaw and Wiltz joined in singing songs like "He's Got the Whole World in His Hands" and "Lord, How Come Me Here?"[67] It was a rainy Saturday as they traversed the Westside and Eastside Trails with a group of about fifteen to twenty people. Sims-Alvarado provided context, telling stories of the neo-Nazi movement and the rise of the Columbians during the civil rights movement. I was present that day, observing how the collaborative performance linked the "body" of the exhibition to the "spirit" of the movement.

Strategic song choices that reflect a blues-narrative reality allowed for the ghost's voice to be heard. The lyrics to the spiritual "Lord, How Come Me Here?" repeat a refrain of absolute despair: "There ain't no freedom here, Lord / I wish I never was born." In an interview with radio station WABE, Alilaw says that the song was chosen because it evokes the emotions of "despair and even hopelessness that can be found in the midst of struggle and pain and hardship." She continues, "the imagery we have of the people who fought and did everything that they could during the civil rights movement is one of strength and endurance. . . . We're on the other side of that, but there was this despair and this depression and I think that all of that needs to be expressed and needs to be healed."[68] In her explanation, the sopranist considers that historical trauma, something that AoAB and other public-art entities attempt to repress from the public, must be made visible and witnessed so that we may see the tear in the fabric and find a way to mend it. Rather than forming a binary between violence and triumph, Alilaw considers the necessity of displaying struggle and strength. Through the collaboration of the spiritual, expressed musically, with the historical, they broke through the mask, proving that there is an alternative method to public-art making.

So much effort has been spent to assuage, rescue, and protect white lifeworlds; even acts seeking to redeem the past focus on pacifying the villain rather than saving the victim. This framing invites the public to view the world as one intent on protecting white life, no matter the cost to humanity. It naturalizes the racial order of our circumstances. The moral mask gives the perception that something has been done to improve the plight of the marginalized without any actual transformation. There is an alternative, but it often requires us to step outside the embedded dominant patterns and ideologies. Lorde reminds us, "the master's tools will never dismantle the master's house. They may allow us temporarily to beat him at his own game, but they will never enable us to bring about genuine change."[69] So instead of working with the master's tools, we can do as Ellison, Wright, and Woods exemplified for us when they redeemed the blues genre—a music created by the oppressed and not the oppressor—as a rhetorical strategy for relieving the burdens of the sacrificial victim and placing them back onto the oppressor. In this section, I will do the same, considering the freedom song genre, the music of the activist, as a rhetorical strategy to form a hopeful and motivating community around the victim as they press forward for liberation.

In chapter 2, I discussed the ways the blues provide for Black agency, allowing their belief in liberty, freedom, and opportunity to grasp the core of America and wring it toward socially equitable practices. The blues, then, is a way of knowing. It is an amalgamation stemming from Louisiana that incorporates Native American traditions, cultural, linguistic, and religious practices of West Africans, and Afro-Haitian revolution-minded poetry and architectural styles with sacred communal spaces, Congolese dance, and the community forged in New Orleans. The blues, which extended to "Jazz, R&B, Soul, Funk, and Hip Hop," developed a "song movement" that built "new communal bonds."[70] As Woods describes,

> Crafted from the deepest imaginable psychological pain, the auction-block renaissance gave to the Blues its irrepressible will, its indestructibility, and its malleability. This new profound working-class knowledge system became the lifeblood of the people imprisoned on the plantations outside the city. The new ontology, epistemology, and praxis that emerged among them is the Blues. Although there are hundreds of dialectics and dozens of regional, religious, ethnic, and gender identities embedded in the Blues pantheon and its extensions, the central ethical core is the creation of a socially just and sustainable society in the bosom of a social structure dedicated to economic monopoly and the exploitation of Black working-class communities, families, individuals and traditions.[71]

Woods's work exposes the blues epistemology as a philosophical system evolving in the South after the Civil War, where the Black working class established the keys required to build a new North American commons focused on "social justice and sustainable human, community and cultural development."[72] Freedom songs are an extension of the blues pantheon.

When I say "freedom song," I'm referencing those protest adaptations of African American spirituals and gospel songs, like "Ain't Gonna Let Nobody Turn Me Around" or "We Shall Overcome." Even the more recent "Glory" sung by Common and John Legend or "Freedom" by Beyoncé and Kendrick Lamar harken to the inspiration of freedom songs. Martin Luther King Jr. describes the freedom song as "the soul of the movement."[73] The soul is the mediator between the spirit and the body. It is a place where our emotions and our thoughts embrace. One of my criticisms of the exhibit was that it provided sensation without feeling. The gist of it is it lacked soul. Soul is a form of the erotic. It "provides energy for change."[74] It is a revolutionary source that African Americans have used for the past four hundred years on these shores to motivate them and provide the power needed to continue. Soul is the heartbeat of the Black Mecca. When you remove the soul from public art, you gentrify American culture and history. This cultural gentrification dulls the senses, making it easier for developers to come into demotivated spaces and displace the residents. Public art that combats gentrification, segregation, and oppression must have soul.

Since romantic lyrics rescue white people from dealing with the guilt of systemic racism, they manage to bring symbolic closure to the current racial issues in the environment. Romanticism does not serve the communities that are being gentrified. If we are not mindful of these detrimental results, public art will maintain the myth of a moral America and keep us from ever cleaning up our most significant issues. As Fanon puts it, "The white man wants the world; he wants it for himself. He discovers he is the predestined master of the world. He enslaves it. His relationship with the world is one of appropriation. But there are values that can be served only with my sauce."[75] Freedom songs are a bit of that sauce. So as an alternative to gentrifying romanticism, what if we were to use freedom songs as a rhetorical strategy in public art and urban redevelopment to keep the soul? Every Black musical genre has had its freedom song, from gospel to funk rock, reggae, rap, and hip-hop. Songs of freedom are indelible to African Americans and the oppressed. What makes it a freedom song isn't just the rhythm but also the lyrical code. As MLK argues, "I have heard people talk of their beat and rhythm, but we in the movement are inspired by their words."[76] Understanding the rhetorical success of a freedom song's message offers key strategies that can be applied to public-art exhibitions to make immorality plain and influence participation in change. As a rhetorical strategy, freedom songs would bring hope to activists and disrupt the antagonist by (1) bringing visibility to the invisible, (2) invigorating an activist collective identity, (3) providing emotional renewal, and (4) creating new opportunities for engagement.

First, the words sung during protest marches made the marchers visible, as Julius Lester attests freedom songs "comfort the disturbed and disturb the comfortable."[77] They are meant to break up the space and cram it with determination. An activist recalls, "the song made sure that the sheriff and his deputies knew we were there."[78] The marchers made the songs fill the space instead of allowing it to fill them. For the public exhibit to reflect reality, it might have to cause a disturbance. When Alilaw and Wiltz chose to sing a song of despair and hopelessness, "Lord, How Come Me Here?," they were filling the space and causing a disturbance. Though it, like all forms of education, has its challenges, the overarching goal of this strategy is to teach new generations how to live in a diverse society, allowing them to fill up the environment so that the old ideology has no room. During the Our Walk to Healing event, when Sims-Alvarado narrated the neo-Nazi history along the east side of the trail, she filled the space with truth, no matter how uncomfortable.

Simply embedding the memory could lead to desensitization, so exhibitions should also teach people how to participate. The second characteristic of a freedom song is that it is participatory. During the civil rights movement, activists sang them at demonstrations. Black Lives Matter protestors have moved contemporary songs of freedom to social-media activist spaces, adding dance and performance to participate in Kendrick Lamar's "Alright" and he and Beyoncé's "Freedom" on Twitter, TikTok, and Instagram. For an exhibit like the civil rights open-air museum, this could be materialized by sharing the images of direct-action-protest support on both sides of the trail rather than leaving the direct-action education to a predominantly Black population. Freedom songs teach everyone how to protest, and what makes them particularly special is that you don't have to be Black to sing them; you just have to understand racial history. A goal of freedom songs is to be able to integrate allies of other ethnicities and races into the movement as a method of "working toward interracial unity."[79] This can occur in freedom songs because a new collective identity as activist is produced through participation.

Third, the freedom song is the expression of the sacrificial victim to posterity. The activist sings, "I woke up this morning with my mind stayed on freedom."[80] Freedom is a future promise. Thus, the songs connect the past and present struggles to something forthcoming. The songs are wrapped up in their history but courageous in their hope. Hope is the want for something you do not yet have but consider a probability. In freedom songs, "the ghost presents itself as a sign to the thinker that there is a chance in the fight for the oppressed past."[81] For African Americans across this nation, freedom is still a hope. It has not been accomplished. Therefore, any exhibit narrating the civil rights movement in Atlanta needs to connect to what is still left to accomplish. We cannot symbolically close the goals of the movement. Those goals were transformed for new generations into the Black Power movement and, later, the Black Lives Matter movement. Though the methods may be altered, the goal for freedom is still the same, and civil rights are at the heartbeat. Freedom songs have no natural end. Their choruses can be repeated and reconfigured over and over until freedom is won. A civil rights exhibition should reflect the same.

Finally, freedom songs are particularly useful for engaging an audience with the immoral because they require you to pick a side. One song performed during the movement literally asked, "Which side are you on?"[82] There is only one right side, and that is determined by the theme, the moral lesson the song came to tell. The singers adapted the song from the 1930s labor unions movement to reflect the case for civil rights singing: "Oh tell me, Mayor Allen, Where is your heart? / We are all children of the Almighty God."[83] The address to Mayor Allen, refers to Mayor Ivan Allen of Atlanta, who supported the civil rights movement after being moved by demonstrations from African American students about the hindrances of segregation and his own conscience being awakened by his relationships of "mutual respect and support" with Black leaders. Mayor Allen was the only southern mayor to support the 1964 Civil Rights Act.[84] He picked a side. The song continues to chide listeners, asking, "Will you join the Ku Klux Klan or Martin Luther King?"[85] Such refrains remove options for ambiguous choices that attempt to maintain some middle or compromising line. Similarly, in the case of a narrative exhibition, it must choose a human character to play the protagonist and the antagonist. The only way audiences can choose what side they are on is to see both sides clearly and know which one is considered immoral. The antagonist was hidden in the AoAB open-air museum as if all these Black folks were fighting an apparition. However, by choosing and putting on display the antagonist, the exhibit's authors designate a guilty party and pick a side. So as the song asks, "Which side are you on?"

Though this exhibition was temporary, a more permanent display on Atlanta's entire twenty-two-mile loop could force a reckoning with other Lost Cause memorials, like Stone Mountain but only if it has a courageous soul, willing to uncover the tragic face. Freedom songs are a direct reflection of the civil rights movement strategy. Direct-action, nonviolent protest was largely successful because images of peaceful protestors being broken and abused by police officers and white men in masks caused the North to grow sympathetic to the Black cause. The soul of the movement identified with public humanity, leading them to become participatory allies. So why, when honoring these protestors, would we remove the photos of the brutality they faced from the attention of an affluent public? They need to see the image of Harold Sprayberry, spraying insect repellent in the air as one hundred Black students staged a sit-in at a local Atlanta restaurant. They must view state troopers passing out billy clubs in preparation for Atlanta University Center student marchers at the Georgia state capitol. They must see a police officer grabbing a woman demonstrating in downtown Atlanta. They should know of the man ordering comedian Dick Gregory and John Lewis to leave a restaurant across from the Rialto Theater in Atlanta. When we exclude these images, we disavow the truth to proclaim a myth. We close doors on a continuous movement. We remove power from today's activists and empower the white supremacists at Stone Mountain. When Atlanta's history is culturally gentrified, its soul is lost.

CHAPTER 4

SO, THE BLACK MECCA TURNED TO BEER TOWN, OR AMERICAN TRAPPIN'

On June 12, 2020, Rayshard Brooks, twenty-seven, fell asleep intoxicated in a Wendy's drive-through line in southern Atlanta. He was blocking other customers. Police officers were called to the scene. Officer Devin Brosnan arrived and was able to wake him and get him to pull into a parking space. Then, Officer Garret Rolfe came. Rolfe questioned Brooks for about twenty-seven minutes. Brooks asked if he could leave his car and walk home. Rolfe then performed a sobriety test. At 11:23 p.m., Rolfe told Brooks he "has had too much drink to be driving."[1] He pulled out his handcuffs and attempted to make an arrest. At this point, the reasonably calm scene turned as Brooks, still inebriated, grabbed Officer Brosnan's Taser and punched Officer Rolfe. Officer Rolfe fired his Taser as Brooks ran away. Rolfe continued behind Brooks and reached for his handgun. Nearly eighteen feet away and still running forward, Brooks reaches his arm back to fire the Taser he'd stolen from Brosnan. Officer Rolfe shot his gun. Two bullets hit Brooks in the back, and as he bled out on the ground, Officer Rolfe kicked him, and Officer Brosnan stood on his shoulder, leaving him there for more than two minutes without medical aid. Brooks died after surgery at a nearby hospital.[2] This is what happened to an inebriated Black man who fell asleep in a Wendy's drive-through line. Even after spending more than forty minutes talking to Brooks and understanding that he was a parent celebrating his daughter's birthday that week, the officers failed to recognize Brooks as a human needing protection from himself while under the influence. Instead, the cops believed that their own lives were in danger as the Black guy ran away from them at the moment he was killed. They argue that they "had the right to use force to prevent [Brooks] from 'imminent use of unlawful force against them.'"[3] The claim is backed by "individualist ideology," supporting self-defense over the community and citizen protection.

One hundred and fourteen years prior, white people in Atlanta also deemed Black men drinking a threat, leading to the death of "between twenty-six and forty-seven black lives" in the 1906 Atlanta race riots.[4] At that time, Black men were accused of sexually assaulting white women. The white power structure pointed to Black dens and dives as the cause of Black men's alleged unhinged attacks against white women. Over three days from September 22 to September 24, mobs of white men brutally attacked unassuming Black people across downtown and into nearby suburbs. In the city's response to the events, police chief Henry Jennings ordered all Black-owned businesses closed. Members of an advisory council of white elites, supported by some Black elites wanting interracial harmony, targeted bars serving alcohol to lower classes of any race.[5] The unverified accusations against dens and dives were a means to suppress Black culture, inhibit their freedoms, and maintain the veil. The events overtly follow the worldview of racialism, holding up racial divisions to protect white individualism.

Today, white individualism is still the focus of protection, identifiable in our redeveloping cities as exclusionary redevelopment trends hold up "patterns of racial and class segregation," creating enclaves of new developments "adjacent to but vigorously disconnected from poor, mostly minority neighborhoods."[6] This is evidenced by Malt Disney, a nickname for the new brew and beer playland on the west side of the BeltLine trail. The Westside Trail opened to the public in September 2017, with a new facility catering to the craft-brewing subculture. The Lee + White complex—a collection of fourteen consecutive warehouses dating back to the 1950s—covers three acres of land along White Street with a prime location down a half mile of the trail. Once known as Warehouse Row, it started to transform after developers purchased it in 2017 and breweries found their home in the space. As of 2021, the repurposed warehouses are home to seven drink-focused locations dedicated to the art of fermentation.[7] As you'll see in this chapter, Malt Disney's position in the space forms a culturally gentrified enclave in the primarily Black residential neighborhood while leaving the critical space of Black culture invisible to people visiting the complex or walking the BeltLine. I began this chapter by recounting the events surrounding the death of Rayshard Brooks and the Atlanta 1906 race riots as they serve as points of caution and contrast for this chapter's inquiries about the emergence of the three-acre space dedicated to beer culture in the middle of West End. This type of gentrification is a form of cultural violence against a group's built environment, or, as put by local artist

Shanequa Gay—a recorder of West End's Black culture—what they are doing at the intersection of Lee Street and White Street "just feels like an invasion."[8] Although it doesn't physically harm or kill individuals, the intrusion into a neighborhood that has been a Black community for more than fifty years legitimizes racialism and its supporting structure.

In this chapter's first and second inquiries, I want to answer how changes in the gentrifying built environment, such as new craft breweries, keep Black people in the space between permission and exclusion. To do that, I open us up to thinking of cultural gentrification through the concept of "American individualism," where some individuals at drinking establishments enjoy freedom while others are an assembly of phantoms shaping that freedom. Individualism is a moral, political, and social way of thought that prioritizes personal autonomy, choice, and merit. Individualism suggests that outcomes in life are dependent upon individual value and sacrifice. Under this conception, hardworking white individuals are deserving of an alcoholic beverage. And to sustain this argument, a narrative of Black irresponsibility while drinking is amplified.

Though today's recollections of the temperance movements in the United States omit the racial past, history tells us that the move to prohibit the production, sale, and distribution of alcohol in the United States was primarily publicized by using racial stereotypes that presented Black men, Native Americans, and working-class European immigrants who drank as "insular drunks" and a threat to the white middle class.[9] Before the Atlanta race riots, prohibition hadn't made much traction in the South, and no southern states were dry.[10] However, with the association of white women's rapes with the image of uncontrollable Black men drinking, Georgia became the first southern state to go dry in 1907. During the time of national Prohibition, 1920–1933, there was "uneven enforcement" where "Mexicans, poor European immigrants, African Americans, poor whites in the South, and the unlucky experienced the full brunt of Prohibition enforcement's deadly reality," while "the urbane elite" could be found "sipping cocktails in swank, protected nightclubs" and speakeasies.[11] While drinking is typically viewed as immoral, white individualists maintain their sense of self and flaunt their higher social status by standing out from drinking Black males.

As Morrison attests, American individualism depends on the "Africanist population" to make meaning of white identity as "not enslaved, but free; not repulsive, but desirable; not helpless, but licensed and powerful; not historyless, but historical; not damned, but innocent; not a blind accident of evolution, but a progressive fulfillment of destiny."[12] We are the phantoms upholding their conquest. The American individualist depends on racialized inequality and white-supremacist structures to boost their self-esteem and enhance their social status. Even once free of slavery, Black people have never been able to "safely show the braggadocio" of free men. "White Americans, however, can violently reassert their privileged identities and institutionalize them in cultural rituals and social structures," including "segregation, physical violence, and racist speech-acts." In this way, American individualism has a "dependence on structures of exploitation" to maintain the "personal freedom and well-being" of white people.[13] The killing of Rayshard Brooks and the Atlanta race riots are direct, violent acts that support this proposition. But culturally violent acts for upholding white individualism (like cultural gentrification) are vital for us to assess. Like the previous chapters, I am interested in the actions that maintain Black invisibility (like American individualism) and the strategies for humanizing us. The emergence of beer culture in Atlanta in the mid-nineteenth century and its reinvigoration in craft-brew culture in a contemporary gentrifying Black Atlanta neighborhood are examples of white individualist repossession of space and the patterns that create and re-create ghosts.

In the second section, I follow the ghosts, pulling together their stories connected to drinking culture in Black lifeworlds and white lifeworlds in Atlanta. Looking out at the changes happening in the West End, one child asked Angel Poventud, an activist volunteer along the Atlanta BeltLine, "Are they building it for white people or the Black people?"[14] His question is not out of the ordinary when considering the changes in the built environment. Wondering about belonging in a space is part and parcel of the complex nature of urbanism—that while the development is attractive, there's a feeling of exclusion that cannot be shaken. When it comes to humanizing the ghosts of cultural gentrification, following the history of the built environment—the space the young boy set his eyes on—can allow us to find the traumatizing experiences that explain the feeling of being between permission and exclusion in a neighborhood. Residents across southern and southwestern Atlanta ask the same question that the young man asked Poventud as they brace themselves for the BeltLine trail construction across these historically Black neighborhoods at different rates. They have already seen the significant changes in the first large portion of the BeltLine trail that opened in 2012 on Atlanta's east side. Before it officially opened, speculation on the BeltLine's promises was one of the major drivers that shifted the demographics of the Old Fourth Ward neighborhood, where Martin Luther King Jr. grew up. In the first decade of the twenty-first century, white residents increased from 16 percent to 34 percent between 2000 and 2010, and average home sales increased from $126,000 to $290,000 over the first eighteen years of the century.[15] Visible transformations in the built environment accompanied the fast changes. An old Ford factory was converted into loft apartments. The Sears, Roebuck and Co. warehouse became Ponce City Market, a 2.1 million-square-foot mixed-use space of boutiques, gourmet eateries, offices, and apartments.[16] Then, in 2018, New Realm Brewing—the first brewery with a full-service restaurant on the Eastside Trail—was opened in an old warehouse space.[17]

There are a few sure signs that your neighborhood is already gentrifying: that new craft brewery, the yoga studio, hipster café, health-food store, and boutique shops, which ring the alarms for those who may not have already been leery of the reduction in government housing, the opening of a charter school, and faster home sales happening before those businesses come in. People of color in gentrifying neighborhoods are often aware of the signs but find little power in staving off the influx of new, wealthy investors eyeing their community. When residents alarm government officials that speculation is inciting displacement, the kings and queens of capital have already staked their claim, giving long-term residents the sense that their need to get back on the move could be delayed, but it is undoubtedly inevitable. What if these signs of gentrification have more to them than meets the eye? How might some details of the changing built environment harbor the façade of diversity and inclusion? As of 2018, "an outlay of $500 million of mostly public BeltLine money has generated $4 billion in private investment, with a further $4 billion planned or proposed."[18] In my inquiry, I turn to the private investments that have spurred the iconic symbols of gentrification on the West End—that of Lee + White.

The feeling that something between alcohol and African Americans was causing Lee + White to feel more exclusionary than permissive led me through this chapter. Recognizing ghosts takes effort. For this researcher, my senses question why Malt Disney feels foreign and "not mine" even though I'm American. Hauntings are made of tensions.[19] From that sense of tension between permission and exclusion, I know I'm in a space where ghosts may live, and somehow, I must reconstruct the world that the spirit conjures. There's an oppressed past here, and as Gordon encourages, we must fight for it because how we "grapple with history is intimately tied to the very things themselves, to their variable modes of operation, and thus to how we would change them."[20]

Craft breweries may seem like a fad to the greater Georgian public. However, as soon as you think you've just stumbled on a new, hip spot to talk about on social media, you find yourself, or at least I found myself, in the middle of the Atlanta 1906 race riots, where Black drinking establishments were condemned, leading to prohibition across the state. In this lies the tension: craft brewing has historically been a white male industry and social space. It has made its mark on West End—a majority-Black, low-income neighborhood—since the white flight in the 1960s and '70s. West End is coined by some of its residents as a Black Mecca in and of itself. But this area is transforming through cultural gentrification and a 78 percent increase in home values from 2000 to 2018.[21] And the breweries wouldn't be such a problem except that Black people have a long and sordid history with alcohol in America. While Black breweries exist, at the time of this writing, none reside at Lee + White in this predominantly Black neighborhood. The dominant culture is taking control of the space. Because we understand our racial nature, we know that being completely free, unapologetically Black, and vulnerable in Lee + White could be a safety risk. So we either assimilate, accommodate, or segregate ourselves.[22]

The third inquiry of this chapter regards humanizing the ghosts by humanizing Black people for themselves. The built environment can incite exclusion and dehumanization, but what can Black cultural developments utilizing the blues tradition tell us about redesigning neighborhoods that reinforce the equality of humanity rather than individual autonomy? Clyde Woods argues that the blues tradition combats racial and economic monopolies and imagines a new world order that affirms Black cultural and intellectual traditions. There are three pillars to the blues tradition. The first and second, we've addressed in previous chapters; they are social and philosophical imperatives in spiritual songs and the philosophies that guide freedom movements. The third pillar comes out of the first two. It is "an ethical development agenda that opposed slavery, racism, and monopoly in all of their manifestations." Woods argues that this agenda promoted "social justice and sustainable human, community, and cultural development."[23] A particular expression of the blues tradition is native to Atlanta, and in its evolution, I argue it can manifest the third pillar. I'm referring to trap music. In the third section, I take elements of trap-music culture as a form of the blues tradition that makes way for Black self-consciousness and humanization.

THE ISSUE OF AMERICAN INDIVIDUALISM

As a part of the cultural gentrification process, West End is undergoing a transformation of its leisure spaces. As a characteristic of leisure spaces that are safe for white people but yield huge caution signs for Black people, a brewery and beer-amusement space constitute part of what the West End is being fashioned into. On the surface, modern redevelopment projects would never identify that they are creating "white spaces." Instead, they argue the public goal of redevelopment is to move single individuals into diversified, equitable locations. We know from the discourse surrounding the BeltLine's construction that a community ethic is inherent in its goals. With honorable intentions, the originator, Gravel, argues the BeltLine is a means for bringing diverse people together through an environment that connects us, writing that an essential aspect of the BeltLine proposal was that it "very deliberately links places with names like 'Cabbagetown' and 'Blandtown' together. These forty-plus neighborhoods each have their own history, culture, and politics, and the Atlanta BeltLine connects them across the tracks and down the line, making historic barriers into a new public meeting ground."[24] However, despite these efforts and similar influences occurring since *Brown v. Board* (1954), Atlanta is still a segregated city. And according to research by the Brookings Institution published in 2021, Black residents in Atlanta "are extremely segregated from the rest of the population," as "almost 70% of Black residents would have to move to new Census tracts to produce racial distributions within Census tracts that match that of the larger city."[25]

We should be asking why diversification and integration aren't occurring. Why does gentrification lead to displacement and separation rather than moving *single individuals* to a *universal belonging* within a particular location?[26] I argue that the racial social order and the denial of Black humanity is the most critical feature of American society hindering diversity, inclusion, and belonging. In this chapter, I use Du Bois, Fanon, Morrison, and Ellison to explore the case for the eradication of individualism as part of an effort to expose the presence of ghosts and undermine ongoing efforts to keep them invisible. As political scientist Lawrie Balfour contends, "the story of racial injustice is still importantly a story about memory's suppression"; therefore, I uncover the beast.[27]

In 2016, Gravel stepped down from the board of directors of the Atlanta BeltLine Partnership. He was dismayed that the project wasn't meeting its affordable housing goals.[28] The evidence was clear: the dreams of using the twenty-two-mile path to move the city "past racial, ethnic and class divisions and towards a more cosmopolitan embrace of social difference" would not come to pass if the project continued down the same route.[29] Despite his apprehension, the project proceeded without him and marketed a universalist proposition in its public narrative. Here's an example: At a BeltLine Westside Study Group virtual public meeting in 2021 I attended, another attendee asked whether funds from a new program would be used in proportion to a particular neighborhood's investment in the fund program. The senior economic-development manager responded,

> I think it's important that, as a citizen of Atlanta, we really think of the BeltLine as one project. It's our BeltLine, and the project is used from an economic-development perspective. When these Fortune 500 companies, like Microsoft, when they're comin' and looking at Atlanta and comparing it to other markets around the country, they're going out on the BeltLine, and they're seeing the incredible diversity of our city, and they're falling in love with who we are as a city. . . . So, I think, as a citizen of Atlanta, I definitely see it as a project that rises us all. I definitely want to help us all think about that mindset when we think about the project.[30]

Her statement does not answer the question directly and instead attempts to change the audience's thinking from an individual neighborhood focus to a citywide focus. It is an acknowledgment that the BeltLine tells a story about Atlanta that causes corporate investors to want to put their companies there. She concludes that the story narrated by the BeltLine is one of "diversity." She wants all Atlantans to see the BeltLine as one, not separate segments for isolated neighborhoods. But more importantly, she uses an underlying principle she considers common sense and thereby unarguable—that in a free market, the addition of Fortune 500 companies, like Microsoft, is welcomed as a public good for everyone in this diverse city.

Her argument that BeltLine funds being distributed as needed throughout the project will attract individual investors and support all of Atlanta's citizens reflects a universal ethic, which adopts a principle of movement from *self-acting individuals* to a *community acting for universal good*. This principle is a part of what Brandi Thompson Summers characterizes as a race-neutral policy, which ignores systemic issues and "seeks to replace and revalue the Black space." It's a discourse that assumes "benefits of integration for people of color" but results in cultural gentrification.[31] Even though a walk on the BeltLine will present diversity, in that people of all races, ethnicities, and classes traverse the trails, why are Black people like the little boy I quote in the intro to this chapter asking, "is this for white people or black people?"[32] Why did Shanequa Gay describe Lee + White as an "invasion"? Why do Black people look at yoga studios and craft breweries and see them as signs that eventual displacement is coming? Why are residents concerned that they won't be able to enjoy the changes?[33] If this project "rises us all," why has the Urban Displacement Project at the University of California, Berkeley, categorized numerous neighborhoods throughout Atlanta as experiencing advanced or ongoing gentrification and displacement due to the rapid increase in housing costs?[34] As these businesses move in, the Black residents are steadily being asked to exit the universal tent, stage left.

When it comes to understanding cultural gentrification in the built environment, the experiences of Black people drinking can allow us to articulate an understanding of the oppressed past that hinders the Black bodies from being actualized in space. The ideologies that governed reactions to Rayshard Brooks and led to the 1906 Atlanta race riots, more than one hundred years apart, are evidence of the institutional structure in the United States that keeps "black Americans from escaping the limbo between slavery and citizenship."[35] There is a force working against Black bodies. It is threaded in the normative pattern characterizing individual agents' expected and actualized behaviors. The occurrences prove the reality that Black people know is true, though they wish it wasn't: to survive, don't be found living "too free" in white space. And all space, no matter the population demographics, is white space when white people want it to be. As Du Bois writes,

> [The Black man] realizes at last that silently, resistlessly, the world about flows in two great streams: they ripple on in the same sunshine, they approach and mingle their waters in seeming carelessness,—then they divide and flow wide apart. It is done quietly; no mistakes are made, or if one occurs, the swift arm of the law and of public opinion swings down for a moment, as when the other day a black man and a white woman were arrested for talking together on Whitehall Street in Atlanta.[36]

(Note that Whitehall Street has been a major thoroughfare into West End.) As memory tells us, it is reckless for Black folks to live too free because true freedom drops the veil between Black and white lifeworlds. It humanizes the ghost, upending the racial hierarchy white America depends on for privilege. Thus the "swift arm" comes down to protect this American individualism, which requires Black people to be the "intermediate between brute and man" so as to reassure white people of their own "dignity, freedom, and independence."[37] As Jack Turner puts it in his assessment of Alexis de Tocqueville's *Democracy in America*, "Individualist and white-supremacist ideology, in this regard, structure each other: insofar as one is not black, one is free and independent, and insofar as one is free and independent, one is not black."[38]

My greater concern is where this leaves Black people in terms of keeping a home in Atlanta. Freedom in its sincerest state is an act of vulnerability—that when I am most human, I am also authentic; when I am authentic, I am bound to make mistakes. The experience of being vulnerable is a necessary birthplace to belonging because belonging says you are welcome and worthy as you are.[39] Belonging follows this framework:

> *Vulnerable individual* → enters a space of safety and belonging → identifies herself with the space → *joins the universe* designated by the space.

Since the path to belonging passes through vulnerability, when the "swift arm of the law and of public opinion . . . swings down" on Black people being authentic, integration into the visible society is thrown off. Any space where a person cannot be authentic is also a space where that person does not belong. Rather than vulnerability, Black individuals more readily carry inferiority into spaces, which translates to feelings of being unworthy of citizenship. As Du Bois puts it, African Americans reconsider their demand for freedom, thinking, "suppose, after all, the World is right and we are less than men."[40] This afterthought and feeling of shame have been placed on Black lives through ideological processes that forge a representation of Black people as inferior. The inferiority complex is an African American one. Like Fanon's argument about Antilleans, no one Black person stands out in this regard; all Black people exhibit this mindset. But this weakness is not in the individual's soul but her surroundings. The social system is one of comparison and competition. Thus, individuals find themselves in a geography and society that debase Black culture and Black life, resulting in dehumanization and a loss of self-consciousness for Black individuals. Fanon writes, "Man is human only to the extent to which he tries to impose his existence on another man in order to be recognized by him. As long as he has not been effectively recognized by the other, that other will remain the theme of his actions. It is on that other being, on recognition by that other being, that his own human worth and reality depend."[41] To not be recognized is to be invisible, and invisibility causes Black people to lose self-consciousness. This happens in American landscapes when Black culture is tokenized or overlooked.

Because of inferiority, instead of Black people being enticed to "belong" in white space, we are asked to "assimilate." Assimilation is an act of fitting in that requires you to stop being who you are and be more like the dominant group. African Americans have forged tight racial allegiances as a countermeasure and a means for survival. The racial group invokes counterdiscourses, such as the blues, attempting to steadily remind themselves that they are worthy. They are represented by such declarations as Black Is Beautiful, Black Lives Matter, and Black Girl Magic, among others. This way, Black people recognize each other, even when the dominant society does not.

When unapologetic Black girls and boys start being too free, Black people call each other in. Our elders and our cautious peers give us "the talk." We remind each other of the fatal consequences of Black people having "too much fun" or "moving too freely." We remind each other of the collective importance that we all survive. The oppressive nature of Black circumstances in America has forced us to almost always see ourselves as a racial group. We are what critic Edward Bland has called "pre-individual,"[42] where the stress is on the group and not the individual. Ellison argues that the preindividual state of Black life is artificially produced by society defining whiteness as not Black and rendering physical violence on the entire Black community, not just individuals.[43] Being wholly individual in this world is challenging because, as a person of color, you are treated and addressed in accordance with the social conditions of your racial group. Yet Black people have found an advantage in this production. We have a collective fan club. As Issa Rae said at the 2017 Emmy Awards, "I'm rooting for everybody Black."[44] At the same time, we have collective accountability partners. As scholar Brittany Cooper writes, African Americans "call each other out," as we did Bill Cosby and R. Kelly, reflecting our collective measuring and disciplining of immorality.[45] I argue that individual Black people go into the American landscape with the group inferiority complex. Rather than acquiring belonging in an American universe, they must hold tight to their racial allegiance to survive.

The framework of Black collective group maintenance follows this process:

> *Individuals made to be inferior* → enter a space of unbelonging → *form racial group allegiance* to survive.

This framework is not ideal for composing an American city that embraces its people as "many and yet one." Instead, it reinstates a segregated city and maintains the veil established by our predecessors. The upheaval of slavery, Jim Crow laws, and segregation moved Black people "from one way of life to another, but not from one life to another."[46] With this framework, Black people remain invisible ghosts that service the white hegemony's way of life. Moving to a life *with* white people and not *for* white people requires committing to a goal of transforming Black people's subjective sense of self-worth into a widely recognized objective truth.[47] Consider why modifications to our shared spaces can aid in this transformation. First, according to Fanon, inferiority results from a flaw in our environment. Additionally, self-consciousness demands external validation. Individuals must recognize the environment in which they live and realize their culture within it. This promotes belonging and combats inferiority. However, due to American individualism, our built environments frequently replicate "white spaces" that perpetuate a sense of alienation for people of color.

Even though this is evident, when Black locals speak out about gentrification, persistently exclaiming that these universalist values for diversity, inclusion, and belonging are not developing, those who want to maintain the current process revert to individualist arguments and assert that newcomers and investors have "individual rights." An individual or family can rightfully purchase undervalued property in a Black neighborhood, make repairs, live in it, or sell it. Individual developers can garner land in underdeveloped areas and build luxury houses or retail stores so long as it is within zoning codes, which, as we learned from Blandtown (see chapter 2), they can also negotiate to change outside of the will of the residents. An individual business owner can rent out space in an old factory and use it for his or her brewing company. This is the basis of capitalism, of property, and of liberty. Gay said it best in our interview: "Capitalism requires the new, and capitalism requires the shifting of Black bodies, irregardless of a place being supposedly 'ours.'"[48] And the American individualist views the unfair advantages of societal privilege as the result of independent achievement and excellence and is blind to structural injustices and racism.[49] Their race-neutral discourses commodify Black culture, making the space appealing for the income it can attract and not for its value to current residents.[50]

The biggest issue with redevelopment projects in America is that they are not effectively discussed in racial terms. It's concerning because "what divides this world is first and foremost what species, what race one belongs to."[51] Fanon argues that individualism is the first among many Western values that proves worthless because it has nothing to do with the struggle that people are facing in their lives. The idea of economic progress being available to individuals when they "pull themselves up by their bootstraps" is a fallacy to the sons and daughters of enslaved people who don't enter the world recognized as individuals but as racialized, dehumanized beings. The goal of creating diversity is admirable. But it can disregard laissez-faire racism, the contemporary experience of racial inequality that "relies on the market and informal racial bias to re-create, and in some instances sharply worsen, structured racial inequality."[52] You may recall from economics that "laissez-faire" means "hands-free." It's the classical economic principle promoted by Adam Smith that an economy on autopilot, with little federal-government intervention, allows individuals to freely pursue their self-interests and naturally benefits the larger public. In our modern capitalist marketplace, we think we have put individualism on autopilot, arguing that through laissez-faire economics, the market will adjust itself as individuals make decisions affecting supply and demand. The senior economic-development manager's comment at the BeltLine meeting was a performance of this framing. But in actuality, because of our history, America's laissez-faire economic plan didn't throw *individuals* into a system on autopilot. Instead, it threw *racial groups* in, and it jammed up the system so that poor white people would stay poor if it kept Black people poor too and cemented the white group's power of position.

Our market system is more readily determined by race than by individuals and class because it's a laissez-faire racist system that replaced the biologically based racism of the Jim Crow era. In a "manner appropriate to a modern, nationwide, postindustrial free labor economy and polity," laissez-faire racism can legitimate "persistent Black oppression in the United States." And a "significant segment of white America effectively condones" this form of racism under the laissez-faire ideology of survival of the fittest.[53] America's market system is not built of individuals getting closer to universality. A critical examination of the BeltLine's narrative in the West End reveals that the project is not moving from *individual* to *universal* interest. Instead, cultural gentrification is occurring because, contrary to popular belief, we are not an individualistic nation; we are a racial one. And not only African Americans but all Americans are shifting from *individual* to *group allegiance*.

Generally, Americans move in groups by race. Race-based movement has been encouraged by racial covenants and redlining, which devalue Black property. For that individual family, that developer, and that business owner to be advantageous in a lower-class neighborhood, they must attract wealthier, often whiter, families to the area. This result stems from the American racial economy, which devalues Black property ownership.[54] Gentrification and other movements of the affluent are not solely individual since affluence demands power, and power depends on a group with both social and economic affluence. The individual in a democratic social order is vulnerable to a shift in class and status and even to falling to the bottom. The insecurity of an individual's status "drives individuals to merge identities with that of an exalted group."[55] There is strength in numbers. But in this way, individualism and white supremacy end up working hand in hand. The white hegemony gains economic success and furthers Black displacement by pooling access, power, and voice. Those who belong to the white group can maintain some sort of institutional significance as long as Black people are undervalued. Investors purchased Lee + White, and brewing companies rented it out, betting on the probability of more wealthy, white individuals coming to the neighborhood. Therefore, gentrification is not a conflict of individuals versus individuals but groups versus groups as it is through the white racial group that gentrifiers find an advantage in moving to a Black neighborhood. That's white privilege.

In places like the West End, Black lifeworlds are culturally available there for the convenient use of gentrifiers. As Summers argues, "the incorporation and appropriation of Black self-fashioning, blackness-as-taste, blackness-as-style, blackness-as-struggle, and blackness-as-nostalgia into mainstream markets have created a new medium of racial representation, consumption, and commercial growth."[56] But Black people still maintain an unequal economic and social status. And that inequality is exacerbated by the gentrification that gives the "illusion of inclusion."[57] As local African American brewery co-owner William Teasley explains during our interview, property owners give "limited chances to current residents to open small business and start-up companies in their developments. Every space occupied in Lee + White is from businesses owned by people from outside the community." Additionally, "the outflow of cash from the community and its long-term members" are made worse when attracting outsiders is the main objective.[58]

The American landscape develops its outcasts based on the historical and present association of these spaces with racism, homophobia, misogyny, and classism. These outcasts are out-groups from this idealized universal American identity. As Ralph Ellison wrote to foundational rhetorician Kenneth Burke in a private letter, "I certainly agree with you that universalism is desirable, but I find that I am forced to arrive at that universe through the racial grain of sand."[59] Ellison argues that what exists is a racial–universal dichotomy. He says, "to throw away the concern with the racial . . . would for me be like cutting away the stairs leading from my situation in the world to that universalism of which you speak."[60] In this case, Ellison acknowledges that African Americans cannot throw away race if they ever want to be humanized. As Bryan Crable summarizes, America's problem, according to Ellison, "is not the quest for the universal; rather, the problem lies in the attempt to disguise racial bias behind a 'universal' ethic, in seeking to 'transcend' racial identity by ignoring race-based privilege—and racial injustice."[61]

The race-based privilege here is defined as the continued use of whiteness to gain an advantage. We live in a world where white "individuals" benefit from opportunities that people of color don't receive simply because white people are not Black. That is the definition of "whiteness." Whiteness is rhetorically constructed as power, as not Black, Latinx, or another ethnicity, as not having any other bloodlines, as without other labels.[62] By constituting white in terms of every race it is not, we rhetorically devalue all other ethnic groups. "This is a characteristic of domination."[63] And so long as it continues, the racial stairstep is one that people of color will always have to overcome before their worth can be seen as valid objective truth. Brittney Cooper articulates this experience eloquently, writing,

> Before we fully learn to love ourselves, all people of color in the United States learn that we are supporting characters and spectators in the collective story of white people's lives. The stories we watch and read ask us to put aside their whiteness and relate to their universal human struggles around conflict with the world, the self, and others. The problem is that only the experiences of white people are treated as universal.[64]

In this light, the "universal ethic" that Americans seek stems from a white individualist conception of the universal, making the starting point for a collective American identity racial and not individual. When this individualist myth becomes a part of the development plans, consciously or unconsciously, irrespective of intent, it impacts cultural gentrification. It can discourage the cultural citizenship of diverse groups within the space. This is further reinforced by contemporary Western nostalgia for an idyllic sense of place—one that speeds our spaces backward to a time of white idealism. The Western view is that because of the global village, there is no longer a sense of their idealized local places inhabited by coherent and homogenous communities.[65] Thus, part of the urban revitalization process includes moving backward to that mythic place. It's part and parcel of the phrase "Make America great again," and it goes beyond partisanship. The individualistic fallacy sounds like "I'm not racist. I'm a good person. And everyone is invited into my restaurant, studio, café, store, or bar created in the form and style of the 1950s." The focus in this statement is the intent and not the impact. White individualism and colorblind racism make it easy to consider that the past that gives white people lovely recollections garners the same sympathies from people of color. Bringing a primarily beer-focused establishment into a Black neighborhood and not having any of the already few Black brew owners included in the space makes Lee + White a service to a white sense of place. As more people become nostalgic for an idyllic Western sense of place and use a past that has not had its moral reckoning to determine the future use of the space, our revitalized landscape reinforces historical exclusions and recollects traumatic moments of racism, sexism, and genderism. This is further detrimental to the collective identity of African Americans as a group, proving why America is a racial, not an individualist, nation.

A close rhetorical analysis of cultural gentrification helps us to see better that we are not individuals becoming more universal but individuals reinstating racial allegiances so repetitively that they trap us. And a continued justification of urban redevelopment based on individual rights will keep us there. The BeltLine cannot create a universal community in

Atlanta by ignoring the racial stairstep—the historic barrier we have to cross to form the public meeting ground Gravel envisioned. We do not have the privilege of being oblivious of history or of how our environment's narrative structure perpetuates the unbelonging and uncitizenship of people of color in the United States. We cannot leap over four hundred years of oppression and discrimination against Black people and the abuses of Native Americans. We must be deliberate in all our actions and take every step through and out of racism. We require an "effective eradication of the superstructure" left by colonialists, imperialists, and enslavers.[66] Individualistic Western values that seem to elevate the soul must be silenced and the "spiral of violence," broken.[67] Black voices must stand up, proclaiming they are equal. Black culture, as an expression of real-life struggle, must be visible in our surroundings.

This chapter takes up this issue in observation of the spatial narrative produced by the Atlanta BeltLine as a location outside of homes and places of employment where people interact and engage with diverse others. Suppose we regarded the BeltLine trails as a representative place for the city of Atlanta. In that case, we could think about how it creates places of remembrance (like museums and memorials) and areas for recreation and performance that let locals and visitors express their individual and group identities. As the built environment of Atlanta shifts with new capital investment in luxury housing, gourmet restaurants, yoga studios, and hipster cafés and bars, we must review the historical narratives associated with these places to understand how their inclusion could solidify the exclusion of African Americans from cultural belonging. The narratives established by these locations can engage memories of an American past that could be archetypal for the dominant group while they are damaging for the historically marginalized. As the research of this chapter suggests, the alcohol and beer industry in Atlanta, Georgia, and the nation has a history of criminalizing African Americans and empowering white Americans toward the exclusion of Black bodies from space.

This is the case in the West End: the history of the neighborhood's formation represents the reality in America that it is a nation of groups, ever increasing their racial allegiance for self-protection. The framework for white allegiance follows this process:

> White people fearing inferiority → use power to create spaces of belonging → reinstate white racial group allegiance.

The framework for Black allegiance follows this process:

> Black people made to be inferior → forced to assimilate to white space → reinstate Black racial group allegiance for survival.

What I seek to reveal as I dive into the history of West End and the historical admonishment of Black drinking culture in Atlanta is that because of the allied connection of power to the white race, the reality of the racial-universal dichotomy in America, and the upholding of American individualism, acts that on their face pursue universalism lead to further racial segregation.

CULTURAL GENTRIFICATION OF THE WEST END

West End is home to numerous sites of Black memory: a homage to Black art in Hammonds House Museum, a revolutionary Black spirituality at the Shrine of the Black Madonna, and the recovering of the beneficial aspects of Black soul food at Soul Vegetarian. But if you were to walk the Atlanta BeltLine trail around the complete and incomplete chartings of its path, those locations would not be in view. As the BeltLine trail continues production with sidewalks and the eventual streetcars/trolley system, a new transport route is being forged. According to its own "universalist" goals, the BeltLine would provide new access points into neighborhoods around Atlanta. The latest gateway to the West End puts white life on the front street, in the public's view. As if turning back the hands of time, the mobility imposed by the trail focuses on a white idyllic past that would gentrify much of the Black cultural productions in the area. To understand how cultural gentrification is imposed, I reconstruct the world the ghosts of Beer Town's past conjure. I begin at the start of the West End, recovering the narrative process by which the white ideal home was established as a reflection of the circular nature of America's racial reality.

HOW THE WEST WAS WON: THE FORMATION OF THE WEST END AS A RACIAL, NOT INDIVIDUALIST, PURSUIT

The formation of the West End from germination to growth is a representative anecdote of anti-Black racism promulgated in space. From a tavern to the first brewery in the city, beer became a staple in the new settlement. It just as quickly became a force for opposition between the secular and the sacred, and between Black and white, defining movement through the social environment. If not truthfully acknowledged, the narrative could present itself as individuals seeking communal prosperity rather than a racial group satisfying desires by constructing an allegiance into the landscape.

In 1830, Atlanta, known as Terminus at the time, was mainly a forest area, best described as a frontier with trails and dirt roads traveled by Native Americans, early settlers, and traders. In 1836, the state's general assembly voted to expand the Western Atlantic Railroad to link the Port of Savannah and Tennessee. But even before the passage of the act, white settlers moved into the area. As traders used local dirt roads to move between settlements, there came a need for a hotel. Charner Humphries (1795–1855) had a plantation, with twenty-five to thirty enslaved people, south of the area and ended up opening the community's first tavern,[68] as well as a racetrack north of the site (in today's location of Spelman College).[69] He painted the two-story tavern white. Being the first painted house in the county, the tavern was named Whitehall or White Hall.[70] Whitehall Tavern was known to be the only hotel for travelers from southern Georgia to Tennessee.[71]

The tavern became a metaphor for mobility—mainly, white freedom of movement. The tavern's location, on Gordon Street and Lee Street, reflected the dominant movement of people into and out of the budding neighborhood. Native Americans initially routed the trails, and after the land was taken from them in 1821, white settlers used the routes as they were the paths of least resistance in the heavily forested area.[72] A former resident described Gordon Street as "being an old Indian trail; where the Cherokees used to travel, where the intrepid white man pushed his trade; and the hardy back woodsmen were accustomed to take lodging at night."[73] White settlers used Gordon Street as the main road west to Decatur, Georgia. The crossroad, Lee Street, was the main road to go south to Newnan. A north-south highway developed in 1848, west of Lee Street, became the main highway under the name Whitehall Street.[74] Because of its location, the tavern was also the place to deliver and pick up mail. Soon the neighborhood also had a name: Whitehall, drawn from the inn that functioned as its central point of social interaction and movement.

The tavern's social features and location made it fundamental to forming the neighborhood's culture in its early years. It functioned rhetorically as a zone of contact where settlers, militiamen, and travelers could go to and experience "public symbols of the ideals and aspirations—and thus the identity—to be shared by every citizen" and member of the fledgling community.[75] According to the 1931 unpublished manuscript of Wilbur G. Kurtz, which chronicles the interview he had with Humphries' son-in-law, the tavern was an important social space. It had eight rooms, generous hall space, a porch, a dining room, two fireplaces, and a kitchen, where cooks "prepared wonderful concoctions before a fire-place, with a battery of 'spiders,' pots, pans, and portable ovens."[76] West of the house was a horse stable, and across from it was Charner's store, where he sold rum, which was the "merchandise in demand in a frontier community."[77]

The tavern was the place to go for the county's Muster Day for annual militia enrollment. During the event, able-bodied men would take part in drills of marksmanship. The winner would get the yearling cow, which was eaten with a potent form of brown October ale,[78] a type of beer made using top-fermenting yeast.[79] A whiskey barrel was also standard. And Humphries kept drinks on tap, and cash customers could drink on the house, while visitors were expected to pay a nickel or dime.[80] In this way, a fresh, local whiskey or ale was the staple of the Whitehall neighborhood. Whitehall Tavern stopped operating after the Civil War. Some say it was taken down and the timbers were used to build a house. Other accounts are that it was burned during the war.[81] Regardless, its memory persists because it provided a place where new settlers could encounter each other and come to comprehend what it meant to be a southern American.

Beer was significant to the social functioning of Atlanta and Whitehall, particularly in the 1850s. Indeed, considering the conservative manner in which the South contemplates beer and alcohol policy today, it is hard to conceive of this past, but taking the past into account provides at least one view of the idealized sense of place white hegemony yearns for today. The proclaimed godfather of Atlanta brewing, Edgidius "Edgion" Fetcher, got his start in Whitehall. Brewing came to the United States and Atlanta with an increase in German immigrants in the mid to late 1800s. They brought a brewing technology that allowed the production of lager beer and fueled local beer production in Atlanta. Fetcher and his brother migrated from Germany to Atlanta and opened the first brewery near Howell Park, on today's White Street and Westside Trail. Though the name and exact location have been lost to history, it is known that Fetcher's brewery stopped operating after the Civil War.[82]

After the war, the city put a license tax on bars. Being outside the city limits, Whitehall didn't need to heed the tax, and an increasing number of bars opened in the area. According to historian Cornelia E. Cooper, there were at least seven bars and two breweries in Whitehall at one point. One brewery was located on today's Lawton Street (cross street unknown), and the other was across from the Candler Warehouse, once the largest cotton warehouse in the city, located near today's West End MARTA (Metropolitan Atlanta Rapid Transit Authority) Station. Pre–Civil War Whitehall's breweries and bars led to the production and distribution of alcoholic beverages in the area. It could have made out to be the Malt Disney of the era until post–Civil War Confederate angst led supporters to seek the construction of a New South for white America. The strategy of exclusion and regulation of Black people and the federal troops eventually led to cauterizing the beer and liquor industry in Whitehall and then to the rest of Atlanta.

By 1870, the Whitehall neighborhood was home to three hundred Black people, which was almost 50 percent of the population. The influx of freed men and women in the area occurred because of the presence of federal troops at the McPherson Barracks, the previous location of Humphries's racetrack on the northeastern end of the neighborhood, which would become the site of Spelman College after troops left in December 1881. The barracks became a refuge for freedmen and spurred early diversity in the neighborhood. But such integration of the newly freed into white space was short-lived as Confederate sympathizers strategized to make Whitehall more exclusive.

The postwar environment inspired Confederate supporters to take control of the future of the neighborhood and its culture. West End's history after the Civil War reflects the designation of the space as a white middle- to upper-class hotbed. George Washington Adair (1823–1899), first a slave trader and then a real-estate broker after the war, sought to sell land he purchased in Whitehall and attract white middle- to upper-class residents. As Timothy J. Crimmins chronicles, Adair's plan included a process of exclusion that started with renaming the neighborhood, designating its boundaries, and naming its streets in commemoration of the Confederacy. First, the McPherson Barracks, where freedmen were taking refuge, were excluded from the official neighborhood limits, as was the future Atlanta University Center. Second, the name West End was chosen by Adair based on the name of West End in London, a fashionable commercial and entertainment center. The name symbolized what Adair hoped Whitehall would become for the city of Atlanta. Third, Adair and early property owners created social distance by changing street names to commemorate Confederate forces, including Stephen Lee (commander in chief of the United Confederate Veterans), General John B. Gordon (Confederate general), Brigadier General Turner Ashby (Confederate general), and General Alexander R. Lawton (quartermaster general of the Confederacy).[83] Except for Gordon Street, these street names are still present within the neighborhood limits today. They reflect the hegemony's consideration of symbols in the built environment as an association for identification with the place. West End, from the start, was to be recognized by the culture and values of the Confederacy, thus excluding African Americans in the representations of place.

The next step to distance the neighborhood from unwanted others included finding a way to not only isolate the federal government but also regulate federal soldiers who frequented saloons in West End. This led residents to seek state incorporation, allowing them to tax liquor dealers and manufacturers. Licensing would help save the town from getting a bad name because of "unruly behavior" from alcohol consumption.[84] The neighborhood that was all wet quickly "dried up." The legislature applied for state incorporation in 1868 and was granted the charter, allowing them to tax liquor dealers and manufacturers.[85] In 1878, the neighborhood secured a charter to forbid the sale of intoxicating beverages. In 1893, its need for a fire department and other protections led to West End's annexation by the city of Atlanta. The city pledged to continue West End's prohibition of alcohol. What we learn is that white residents were willing to forgo their alcohol use to inhibit the federal government from assisting freed Black people having any.

Seeking to attract new white residents, Adair and other property owners sold land for less than its worth, supported the Atlanta Street Railway, and promoted the neighborhood as a great place for businessmen who worked in the city. In particular, setting up ease of mobility of people into the area was essential to neighborhood growth, according to Crimmins.[86] The Atlanta Street Railway—a trolley line—was formed, running west to Lee Street and south to Gordon Road.

Adair invested in the railway company, building capital and power for the development of the new town. Crimmins describes that the location of the railway on the original main arteries made the Gordon-Lee intersection a commercial sector, where men working in the city could take a trolley home. Victorian homes were built along the streetcar route. In addition, the lower cost of property made for an excellent investment, increasing the wealth of early financiers. This information reveals that strategic plans regarding the movement of people in the neighborhood affected its growth and determined the types of people—primarily white businessmen—that would enter West End, making it an upper- to middle-class space dominated by white males. Former Atlanta mayor Evan P. Howell described the neighborhood in 1890: "West End is emphatically a residence community. There are no manufactories with soot and dust, no paupers, but a thrifty, well-to-do class of people, who generally own their homes, who have their garden, their flower yards, their horse and cow and fowls, and, who, away from the noise and dust and strife of the great city, live in quiet and comfort."[87] This description reflects the initial culture and purpose of West End as a space outside of a working-class city and set apart for middle- to upper-class white life. West End had formed its own social distance from African Americans, the federal government, and lower-class whites. By 1890, the population had risen to one thousand, with very little growth in Black bodies, as the Black population went from 50 percent of the neighborhood in 1870 to 33 percent twenty years later. By 1930, only 15 percent of the population was Black, and their homes were closer to Spelman in the northern portion of the town.[88] Then, Interstate 20—an expressway running east to west—was designed in the late 1950s and constructed in the 1960s. It ran through West End, separating the northern portion of the town from the southern half. It was promoted to West End residents as a suitable means to keep Black students and faculty at the historically Black colleges north of the neighborhood out.[89] West End was an identifiable white space in a diversifying city. White individuals were finding belonging and reinstating white allegiance through their use of space.

The city was doing the same. While West End promoted the temperance movement within its neighborhood, the larger city was having a temperance movement of its own. In the early days after the Civil War and into Reconstruction, alcoholic beverages were a crucial factor in separating people—the rural from the urban, the sacred from the secular, the Confederacy from the federal government, and white from Black. With the clear intention of identifying post–Civil War West End with a southern Confederate identity, the early developers sought to use its stance on alcohol to identify its old southern values. But more broadly, the war over beer and alcohol in the city and Fulton County, in which it resides, brings to attention the widening racism against African Americans, Jews, and German immigrants. As Ron Smith and Mary O. Boyle state, "Prohibition had become a battle over not only alcohol but also more generally about who was a 'real American.'"[90]

The temperance movement in Atlanta started before the war and was reignited after the war as alcohol consumption increased. The move across the United States was spurred by the argument that consuming alcohol led to domestic violence and economic ruin. Before West End's incorporation, from 1885 to 1887, Fulton County (where Atlanta is located) was voted dry. Under the local option law, whiskey and spirits were banned, while local wines could be sold. Breweries could continue to brew beer, but it was illegal to sell it within the county. The dry law was short-lived. By 1887, another vote brought the county back to wet status. But as stated before, as a part of their annexation, West End was able to maintain prohibition. Alcohol—particularly African American and Jewish immigrants drinking and selling alcohol—became the scapegoat for white violence against Black bodies, leaving Black people to carry shame for public drinking.

ATLANTA'S RACE RIOTS

Atlanta's elite developers perceived a model of racial cooperation as a threat to the New South and a rejuvenated white space that would rise out of the Civil War. "Blacks were transformed, as whites perceived their collective future, from permanent productive members of the New South into destructive obstacles to the realization of a revitalized white South," writes historian Gregory Lamont Mixon.[91] As such, violence against Black bodies was a tactic by Atlanta elites for maintaining white supremacy. Anti-Black fervor increased in 1904 as many white people feared "racial equality" and expressed anxiety about the ability of the legal system and white paternalism to regulate Black bodies in the industrializing and urbanizing South. By the summer of 1906, the angst had grown to a boil, leading white people to seek violence and scapegoating to restore racial order for their state of "white crisis" in what is now known as the Atlanta race riots.

Two types of white-fear-inducing stories proliferated in the *Atlanta Constitution* and *Atlanta Journal* newspapers in September 1906, encouraging immediate vitriol against Black Atlanta: (1) accusations of Black sexual assaults against white women and (2) allegations that Black drinking establishments were the cause of the alleged attacks on white women.[92] Papers published on the Friday and Saturday before the race massacre claimed that the "City License Inspector Ewing found pictures of nude white women openly exhibited in Black clubs on Decatur Street."[93] In the nineteenth century, Decatur Street—east of West End toward the city center—was a white prostitution district. However, by the 1900s, Black prostitution entered the area. Black-owned "dens and dives" were available for cheap lodging and drinks.[94] In addition, Jewish businessmen and businesswomen served alcohol in integrated saloons. The street included "Colored Saloons," as well as Chinese, Greek, Italian, and Syrian businesses.[95] Segregation forced Black people to be served in the back. An *Atlanta Journal* article described it as the "street of shame," where drunken people joined with criminal whites, smelling like old beer, assorted drinks, and grease used for frying food.[96] With the newspaper's increased focus on the vice of Decatur Street as a threat to the sexual safety of white women, on September 21, the day before the riot, the operating licenses of twenty-two Black restaurants were terminated.

Then, on Saturday, September 22, 1906, a new headline reached the newsstands, asserting that four white women were assaulted with at least one "black brute" suspected, one Black man arrested, and another unidentified person on the run. Mixon writes, "The papers claimed that white women were prisoners in their own homes because the streets were flooded with 'black beasts.' The slightest touch or even movement in the shadows prompted many of Atlanta's white female population to scream first and assume they were assaulted by the infamous black brute."[97]

The alleged assaults justified the white brutal and indiscriminate attacks on Black bodies from September 22 to 24, 1906, which led to the killing of approximately twenty-five to forty-seven Black people.[98] The vigilante mob gathered at "Marietta, Peachtree, Whitehall, Decatur, and Broad streets," starting their attack on Black people on Decatur and Marietta Streets, even though the alleged sexual assaults occurred in a mixed residential area of Atlanta and Dekalb County.[99] Outnumbering Black folks on the streets at least two to one, the white mob was armed with "clubs, iron pipes, and brick bats."[100] They continued to areas where Black people were isolated and could be outnumbered. The mob attacked street cars as Black individuals were riding trolleys downtown. Black people were prohibited from buying arms, but Black women fought back with umbrellas and hair pins, while in more densely populated Black neighborhoods, they retaliated against white streetcar riders. Some solitary police officers attempted to protect Black people against the rioters when it was easy, but "mass police efforts to maintain order usually were overwhelmed by white power."[101] Some joined the rioters or aided efforts by staving off Black retaliation. For instance, Sheriff John W. Nelms gathered 150 white business and professional men from the West End to keep Black people from fighting back. Atlanta's National Guardsmen started coming out to quell the rampage early Sunday morning. They took control of the streets from Sunday to Tuesday "not to suppress the riot but to prevent Black retaliation."[102] Black people found seeking vengeance were rounded up by the Georgia militia.

In the end, the riots utilized to reinstate white control over Black bodies inevitably worked to reinforce white supremacy in Atlanta. This is evidenced in the ways punishments were divvied for the events. One white police officer died, and sixty or seventy Black people were jailed for it. Alex Walker, however, was the only one convicted of the officer's death. He was sentenced to life in prison, while "no white rioter received a sentence as severe as life imprisonment for killing a black person during the riot."[103] In the aftermath, segregation was reinforced in businesses and social life across the city, and Black folks were disfranchised, losing political power until the 1940s.

Walter White, then the thirteen-year-old future president of the National Association for the Advancement of Colored People, provides insight into the ideological underpinnings that emblazoned these events. During the riots, he attempted to protect his family home in Darktown, a Black district in downtown Atlanta. White, whose complexion could pass for white, used his fair skin advantageously to purchase weapons. He and his father watched vigilantly as a mob approached their two-story home. However, before they had to fire their weapons, a friend distracted the crowd by setting off a volley of shots from a brick building. The group of white renegades went in the other direction. But in the experience, White learned something about his identity. According to his account,

> I was a Negro, a human being with an invisible pigmentation which marked me a person to be hunted, hanged, abused, discriminated against, kept in poverty and ignorance, in order that those whose skin was white would have readily at hand a proof of their superiority, a proof patent and inclusive, accessible to the moron and the idiot as well as to the wise man and genius. No matter how low a white man fell, he could always hold fast to the smug conviction that he was superior to two-thirds of the world's population, for those two-thirds were not white.[104]

In this experience, White finds himself as a living ghost, a phantom existing for the reestablishment of white superiority. In his words, we also see the more significant critical assessment of the riot: white people instituted a witch hunt against Black people to protect white personhood and maintain segregation.

Rather than Black people being victims of white hate, Black people with beer and alcohol were sanctioned as threats, establishing the drinks as symbols of separation of Black and white folks and regulation of alcohol as a means of controlling Black bodies. Black men were codified as animals after white women, degrading Black masculinity. Meanwhile, Black women were marginalized in a narrative concerned with protecting white women from the mythic predator. The *Atlanta News* articles argued that Black people needed to be subdued for white safety.[105] The implied causation between Black drinking and rape provided support for closing Black dens and dives, reinforcing the need for prohibition across the state. Newspaper articles throughout the South used the race riots in Atlanta to encourage the closing of Black establishments. The editor of the *Atlanta Journal* encouraged the prevention of licenses being given to any man, white or Black, who would sell alcohol to Black people.[106]

Atlanta's national humiliation was thought to be caused by Black people drinking.[107] Over two hundred Black and white elites came together in a combined meeting in the city council on the Tuesday after the riots died down. In the forum, the cause of the riot was determined to be the "low dives," which included saloons, dens, and clubs. Because these businesses were made into the scapegoat, carrying the sins of the attackers, they had to be removed from the city. The group declared that they must be closed. The dens on Decatur and Peters Streets were targeted. In addition, by the end of the month, a grand jury condemned the *Atlanta News* for inciting the riot. From October 1906 to January 1907, white Atlanta defined "Law and Order" and reestablished conservative rule to solve the race issue.[108]

The vision of a drunken Black man was enough to spur white people to agree to prohibition, regardless of their own pleasure from the drink.[109] All the fervor against Black alcohol establishments provided fuel for temperance, and lawmakers wrote new legislation for Georgia-wide prohibition. In 1907, the Hardman-Covington-Neel Bill made statewide prohibition mandatory.[110] This racial history reflects the intense passion that southern white people had for policing Black bodies and returning to a white-dominated region. It is a part of the shame placed on Black individuals and the privilege given to white individuals. While white Americans may have an idyllic perception of the freedom from alcohol regulation in the pre-temperance movement era, African American collective memory holds on to a more traumatic conception of the past and present racial dichotomies—times when alcohol was used to separate the races. These moments inevitably affected the future of African Americans in the brewing business, which I will discuss in the following sections. But first, I turn back to the West End to understand how the white, exclusionary neighborhood eventually became a mecca of Black culture.

AFRICAN AMERICAN ESTABLISHMENT OF WEST END AS A BLACK MECCA

Because of white racial allegiances embedded in space, Black communities combat historical exclusion from the celebrated landscape of the United States by attempting to form their own home. When a culture sees a substance of themselves in a public place, they are more likely to identify with it, transcending any other differences between themselves and differing others and becoming a part of the group. In this way, identification with place occurs when the sites yield to the people's language, featuring their attitudes and values.[111] The invitation to join the collective does not come unless you can create and publicize your cultural symbols of representation in that location.

By 1930, the West End population totaled 22,882, with 15 percent being Black. The majority of the small Black population lived at the northern edge of the neighborhood, closest to Spelman College, which was founded as a seminary for Black women, moving from its location at Friendship Baptist Church to the old McPherson Barracks location in 1883. Though Adair and early West End developers had successfully made West End a "homogeneous, well-to-do white community" in the early twentieth century,[112] the civil rights movement—specifically, the 1954 *Brown v. Board of Education* ruling against separate-but-equal laws in schools—began the integration of all areas of society. In the 1960s, once they could access housing in West End, Black people increasingly moved there. In response, white residents fled to areas north of the city center, reflecting retaliation to integration and the white privilege of mobility in and out of areas at will. By 1976, West End's Black population made up 86 percent of the residents. Whereas Whitehall Tavern

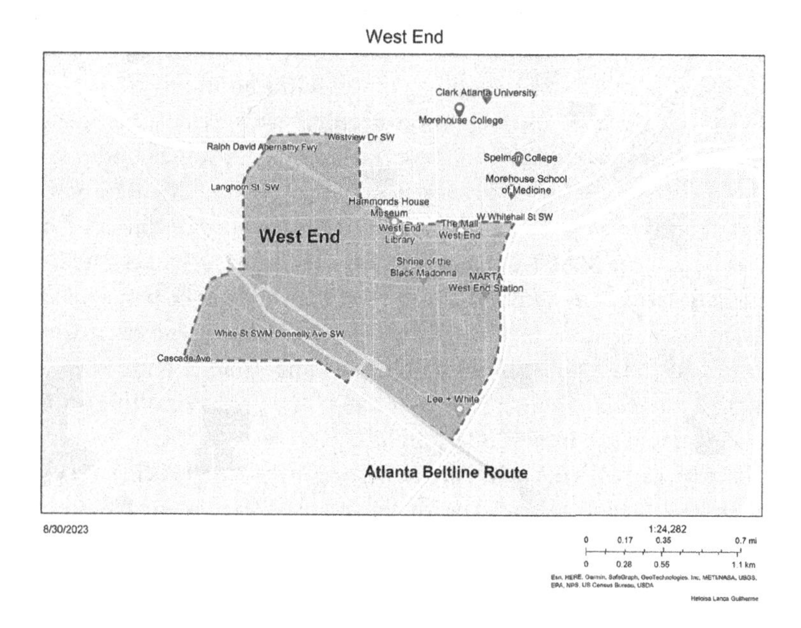

Map of West End with a focus on the northeastern corner and Black cultural sites of memory developed from 1908 to the present by Heloisa Lanca Guilherme. The dashed lines mark the boundaries of West End. The solid line marks the Atlanta BeltLine trail segment as it goes through West End. Point icons represent various sites of memory and Lee + White's location, which extends about a half mile along White Street.

and the trolley system brought white businessmen to the area in its early years, it was a mall and public train system that would become the nexus of Black movement in and out of West End.

A look at the deep map of West End's sites of memory shows that they are all located in the northeastern corner of the neighborhood. This is the same area that eventually developed into a commercial center in the early twentieth century around the original location of Whitehall Tavern. Although white consumers and businessmen gradually stopped visiting these locations, a more modern transportation system cemented the Gordon-Lee intersection as the gateway for in-and-out traffic in the late twentieth century. The mall increased the neighborhood's appeal to visitors.

As white wealth left the neighborhood, the city of Atlanta and the remaining white residents wanted to revitalize West End. The City of Atlanta Housing Authority invested $14 million, including federal dollars, to clear out 103.1 acres of land of older homes and commercial spaces for new construction, including a new mall.[113] The Mall West End was built on 14.9 acres and opened in 1973.[114] It connected with the already present

Sears, Roebuck and Co. store on Gordon Street (now Ralph David Abernathy Boulevard). Richard A. Dent was named mall manager, becoming the first Black director of a shopping center in the South.[115]

Even with the mall opening, it was necessary to provide a new generation with a means of getting to these businesses. Consumer traffic to the mall was encouraged by the development of the West End MARTA Station, which opened in 1982, bringing commuters to the neighborhood by both bus and train. The MARTA Station was constructed between Lee Street and Whitehall Street, across from the Mall West End. The public transportation directed traffic of students and faculty from the Atlanta University Center of historically Black colleges north of the neighborhood into the West End, making it a popular area for college students and professors. This brought in new, young Black professional families.[116]

However, there is a difference between being *in* a place and being *of* a place. Though white people migrated north, they were still represented in the built environment, leaving behind symbols of the racialized past, perpetuating anti-Black narratives. Many of the locations African Americans now call sites of memory for Black culture were originally resurrected for the supremacy of whiteness. The hostile history worked in opposition to the rhetorical purpose of shared public space, which, according to rhetorician Gregory Clark, is to "present images of actions that 'awaken a disposition' in the individuals who compose a community to act together upon values that constitute their common identity."[117] If the "common identity" of Black Americans needed to be "awakened" to foster belonging, new narratives had to be inscribed in the space. Thus, Black residents had to story the built environment in a new way by removing some of the relics of the white-supremacist past and providing counterhistories that center Black people as not only human but also worthy of visibility. The new Black residents did precisely that.

In 1991, Gordon Street, once named for a Confederate general, was renamed Ralph David Abernathy Boulevard (RDA), recognizing the civil rights leader and reverend who led the West Hunter Street Baptist Church on the main street. And in 2001, Ashby Street was renamed Joseph E. Lowery Boulevard after the civil rights movement pioneer. The name changes also reflected the shifting environment of Gordon Street and Ashby Street since African Americans became the majority population. Visible along the drive down RDA and west of Whitehall Street are the Mall West End, Soul Vegetarian, the Goodwill Thrift Store, and the Shrine of the Black Madonna—just a few of the locations that are key to Black collective identity in the space. The sites form a nucleus for the neighborhood, providing visibility to the diverse elements of African American culture that are supported by many of these locations, revealing how a space initially planned to be a white enclave could be transformed into a metaphorical origin for Black life after the civil rights movement. Beyond the renaming of Gordon Street to RDA Boulevard, the symbols centering Blackness are represented materially in the built environment with the shift of Uncle Remus library name to the West End Branch, the subsequent counterhistory of the Wren's Nest and Uncle Remus stories, repurposing of the Gordon Theatre to the Shrine of the Black Madonna, and establishing the Hammonds House Museum, all of which I'll discuss next.

One of the most controversial issues to hit West End was the push by Black residents to remove the name Uncle Remus from the local library branch. The original name recognized the internationally famous nineteenth-century American writer of the Uncle Remus stories, Joel Chandler Harris, who lived on Gordon Street. Harris fashioned the fables after stories told to him by George Terrell, an enslaved person on the Turnwold Plantation near Eatonton, Georgia. The narratives, including talking characters like Br'er Rabbit and Br'er Fox, became highly controversial to Black people, who recognized the white author's retelling of stories he heard from an enslaved person as a white framing of Black life and appropriation of Black work. The library itself represented the hypocrisy of racism. The caricature of Uncle Remus was used as the fictional Black narrator of Harris's stories. The library was named after this Uncle Tom–like character representing stereotypes of the obedient Black servant eager for the approval of white people. Still, at the time of its opening at its current location in 1949 (it was first opened in 1913 at Harris's home),[118] Black people were not allowed there. After the *Brown* ruling, residents throughout Atlanta fought against integrating Atlanta public libraries, with the main branch not being integrated until 1959.[119]

By the 1980s, the Uncle Remus Branch, still using the controversial name, was hosting heritage events to recognize Black history. Harris's book, though still available, was rarely used until tourists of Harris's home, the Wren's Nest, came in the summer. Black residents considered the name Uncle Remus evermore offensive, so they petitioned for the name change. In 1982, the Atlanta Public Library Board voted to change the name to West End Branch. The decision was made with a clear majority among trustees, voting seventeen to thirteen, but there was an uproar of dissent from people outside the Black community. One person argued that the stories are "a compliment to black people" because "Joel Chandler Harris loved them and appreciated them and wrote in their own dialect of the time."[120] Such comments reinforced the racial ignorance represented by the Uncle Remus stories. In an opinion piece, name-change opponent Waights G. Henry Jr. wrote that Harris did for Black people what Homer did for the Greeks by preserving their thoughts and folklore.[121]

While Henry felt that the name change buried the Black past, the Black residents of West End, like Michael Lomax—an English teacher at Morehouse and Spelman—considered it offensive to recognize a history reflected in a "stereotyped character [Uncle Remus] from the old plantation school of southern literature."[122] Henry failed to acknowledge that Homer had the privilege of getting credit for his work while African Americans did not. Removing Uncle Remus from the library name was a step toward forming a built environment that was inclusive of Black thought and Black people.

In addition, activists shed light on how Harris's stories had been used to whitewash slavery in a revisionist history to make the past more acceptable, leading libraries across the nation to remove Harris's books during the civil rights era. It also forced the Joel Chandler Harris Association to rethink admission policies that excluded Black people from patronizing the Wren's Nest, a museum opened at Harris's home after he died in 1908. Named the Wren's Nest for a wren that nested in the mailbox in the late 1800s, the national historic landmark housed the library before it moved to its current location in 1949, where it continues to get visitors interested in the author. The Harris Association was able to purchase and preserve the land with the aid of money from former US president Theodore Roosevelt and business tycoon Andrew Carnegie.

In his day, Harris was seen as a progressive leader. Although he did not advocate integration and held high regard for the Old South, he did support Black education and the right to vote. Though Harris's stated goal was toward "the obliteration of prejudice against blacks . . . and the uplifting of both races so that they can look justice in the face without blushing," the museum formed in his honor excluded Black patronage until a court order in 1968 forced integration.[123] Nonetheless, the museum's image and Harris's memory had been tarnished, and a loss of subsidies from the city kept the museum from getting necessary upgrades. In the 1980s, the association, run by one hundred white women, was forced to broaden its membership to men, reframe the Uncle Remus stories in the media to restore its popularity, and fundraise for nearly $300,000 worth of necessary improvements. The association was also advised by West End Neighborhood Development president Cleta Winslow that they would need to emphasize Black people's contributions to Harris's work if they wanted to improve its image. The 1982 elected association president, Gloria Baker, sought to "transform the decaying house into a museum that all citizens of Atlanta, black and white, can be proud of."[124]

Furthering these efforts, in an *Atlanta Constitution* article, characters like Br'er Rabbit were positioned as more worthy of remembering for their African origins than the invented narrator, Uncle Remus. He was likened to an Uncle Tom. Harris was characterized as a folklorist who did not intend to be condescending in using a Black southern dialect in his writing.[125] In addition, the Wren's Nest stopped screening new members, opening membership to all interested parties.[126] These actions toward inclusivity, though still in recognition of a controversial and offensive history, were spurred by Black West Enders' need to form a built environment that invited their identity and accurately documented the troubling and traumatic history that brought them there. African Americans' public condemnation of the work, which was national in scope, resulted in a drop in patronage at the Wren's Nest and the removal of books that were once required school reading from the Atlanta public school curriculum.[127] Once these issues were brought to light, the library transitioned from a site that retracted the Black experience to one that invites the Black experience. In addition, the Black story of resistance became a part of the narrative of the neighborhood. They are now symbols of Black resistance to a social order that attempted to romanticize and appropriate their past. The sites support a coordinated effort to overcome the oppressive past and establish a shared future.

Such changes were also evident in the use of past buildings to reflect diversity in Black religious thought and theology, which work as "constitutions," expressing a shared reality and establishing the "expectations and conventions" of the "social order."[128] In the *Lit without Sherman* exhibit by artist Shanequa Gay, art and audio recordings of residents give a glimpse of a West End full of religious diversity, from Rastafarians, Muslims, and Christians to Buddhists. However, the Shrine of the Black Madonna stands out as a critical collective site of memory for West End residents because of its community work and its prime visible location on RDA Boulevard. The Shrine of the Black Madonna, made up of adherents to a denomination of the Pan African Orthodox Christian Church, opened a location in 1975 on the original site of the Gordon Theatre. This segregated theater opened in 1940, with this community film emporium seating 1,300 people.[129] During a time of racial unrest, forty members of Detroit's Shrine of the Black Madonna transformed a facility designated as a white space for entertainment into a center for Black empowerment. The theology of the Shrine became popular in the 1950s and '60s. It centers Black people in Christianity and Jesus as a Black Jew to address the needs of a "black revolution," according to Albert B. Cleage, who started the church in Detroit.[130] Christianity, a religion sometimes vilified as a "white man's religion," is recognized as a "black man's religion" within the Shrine of the Black Madonna.[131]

In the West End, the Shrine operates a bookstore and holds programs for the community. Many programs are centered on restoring African American identity and Black history. As such, it represents one of many segments of Black theology and political thought that are produced in efforts to reinforce Black identity and humanity in an anti-Black world. The Shrine of the Black Madonna buttresses a revolutionary-based theology in a space expected to conserve white ideology at the exclusion of others. It forges transcendence for African Americans with the West End space by (1) identifying a shared substance, Black trauma, and oppression, (2) providing resources for understanding the shared attitudes, like Black history classes and a Marcus Garvey Day celebration, and (3) establishing shared expectations for the people. In this way, theology works within the site of memory to provide a construction for the future.

Along with transitioning the space from being a segregated white space, West Enders cemented Black culture as an acceptable representation of Americanness. The visibility of Black culture continued to be reinforced in the built environment of West End as African Americans formed their own spaces for visibility. One such location continues to enforce its mission of honoring Black art and culture. This is the Hammonds House Museum, stationed in one of the three oldest houses in the historic district. Located just four miles west of the Mall West End, Hammonds House is named for Dr. Otis T. Hammonds, a Black doctor and retired chief of staff and anesthesiology at Southwest Community Hospital (now the Atlanta Center for Medical Research) in Atlanta who owned the nineteenth-century Victorian home. After he died in 1985, the Fulton County Board of Commissioners, led by Michael Lomax, purchased Hammonds's home to turn it into an African American research library. When the library board declined, the building was established as an art gallery, which was fitting for Hammonds, who both had a distinguished medical career and avidly participated in art preservation, collection, and support of Black Atlanta artists. Hammonds's collection of 250 artworks from Haitian, African, and African American artists was included in the home purchase. Since its opening, the museum has served as a gathering place for viewership and participation in Black culture, holding temporary exhibitions, jazz brunches, Kwanzaa celebrations, an awards gala for advocates of Atlanta's arts, and other art-inspired events. In 2018, the museum celebrated its thirtieth anniversary with an educational symposium that highlighted the impact it has had on West End and metropolitan Atlanta.[132] As a staple site of memory for Black Atlanta, the Hammonds House placement in an 1870s residence in the previously white-exclusive enclave reflects a transition of periods and the significance of West End to Black post-civil-rights-era history. In addition, when juxtaposed to the Wren's Nest, the Hammonds House shows what happens when Black artists are credited for Black art. These artists can communicate symbols that connect with other Black people through shared experiences. As a site holding these rhetorical symbols, Hammonds House contributes to the conscious and unconscious connectivity people have when images "symbolize a shared way of seeing and, ultimately, being" in the world.[133]

West End continued to draw witness to a generation of art and style in the 1990s as it became a congregating location for Black youth of the 1990s to celebrate music, dance, and hip-hop. A small club in West End was central to the Atlanta hip-hop scene and the life of its artists—Club 559. It's closed now, but for its lifetime, it was considered iconic to Atlanta's nightlife, particularly the promotion of Atlanta's Black music artists. Located on 559 Ashby Street (now Joseph E. Lowery Boulevard), the club was credited for turning songs into local hits. To visitors coming into the neighborhood, "559 was a club in a then-unfamiliar and seemingly dangerous part of town they typically avoided. But to locals, it was a place where they could physically release all of life's stressors through dancing," journalist Jewel Wicker writes.[134] Local Atlanta artists like Lil Jon & the Eastside Boyz regard the West End club and its regular influx of partygoers and dancers as the source of many of their songs' inspiration.[135] Club 559 was particularly significant to the local scene. Still, it brought in outside visitors during the annual Freaknik weekend, where nearly eighty thousand Black youth and college students gathered for concerts, parties, and events during spring break. The Freaknik events were expansive, taking place on Memorial Drive and Grant Park (south of the city center) to Midtown (north of the city). With its proximity to the Atlanta University Center and Black college students, the Mall West End and Club 559 were popular sites.[136]

These, among other changes that Black West Enders made in the area, exemplify some of the symbolic actions African Americans take within privileged white spaces to form community and collective identity through both function and location. Functioning to renarrate Black history and culture within an anti-Black space, sites of memory draw witness to the traumatic past that brought them there and the hopefulness of a future for the African American historical trajectory. Locating the sites of memory close to the MARTA Station—an area where people enter and exit the neighborhood—gives visibility to these stories so that the memories may be remembered repeatedly. As we move further into the twenty-first century, we'll see how repatterning of movement along with redevelopment from Atlanta BeltLine Inc. plans are poised to shift the visibility of these sites and accentuate white spaces of appearance. The threat of the dominant hegemony entering an identifiable metaphorical Black space is that the people may lose the power of production and distribution of their own culture in the area, leading to their invisibility and exclusion from cultural and spatial belonging.

THE MAKING OF BEER TOWN: DISGUISING RACIAL BIAS BEHIND A UNIVERSAL ETHIC

Because of white privilege and laissez-faire racism and how it permeates the entire structure of our society, actions that on the surface could be defined as individuals seeking personal advantage or even some universal benefit are almost always attributed to a racial advantage when the racism of the past is made invisible in our processes and performances of renewal. This is the case of Malt Disney in West End. Pursuing the new haven for the craft-brewing industry along the Atlanta BeltLine's West End Trail will further segregation because it skips the racial stairstep. The racial stairsteps it must cross include the historical abuses against Black people in the alcoholic-beverage industry in Atlanta, the strategized development of West End as a white enclave after the Civil War, the use of transportation routes to curtail Black economic growth and support white success, and the deliberate appropriation of Black history and artistic culture in early West End. When we do not acknowledge nor seek to rectify every one of these oppressive abuses before breaking ground on spatial reconstruction projects, we reinstitutionalize the racist ideologies of the past and dehumanize Black life and identity. As I will present in the following section, Lee + White is poised to render Black culture in the West End invisible, lead to alienation of Black identity, and repurpose the space for white lifeworlds.

Atlanta BeltLine Inc. began officially studying West End in January 2009 with a kickoff and community meetings to help formulate the land use and design plans for the Westside Trail. Remember, for gentrification to occur, it relies on impoverishment and negative stigmatization, which forges a dystopic narrative that favors revitalization and redevelopment,[137] relegating the real life and community to invisibility; reporting strategies to assess the impact of the Westside Trail on local neighborhoods built this narrative context. The West End neighborhood they researched confirmed the underresourced area's lower income and poor attributes. Metrics collected between 2008 and 2014 show that the West End population was 4,341, the largest of the twelve neighborhoods impacted by the Westside Trail. West End was 90 percent African American and 4 percent white, with a median household income of $21,727. These metrics show that 34 percent of people in West End were living below the poverty line, which was 9 percent higher than the Atlanta average at the time. The majority of homes (76 percent) were renter occupied.[138] The dynamic youth and hip-hop culture that had once proliferated in the neighborhood also changed. After a seventeen-year run, the last Freaknik was held in 1999. The Black college spring break that had nationwide attention was canceled as the event became more sexualized and violence and crime activity around it increased. The West End Sears, Roebuck and Co. closed in 1992, leaving Mall West End without a major department store to carry it.[139]

Such changes, along with the effects of urban sprawl, attracted "urban pioneers" to West End before the BeltLine came to fruition.[140] White speculation began in the late 1990s, but gentrification started with home-value adjustments rather than new business shifts. The *Atlanta Journal-Constitution* reported in 1997 that investors were buying dilapidated homes and renovating them for sale. Home sales in zip code 30310 (which includes West End, Stewart Avenue, and Sylvan Hills Neighborhoods) were the highest in the city, having sold upwards of 697 homes in 1996. Most sales came from house flippers, who buy a house, restore it, and sell it again—sometimes selling one home two or three times in one year. These homes were selling for the cheapest price at an average of $38,397 per home, compared to an Atlanta-wide average sales price of $158,406.[141]

By 2002, the West End area saw the median home-sales prices increase by 28 percent, and renovated homes were selling for $150,000 to $260,000. The West End was of particular interest because it already had restaurants, grocery stores, and a shopping mall.[142] In conjunction with gentrification, between 2006 and 2007, auto theft in Zone 4, including West End Atlanta, increased by 36 percent, followed by larceny, burglary, and robbery. Some argue that the increased crime was perpetuated by the hopelessness attributed to displacement, homelessness, unemployment, and drug abuse.[143] The strategy of flipping the homes is a part of the stages of redevelopment, in which investors seek to "change the neighborhood's racialized and classed stigma to attract more affluent populations."[144] And they did attract them. As Gay recollects:

> I remember the most peculiar thing I had ever seen in my life was a white person jogging with their kids and a dog. Something like that captures your attention because it's just that weird, right? I'm staring at this family, jogging and being content in the West End, and it looks so foreign. It looks so foreign. It's like, white people over here that comfortable in the West End, of all places. It was just a representation of, you know, the space being gentrified because there was a point in time nobody barely, you know, would be, much less walking. Nobody would find comfort or freedom in being present in the West End without, you know, kind of looking over your shoulder. Not jogging. It just seems so absurd to me. But it was like the first introduction of, yeah, this area is changing so dramatically that white people feel comfortable jogging.[145]

Though home sales and prices started changing right before the turn of the century, cultural gentrification in West End, coinciding with new white-centric business development, came along with the opening of the Westside Trail and a shift in the gateway to the neighborhood. Rather than addressing the moral issues of systemic racism that led to the degraded state of West End, white privilege pathed the way for cultural gentrification. In this section, we turn to how movement into the neighborhood is being changed, and new business marketing suggests a turn back to the exclusive white past of West End.

In the 1800s, Adair utilized three key spatial strategies to narrate Whitehall as an exclusive white space and increase traffic to the heart of the neighborhood at the main artery of Gordon and Lee Streets. The plan called for changing the neighborhood name and street names to honor the Old South during the rule of slavery, using the Atlanta Street Railway as a means of transportation to and from the developing business and retail district and creating boundaries around the neighborhood to keep Black-populated areas out. Similarly, a spatial change is being made in conjunction with the Atlanta BeltLine Inc. master plan for the Westside Trail. Atlanta BeltLine Inc. is repatterning movement in West End by forming a new gateway to the neighborhood.

The Westside Trail is poised to move the major entrance to the neighborhood from its heart in the northeastern quadrant to the west side of the boundary along White Street. Following the original belt line railway, the Westside Trail runs from the intersection of I-20 and Langhorn Street, across the junction of RDA Boulevard and Cascade, and along White Street to end at Lee Street. Before the BeltLine plan, White Street was encompassed by residential homes on the east of the street, large warehouses to the west of the road, and wooded areas without a clear walking path. A Kroger grocery store is located at the intersection of RDA Boulevard, White Street, and Cascade. Primarily a residential area, this neighborhood segment stood apart from the retail district, where Black sites of memory are located.

As a part of the greater redevelopment strategy, the 2010 Atlanta BeltLine master plan for this larger trail segment organized the space into multiple land-use nodes, which inevitably separate the original gateway to West End and the Black sites of memory from the new developments along the BeltLine. The names used to identify the nodes also capitalize on a rhetorical strategy to differentiate the old gateway from the new gateway. The old gateway is labeled West End Node, while the new gateway constitutes three different nodes in the plan: Kroger Citi-Center Area, Warehouse Row, and Lee/BeltLine.[146] The node names subtly differentiate the West End Node—known for the sites of memory connected with Black collective identity—from the BeltLine Westside Trail.

Unlike the overt separation of boundaries that Adair used to distinguish West End from the McPherson Barracks and the Black refuge area to its north, the Atlanta BeltLine Inc. plans use the subtle shift in nomenclature to distinguish the notorious Black neighborhood from the area nicknamed Malt Disney. This change is a form of romanticization through rebranding that would rhetorically make the site attractive to investors and wealthier residents.

The formation of the trail comes in conjunction with plans to redevelop the Kroger Citi-Center Area and Warehouse Row. The envisioned Kroger Citi-Center Area, Warehouse Row, and Lee/BeltLine are the major redevelopment focus specifically tied to West End as they are of "crucial importance" for making the BeltLine "an active, safe, accessible, and interesting place," the plan reads.[147] The existing Kroger supermarket is expected to be the center of a larger retail node with another multistory, mixed-use building in Kroger's parking lot. The proposal envisions Warehouse Row with mixed-use development and multifamily residences. Thus far, the warehouses in the Lee/BeltLine segment have been utilized by Lee + White, bringing the craft-brewing industry to the frontal façade along the trail.

To bring pedestrian and vehicular traffic to the new businesses, the plan includes improvements to mobility in the surrounding area in conjunction with movement along White Street and the Westside Trial. The intersection of Cascade Avenue, RDA Boulevard, and White Street, which has historically been problematic, will undergo improvements to ease automobile traffic and safety for pedestrians. In addition, regarding the formation of the Westside walking trail, which is already open, other streets in the proposed area are being opened up to make easy access from connector streets to the main artery of the trail.

The West End Trail runs behind Lee + White, lining the warehouse buildings and the backyards of some single-family homes and other industry businesses. The set up allows pedestrians a reclusive walking area, where they don't see the houses along White Street or the Black residents because Lee + White's buildings block them from view. Thus, if you walk the trail from Lee + White to Kroger, a keen observer will recognize it as a small bubble for white visitors and new residents in a Black space that is made invisible. If the BeltLine construction continues its current design, with buildings like Lee + White lining it's paths, a pedestrian that never walks off the BeltLine main trail wouldn't recognize that they have entered a different neighborhood with a different culture or demographic. The placement of trees hides the Black neighborhood from view.

While Adair used the Atlanta Street Railway to bring businessmen from the city into West End in the late nineteenth century, the Westside Trail has become the twenty-first-century gateway to the neighborhood, used to bring young, white millennials into the West End. From a Black West Ender point of view, "If you only carry yourself down RDA, it would appear that all things are well," says Gay. "But if you go down on Lee + White and, specifically, if you go down on Lee + White on the weekend, it looks totally different."[148] Understood through deep mapping of the neighborhood's past, present, and future planned transportation landscape, we can visualize how transportation can be used to instigate contemporary racialization of space in a more covert way. Racialization is constituted by not only the positioning of the new developments but also the types of developments that are making over Warehouse Row in the West End.

From 1830 through the 1950s, the growth of the West End and the formation of the exclusive-white sector blatantly illustrate the story of racist practices in the built environment. However, the production of that racist past is also used to establish present practices by distinguishing illicit racism of the past from present racism. The association of new developments with the term "mixed use," suggests that "all groups have similar life opportunities under neoliberalism."[149] However, through deep mapping and critical analysis of the narrative of the past and the spatial narrative perpetuated in the plans for the West End, we see that the present forms of development use colorblind ideology to reinstitute an exclusively white space and make Black culture invisible within the new area.

The Westside Trail governs the prime locations for spaces of appearance near the Kroger grocery store and in Warehouse Row and Lee/BeltLine. As revealed previously, Malt Disney takes up these locations with Lean Draft House located across from Kroger (near the intersection of RDA Boulevard and White Street) and the Lee + White development along White Street. The adaptive-use project includes four warehouses, a sum of 433,204 square feet and a half mile along the BeltLine. Ackerman & Co. and MDH Partners purchased the properties for $40.3 million from Stream Realty Partners in 2019, which suggests the capital strength expected to come into the neighborhood. According to a press release, along with the breweries that are already located there, the owners have plans to add retail stores and loft offices.[150] The connotation of Warehouse Row as Malt Disney and West End's perception as Beer Town reflects a new era in the neighborhood that shifts the collective identity of the space from how it is recognized in the sites of memory of the Black Mecca.

Let's review. Overt racism in the past used alcoholic engagement to separate race and class. Due to drinking, African Americans and poor whites were identified as lascivious and violent. The West End neighborhood separated itself from the stereotype by prohibiting alcohol after the results of the Civil War freed African Americans. The neighborhood's growth as a well-to-do white enclave was facilitated by prohibition laws before the state or nation had made their own. Then, in 1906, the city of Atlanta utilized African Americans' enjoyment of alcoholic beverages as a grounds and scapegoat for white violence against Black bodies. In these two ways, "the swift arm of the law and of public opinion swings down" on Black people as the history of beer and liquor in Atlanta was used to position Black people as subordinate and instigate an anti-Black social order, placing shame on Black individuals.[151]

Georgia state passed prohibition laws in 1907, and prohibition lasted until 1935. Segregation was outlawed in the 1950s and '60s. All the while, new tactics were instituted to continue the racial order while maintaining an integrated multirace landscape. To carry on the racial structure, developers distinguish the present actions from the overt racism of the past, arguing that the new bars and breweries are open for all and welcoming to everyone. The establishments can accommodate Black people to "fit in" but not necessarily "belong." Invisibility is instituted by not only the spatial location but also the spatial narrative that Malt Disney brings to the West End, reidentifying the scene with white millennial culture, power, and exclusionary traditions.

Research studies into the niche industry reveal that craft beer and craft breweries target a particular market, fostering an exclusive subculture based on age, race, and gender. Craft brewing is used to describe "quality, small batch brewing techniques, a unique group of independent brewers, and the beers they produce."[152] In the 1950s, the larger beer industry became an oligopoly, with the top five brewing companies holding 75 percent of the market by 1975.[153] But the legalization of homebrewing in Georgia in 1995,[154] seventeen years after Jimmy Carter legalized it for the rest of the nation, paved the way for today's craft-beer industry. Then, Georgia's Senate Bill 85, passed in September 2017, made it legal for breweries and distilleries to sell directly to customers, whereas previously they had to sell through wholesale distributors.[155] This created space for a local movement that would market specifically to an expert class of brewers and beer drinkers rather than the masses, leading to the exclusion of women, Black people, and lower classes from the subculture. As Teasley attests, even though the law changed, Black brewers in this space had "no advantages."[156] While industry allies and good folks will help you "learn the tricks of the trade," entering this business requires intensive social and investment capital that is often not readily available to aspiring Black brewery owners to produce, market, and distribute their beers.[157] Access to capital or generational wealth in an industry that requires at least half a million dollars to start up has been the challenge for African American beer brands and impacts where Black breweries are located. But social capital has also been a problem. A lot of commercial and industrial properties are owned by people outside of the community, and they target people like them—someone that's been in business or that they know through their social network—to fill their retail spaces. "Occasionally, they'll reach out to start-up brands, but if you don't have the capital backing, it's hard to move it much forward than conversations."[158]

The effects of giving businesses from outside the local community and its culture a majority stake in the built environment is that it attracts people from outside that neighborhood, exacerbating cultural gentrification. The proliferation of craft-brew-focused industries demonstrates a strategy to bring in young, white millennials without overt segregation within the community. Generally, craft breweries market to young, college-educated millennials. According to a 2014 study, "the typical craft beer drinker is a white male, college educated, ranging between 21 to 44 years in age, and earns at least $50,000–$75,000 a year."[159] Alison E. Feeney presumes that the phenomenon attracts millennials because it fosters a feeling of "sophistication" and has a "prestige factor."[160] Lee + White customers include those of the millennial age group and retirees interested in the beer culture.[161]

Craft breweries are positioned on the Westside Trail as a cultural representation of power and authority for the white population. The brewing industry is important to the American cultural and economic landscape. In the United States, as of 2014, the brewing industry accounted for $78 billion in wages and more than $250 billion in economic output. It makes up about 1.5 percent of the national output.[162] Locally, eleven breweries and pubs opened in Georgia just six months after Senate Bill 85 was passed,[163] joining the already $1.6 billion craft-beer industry in Georgia and representing the economic power this subculture wields in the state.[164] On an individual level, research suggests that those customers who drink craft beer specifically associate it with being a quality product and a form of self-expression that engenders social status.[165]

Power is institutionalized in the industry by not only the racist past of beer and liquor segregation and stereotypes but also the lack of Black people in the industry and lack of Black people drinking craft beer. According to the Brewers Association, in 2020, there were 8,884 craft breweries operating nationally, and 1 percent of those were Black owned.[166] Teasley attests that of the ninety Black-owned breweries that are registered in the Brewers Association, less than a quarter of them are probably open. Further, of the 138,371 jobs available in the industry, only 4 percent of them are held by Black employees.[167] Beyond ownership and employment in the industry, the subculture is almost exclusively white and male. Communications scholar, craft-brew aficionado, and author of the blog series *The Unbearable Whiteness of Craft Brewing*, J. Nikol Jackson-Beckham attests that, in her experience at the Extreme Beer Festival's special session, she was one of five women and the only Black person at the five-hundred-attendee session.[168] While volunteering with the "brew crew" at the festival, she recalls being disconnected from the social atmosphere between the men "who seem . . . to have much more in common with each other."[169] Jackson-Beckham argues that, beyond the festival, the craft-brew subculture "presents a particular combination of openings and barriers to members of the subculture in relation to their many subject positions and contingent identities."[170] Thus, she describes the culture as a tight-knit community that is difficult for outsiders to infiltrate based on race, gender, and age. This social landscape of the community extends beyond the invitation to enter a bar or brewery and includes other activities such as individual homebrewing, professional craft brewing, and craft-brew advocacy on social media.[171] The multiple levels of connectivity serve as manifold barriers to entry and belonging.

Adding to our understanding of economic barriers, William Moore of local Black-owned craft brewery Down Home Brewing states:

> We've taken advantage of [the law change], which has allowed us to use a space, a facility, that was already owned by another brewery to produce our beer. So everyone's like, there's this Black brewery that exists here. And it's out in the market. But at the same time, did we have the budget of your Monday Night, your Sweetwater, your Atlanta Brewing Company, . . . did we have the resources of that and the capital, and maybe even access to funds and everything? No, absolutely not. We did not have that. And so, therefore, you get a situation to where those individuals that are able to utilize their resources and everything. That's when it's like, wow, these big beer brands and these big companies have been able to set up shop, right in the heart of the West End, which is right adjacent to the heart of what once was the civil rights movement headquarters. . . . And I don't say that in a shade way. I'm not doing any shade. I'm just kind of speaking just the facts. It is what it is. If Down Home Brewing Company had the same capital as Sweetwater, which is one of the biggest, if not the biggest brand that's in Atlanta, Georgia, or in Georgia period, then yeah, we would definitely have a Down Home Brewing setup right there and shop where we can have in-house access to capital and collateral.[172]

The multiple levels of barriers for Black people in the brewing culture, including investment and social capital, have inevitably kept the few Black-owned craft breweries out of gentrifying hot spots. This is why locations like

Atlantucky Brewing, which was opened in 2022 by the rap group Nappy Roots, and Black-owned Hippin Hops Brewery, which opened in 2021, are particularly significant. While not located in our study area, West End, these two Black-owned breweries can provide "spaces for people of color who may not feel like they can go to a white-owned brewery because they don't know the lingo."[173]

Malt Disney also reinforces white sense of place and the new neolocalism, which yearns for a bygone era, harkening back to the ideology of "Make America great again" and white supremacy. According to Doreen Massey, the Western view is that there is no longer a sense of their idealized local places inhabited by coherent and homogenous communities.[174] This has led to a contemporary nostalgia for the past, driving a fervor to reestablish local appeal. Breweries are an indelible factor in this past and particularly significant to West End, as described in the previous section.

Atlanta history, in line with the nation's past, shows that breweries were some of the first buildings forged by the white colonists.[175] Taverns were centers for trade, lodging, and socializing. In addition, in the early colonial years, beer with 2–3 percent alcohol content by volume was American's "drink of choice."[176] The saloon and tavern were tied not only to alcohol consumption but also the wealth of the families that owned them, like Whitehall's Charner Humphries.[177] Craft breweries target local tradition in order to gain access to customers in the larger neolocalism movement. This movement suggests that people seek local charm and a return to a local sense of place and a larger landscape.[178] For example, Feeney's research on Pennsylvania's craft-brewing industry reveals that many of the breweries are in areas with historic European influences. The West End's ties to the first Atlanta brewery and Whitehall Tavern provide the neighborhood a significant historical connection. Like the taverns of the past, breweries provide a sense of social belonging for their stakeholders.

Another way to forge a local theme is through naming conventions. Using local names of people, events, or wildlife helps to engage these enthusiasts.[179] Malt Disney reflects back to this idyllic sensibility of life through naming. Let's start with the name Lee + White, which takes on the name of the cross streets it's located on, but in doing so, it also performs Confederate remembrance. You will recall from the origins of West End's street names that Lee Street is named for Confederate commander in chief Stephen Lee. But all memories aren't inherently racist. The owner of American Spirit Works Exchange, a tasting room and barrel-aging facility in Lee + White, was "inspired by old-time grain exchanges, where farmers would come to sell their wheat and barley."[180] The name was chosen to pay homage to that past. The Wild Heaven Beer company offers Stuckeys

Brown Ale, so titled to bring back memories of eating Stuckey's pecan log roll on long road trips.[181] But I ask, whose memories are these? Do the Black residents of West End share this nostalgia? Naming conventions help connect Malt Disney brewers with the new community they are forging in the West End and the past Confederate sentiments. This type of naming is a part of the process of displacement and replacement.

This propensity for the idealized sense of local place caters to a specific past and social framework. Contemporary cultural gentrification relies on racial segregation. The urge for local sensibilities and a sense of place is a retrospective need that takes for granted the white supremacy that made the southern homogenous past what it is. For it to progress, it requires colorblind ideology, forgetfulness of the trauma, and structural racism occurring to people of color. While the Black sites of memory are repositories to contain Black history, without visibility to a diverse community, the past events are forgotten and reestablished based on the economic and class demographics of the region rather than the structural processes that produce them. When placed within the scene of the West End, the craft-brewing industry signifies a shift of cultural representation in the area, transforming who is permitted and excluded. Gay puts it this way: "So the BeltLine is the white line, therefore the wealth line, right? And it's, in my opinion, it's like they're creating this border that decides whether you can get in and get out, who has access and who doesn't." She continues, "Lee + White . . . it's just a representation of what the West End will be here in about five or ten years."[182]

Cultural gentrification along the Atlanta BeltLine trail is dependent upon West End's racist past and the significance of race in the history of alcohol and beer consumption and distribution. Its position along the newest transportation route in the futurist projections of the neighborhood conditions craft brewing to become a significant part of the spatial narrative to the detriment of the memory of Black collective identity in the area. This is how cultural gentrification presents itself in West End: symbols of Blackness have not been eradicated from the space; instead, they are hidden on the edges of the transforming area to make Black life acceptable and usable by new populaces. When African Americans do not see themselves reflected in the built environment along the BeltLine, the substance of their identification with the place is threatened. Being able to fit in would require the dissolution of the Black self and Black collectivity. Therefore, by skipping the racial stairstep, we are again unable to transition to a "universal" community of diverse cultures. America is not made of individuals attempting to foster a universal ethic but rather what may be better described as racial groups trapped.

AMERICAN TRAPPIN'

Throughout this text, I've made an effort to argue that the United States' racialized structure turns Black lives into ghosts, moving them into a liminal space of historylessness to compromise their humanity and equality. Our geography is part and parcel of that process as cultural gentrification displaces our history to the recesses of public memory. In this way, Black people lose self-consciousness and remain unidentified in space. As Fanon argues, the flaw lies "not in the 'soul' of the individual, but in his environment."[183] How can we challenge the social structure that creates these problematic spaces? Some effort has been made toward diversification, a move from the individual to the collective. However, Fanon argues that challenging this world is not a "discourse on the universal."[184] Instead, it is an impassioned claim that our world is dualistic, that we are equal, and that Western values, like individuality, are not eternal because "they have nothing to do with the real-life struggle in which the people are engaged."[185] In a racialized society, personal interest is collective interest. Therefore, we must use our spaces to express reality—the desires, conflicts, and risks that represent the "fundamental values that make the world human."[186] Thankfully, we already have the tools for doing this. I've argued previously that blues music, as a broad genre of the Black music tradition, allows Black people to recognize each other in an expression of the real-life struggles we are engaged in. It's a work of "being for self" to humanize ourselves.[187] It represents Black desires. It is also conflict, and the "conflict and the risk it implies . . . make human reality . . . come true."[188] Using the blues within our shared spaces, we can move toward an ideal where our subjective knowledge of our humanity and equality is transformed into a "universally valid objective truth."[189] Arguing that the blues genre forces suppressed memories of Black reality to be codified in space, in this last section, I turn to a contemporary evolution of the blues genre that is home to Atlanta—trap music.

If Lee + White is what happens when white individuals enter Black space, then the Pink Trap House shows us what happens when Black individuals enter white space. Trap music is a hip-hop genre founded in the South and branded by Atlanta-raised rapper T.I. (Clifford Harris Jr.). The name "trap" comes out of the environment of the artists. Traps are buildings and houses used for illegal drug activity. The word stands as both a warning and a moniker for aspiring "trappers," expressing the difficulty of leaving the lifestyle once you enter. But some trap artists have done just the opposite, challenging the constraints of Black space by using their larger-than-life stardom to crossover into white space, both musically and physically. In this way, trap music is another multidimensional expression of African American desire for freedom. Like other expressions within the Black music tradition, trap music follows the ethical development agenda that opposes "slavery, racism, and monopoly."[190] Trap artists have used this musical exploration to challenge physical spaces by disrupting white space with homages to the music and culture in locations like the Pink Trap House and the Trap Museum.

In 2017, 2 Chainz opened the Pink Trap House in Atlanta as a temporary installation. Imagine a house painted bubble-gum pink, a pink Lambo out front, and a stove with artificial cocaine residue in the driveway plopped onto Howell Mill Road.[191] If you remember, in chapter 2, I discussed that in the early 1900s, Howell Mill Road was a designated marker of white space, separating the area from the Black settlement of Blandtown. When 2 Chainz opened the Pink Trap House, it angered regular travelers along Howell Mill Road, whose complaints were exposed by the press. Rhetorically, the Pink Trap House switched the dichotomy of mobility. At the house, visitors could be seen celebrating hip-hop heritage, taking selfies, listening to sermons, or getting HIV/AIDs testing. Such actions reflect how the space became a location for active Black vulnerability, leading to belonging. While many criticized the event, I argue that 2Chaiz became an "organic intellectual,"[192] articulating the values and interests of the working class. Because of this, the Pink Trap House can be read as an ethical vision to reinforce a multiracial, working-class self-consciousness that can be recruited in a time of struggle. The diverse group of visitors, domestic and international, represent what it looks like to be free to be Black. In reverse, it was the travelers in their cars who were constrained. The fact that the people in the traffic opted out of being a part of this performance was a reflection of the racial allegiances in the United States that favor the restriction of one group at the expense of the freedom of the other. The reality is that if those travelers had exited their cars and joined the events at the Pink Trap House, they would both experience freedom. When whiteness sees itself as equal to Blackness, both become free. By breaking up a racial monopoly in space and affirming Black culture, the Pink Trap House represents the blues tradition in physical form.[193]

Additionally, the Pink Trap House symbolizes what occurs when Black life enters a white space. While Lee + White was able to come into Black space, assert control, and leave Black lifeworlds essentially invisible, the Pink Trap House received much criticism and complaints during its short life on Howell Mill Road because of noise and crowds. When 2 Chainz attempted to bring Black culture into white space as an individual, he revealed a reality of American society: white people can freely move their culture in Black space, but Black people are not able to do the same in white space. Black people will visit white space, attempting to at least fit in, but white people enter Black lifeworlds less often.

Can America move from racialism to a genuine acknowledgment of equal humanity among differing people? Here, I recognize some of trap music's performers and their lyrics as entering a rhetorical negotiation that delivers discourses on the Black lifeworlds' realized struggle and objective humanity. Those former "trappers" who have used rap music to escape from the trap move from the depths of poverty into a new wealth class. They initially move out of the trap as individuals working in capitalist conditions. Being able to move within both class systems to some extent, these artists observe the realities of America's capitalist conception of individual upward progression. Yet despite the seeming upward mobility in tax bracket, the vulnerability of trap lyrics reflects that the artists' lives are caught in the middle—bouncing between the Bankhead and Buckhead, the hood and the high rise, Black space and white space. By placing this dichotomy in lyrical form, trap music appropriately reflects the challenge of American identity's racial-universal reality. It shows the bipolar reality of capitalism and the tragicomic existence of American life.

Trap music highlights this tragicomic reality as successful rappers like T.I. confront the limits of individual success for African Americans. Scholar Regina N. Bradley explains that in the album *T.I. vs. T.I.P.*, the rapper takes on two personalities. T.I. is the corporatized, wealthy businessman; T.I.P. is the dope-boy progenitor of the rapper's upbringing in Atlanta's ghettos. In psychological warfare, Harris places these two personas in conversation, ultimately revealing the displacement of Harris's complete identity under commercialized celebrity. Harris shows that though he attempts to be an individual, success in an anti-Black world requires him to "relinquish control" of himself.[194] This is the consequence of a Black body attempting to make do in a white capitalist space. It leads to personal-identity disaster and dehumanization. Harris reflects the psychological state of entrapment for Black people trying to function within white space. In the end, Harris resembles one of the fundamental values that distinguish trap-music artists; as Bradley attests, "a trap boy refuses to affiliate with or function within a white space."[195]

So what does one do when their world disavows their identity? Trap music has been a part of the effort to put Black culture on equal standing with all others and disrupt "high-culture" and "low-culture" hierarchies. In 2019, T.I. opened the Trap Music Museum, located northeast of West End, a little over a mile from Arthur Blank's Mercedes-Benz Stadium and Bankhead, a low-income Black neighborhood. The museum honors hip-hop artists, expressing that Black culture is worthy of visibility. Spatially, the museum represents the meeting ground of the spiritual and the secular, the slave and the free, the drug life and the celebrity, low culture and high culture. It reflects the synergy that occurs when we embrace the reality of southern life, one that has been for too long identified by a commercialized and romanticized production of the civil rights movement. The Trap Music Museum does not romanticize trap life to make it fit into the mold of high culture. Instead, it honors Black strength, which "is that with the total society saying to us, 'No, No, No, No' we continue to move toward our goal."[196] The goal for MLK's generation is the same for T.I.'s generation: freedom.

In its truest form, trap music is a mode of Black music culture that has not been romanticized or made acceptable to the broader white evangelical class. By honoring the form and fashion of high culture, these rappers allow themselves to perform Blackness within white space, both physically and ideologically. They are replacing the conception of a white individualist society as the foundation for universalism with a concept of a society of equal humans. This is done by not just moving their individual selves into white space but also taking the entirety of the Black spaces they've known and throwing them into white space. Like the Trap Music Museum, trap music is not a means of separating from the racial to become individual. Instead, in trap music, the rapper-singer who has moved up in class is still a part and whole of the racial collective. They don't "wander from the paths of behavior laid down for the group."[197] Because they maintain their connection to Black culture, they legitimate it. They remove the stereotypes of high and low culture and recognize Black culture as a thing not to be demeaned but applauded. They are making it visible.

Trap music has emancipatory potential. Today, trap-music sound has been reappropriated into pop-cultural channels. It gained wide appeal by depicting the bipolar reality of capitalism, as listeners from all cultures in a global capitalist society can identify with it. Trap music is a more aware form of the American identity, and because of this, it can be liberating. Of course, Black culture is only one of many racial groups, but as Jernej Kaluza attests, "it is . . . the paradigmatic example of entrapped identity."[198] When Black identity is emancipated, it defends the emancipation of all marginalized identities.

When we use individualism to describe why and how universal community is produced in our spaces, we are asking people of color to disavow their racial/ethnic identities and be "whiter," thereby reinstating white supremacy. Disavowing your race inevitably leads to an inward battle of identification that when hard fought in the minds of African Americans, leads them back into the dehumanizing chains of slavery and inferiority. Coming into white spaces, like the Lee + White breweries, in many fashions requires me to leave some Blackness at the door if I am to make white people comfortable with my entering. I must be one of those "respectable Black people." These are the rules that white people hate to admit, but Black people know. But we also recognize that we are terrorizing our inner beings every time we try to peel off our Blackness to appease a white demographic. And trap music tells us that when we break through glass ceilings and are invited in white spaces, we cannot and will not leave our race at the door anymore. Blackness will come with us. Trap music is a successful rhetorical form representing an American identity meeting the difficulty of transitioning from racial to universal. Trap music speaks back to the tragicomic reality of American society and says that to emancipate marginalized racial groups, we must esteem their cultural symbols. In this esteem, we place these cultural symbols along the intersections of our spaces and on the gateways and transportation routes to new places. These cultural symbols are no longer denigrated, devalued, or required to assimilate to white codified forms of respectability when they walk through the door. The cultural symbols are given freedom and mobility.

A spatial map of the changes occurring in the West End distinctly shows a shift in major transportation routes as the encouragement for walking the trail and using the future trolley system would make the Westside Trail a major artery for entering the neighborhood. The MARTA, as it is today, may continue to be a segregated form of transportation into the Black side of West End. The map seemingly traps Black history into the northeastern sector of the neighborhood, away from the new gateway to the area. White businesses and social life are placed on the track of mobility, and Black memory is confined, putting white life in the future trajectory of the city and relegating the heyday of Black culture to historical archives. In this case, Black life is constrained and trapped, but what trap-music culture has revealed is that it's not just Black folks trapped. Trap music witnesses the American horror story—we're all trapped by racism.

And let's be very clear here, humanizing our ghosts, recognizing Black bodies as human, requires whiteness to see Blackness as equal. Symbolically speaking, it needs those people in traffic on Howell Mill Road to step out of their cars and visit the Pink Trap House rather than call it in as a disturbance. The onus of racial reconciliation is on white people. But Black people can continue to use the blues tradition for their own self-consciousness and to provide vision to blinded eyes. Trap culture shouts to the reality of America's current identity, "We're all trapped!"

CHAPTER 5

"BUT I AM STILL YOUR NEIGHBOR"

And if the word integration means anything, this is what it means: that we with love, shall force our brothers to see themselves as they are, to cease fleeing from reality and begin to change it. For this is your home, my friend, do not be driven from it; great men have done great things here, and will again, and we can make America what America must become.

—JAMES BALDWIN[1]

In the northeastern quadrant of Oakland Cemetery, between paupers and Confederate burial grounds, is the final resting place of more than twelve thousand Black people in the African American Burial Grounds. Some were born and died enslaved; others were born enslaved and died free. I walked the 3.2 acres after its restoration in the summer of 2022. There, I felt the hope and the "something-to-be-done" calling forth from the spirit of my cultural kin. It wasn't until my work on this book that I began recognizing cemeteries as spaces to learn history without the filters of a curated museum. And a book that follows ghost stories isn't complete without reckoning with the graveyard.

In 1850, needing a space to rest its dead, the City of Atlanta purchased six acres of land and committed it as a cemetery. The area would increase in size to forty-eight acres during the following seventeen years. While Atlanta is notorious for rebuilding rather than preserving, cemeteries are treated differently. As a local tour guide, Victoria Lemos attests, "Cemeteries seem to be the only ground that everyone agrees is sacred. It's rarely sold off to a developer. It can't be turned into condos. When the Department of Transportation projects find evidence of burials, everything must stop." But there are exceptions. And the exceptions "almost always revolve around burials of African Americans."[2] Regarding these exceptions, Oakland Cemetery was no different until recently.

When the cemetery was initially established, African Americans were interred in the northeastern corner of the six-acre plot. It was referred to as Slave Square. But the city required extra room to bury its dead following the Civil War. By 1877, the Atlanta City Council deemed they needed more land for white Atlantans. They ordered the remains of the African Americans in Slave Square disinterred and reburied on the pauper grounds for Black people.[3] In this, we find that even in cemeteries, Black bodies could not rest peacefully for when white people wanted their land back, they would displace the dead, uprooting them to make room for more white sacred space.

From my entrance at the front gate of the cemetery, I followed the path I was advised to at the Visitor Center. I started by walking through the Original Six Acres, a grounds for early white settlers of Atlanta and the original Slave Square, before heading east to the Confederate Burial Grounds. I made my way gently into the Confederate grounds. I looked up through the glare of the sun to see the sixty-five-foot-tall Confederate Obelisk, a monument dedicated to the Confederates that was funded by the Atlanta Ladies Memorial Association. The obelisk, ironically or fittingly, is made of granite from Stone Mountain. While the federal government would not sponsor a commemoration of rebel forces, the ladies arranged for their burial at Oakland Cemetery. When the cemetery expanded to forty-eight acres in 1867, a space was made to lay 9,900 soldiers to rest, only sixteen of them Union soldiers. In this space, I encountered the spirit of those who thought keeping me in bondage was worth dying for. And while some deemed it fitting to memorialize their cause, I fortified my own heart, combatting the hatred and animosity that could fester among foes.

The African American Burial Grounds began at the crossroads where the Confederate Burial Grounds came to an end. In 1866, the city had set aside a section northeast of the Confederate Burial Grounds where African Americans could purchase plots. In the "bottoms," a low-lying space that was prone to flooding, more than 12,300 recorded African Americans were buried.[4] And others that were unrecorded may never be known. The Historic Oakland Foundation found eight hundred unmarked graves in 2016 using ground-penetrating radar. The ghosts of the Black Mecca I encountered there were not dead but rather alive, offering a moment of circular time for me when their past and my present collided. As I wandered through the cemetery, the recently published African American Voices self-guided-tour narration brought their stories to life. I found the graves of such figures as Bishop Wesley John Gaines. Despite being born enslaved, by 1881, he established Morris Brown College as the first and only Black-founded higher education institution in Georgia. I also found Carrie Steele Logan, known as "the mother of orphans," who established an orphanage at her house on Auburn Avenue while working as a maid in the 1880s. The Carrie Steele Orphan Home (now the Carrie Steele-Pitts Home), the first orphanage for African American children in Georgia, was started in 1888 and is still welcoming children of all races. It is now located on Fairburn Road. And I found the burial of William Finch, a tailor who was born enslaved in 1832. Finch stitched a United States flag as a gift to the Union army after the Civil War as a protest to his enslaver's son, who was a Confederate soldier. In 1870, Finch and George Graham were the first Black people elected to the Atlanta City Council. His gravestone, like others, was constructed like an open archway to depict the spirit's journey from earth to heaven. On these grounds, my spirit crossed paths with their spirits. Their job remained unfinished, still pouring crimson through the veins, hearts, and movement of a people who were not at rest.

My rhetorical-critique eyes quickly took over. According to the route I walked, the Black cemeteries and the pauper fields to the north of them appeared to be positioned as shadows of the Confederate grounds and its large obelisk, which were gathered away from the entrance to signify a contrast of white souls, Black souls, and poor souls. But still, there is a different perspective.

As I left the African American Burial Grounds to go back southwest toward the exit, for a moment, I stood atop a high point on the land. I could see the intersection there where the Confederate grounds ended and the African American Burial Grounds started. From this vantage point, having just met with the spirits of my cultural kin, my spirit beheld not a people of inferiority but a people full of hope and promise that persisted for future generations. And as I looked down at the Confederate Burial Grounds, I did not have to fight sentiments of hatred; instead, I had to fight feelings of pity, knowing that while they had sacrificed their lives for the cause of oppression, in the long run of history, the cause of life and freedom will be most honorable. Beholding contrasting memories in the same location exposes a haunting, and a haunting demands action. In the absence of haunting, the traumas that comprise America's past are erased, creating the idea that our hands are clean. At the same time, a haunting may result in my humanization.

The cause for life and freedom is kept alive when pains are taken to remember complex and often-antithetical events. Oakland cemetery has done well to reckon with its history by making notes of the troubling past on informative plaques that are used to educate without romanticizing. In 2016, a $600,000 restoration project was started to repair broken grave markers and survey the gravesites. And in the summer of 2022, the Historic Oakland Foundation, along with the Department of Parks and Recreation, held a ribbon-cutting ceremony commemorating the restoration of the African American Burial Grounds. At the ribbon-cutting ceremony, Mayor Andre Dickens said, "this cemetery is indeed alive." He also described Atlanta's history as "complicated and rich."[5] Our complicated and rich history has been the driving concern of *Ghosts of Atlanta.* And the consideration that our past is alive in our ghosts has been my guide to understanding the complexity of the Black Mecca as a Black homeplace. It's evident that there is still a veil here in Atlanta separating Black and white lifeworlds. And I have asked what happens to Black culture, the Black homeland, and the Black people as a whole when they are displaced to make room for white people? And how do we, Black people, use our special sauce to tear the veil and forge conditions that humanize us, making us alive to the past, the present, and the future of this city?

Ellison proposes that we as a nation need an "ultimate vocabulary" that describes whom we may become.[6] I still believe Atlanta to be the best place to do that. An "ultimate vocabulary," originally defined by Kenneth Burke, is a language, a symbolic action, that allows individuals to transcend their individual statuses and their deep-rooted oppositions and become a part of a community. Ellison's ultimate vocabulary reminds us that the goal "is not to seek a way out of distinction, hierarchy, and order" but "to embrace the responsibility" of our Constitution, of freedom, citizenship, and equality.[7]

Though Burke envisioned this ultimate vocabulary, he could not get out of the dichotomy of Black and white to conceptualize a scheme that would solve America's racial conflict.[8] This is one reason why Kenneth Burke, the renowned rhetorical theorist of the twentieth century, was not the epistemological guide for this book. Burke used Marxism as his closest example of an ultimate vocabulary. He wrote that through an ultimate vocabulary, marginalized people view themselves not as individuals trying to achieve more power but as members of a class destined to play a role in history. They see their role as ultimate and universal. Burke attempts to apply the concept to African Americans, arguing that "the Negro does not become equal to the white by a kind of intellectual 'passing.' He can explicitly recognize that his particular act must be adapted to the nature of his historical situation in which he happens to be placed; yet at the same time, he can view this situation universally (thereby attaining the kind of transcendence at which all men aim . . .)."[9]

In sum, Burke contests that African Americans become equal when they alter themselves to fit the oppressive circumstances and change their perspective to see this alteration as an issue that all humanity must contend with. The problem is that racism is not a dilemma that all humanity is on the receiving end of. Racism is a white man's problem and a Black man's burden. Such a supposition like Burke's allows white people to ignore the problem and Black people to continue carrying it.

The burden isn't light. Thus, African Americans have a penchant for warning the rest of America when the worst of America's identity is showing.

From the start of this book, I recollected on my family's experience at Stone Mountain as a meeting up of ghosts—the ghosts of the Confederacy with the ghosts of my enslaved ancestors. I acknowledged that in this meeting, at a mutual location for both a Confederate memorial (Stone Mountain) and the metaphorical origins of African American collective identity (Atlanta), the traumatic history of the past was made visible. That visibility produced "a something-to-be-done." It brought to the fore the reality that the past's problems had not been reckoned with and that if they were never dealt with, we would live out our lives consistently subjected to the supremacist chains those Confederate generals wanted to keep us under. But if, by some means, we were to see our history for its sad, scary, and violent beginnings, decide that racism and its oppressive results are immoral, and change every aspect of the lifeworlds that put us back in those chains, we could be freed. In this way, I suggested that to free the enslaved and free their heirs, it's necessary to combat every element of our nation's structure, including racist and neoliberal ideology, that keeps them tied in bondage, never connecting to an actual origin and consistently being displaced from their next destination.

That very goal is broad and deep but made easier to grasp when we acknowledge the power of space to both constrain people and make them free and to persuade us to see everyone as equal or convince us that our demographic differences make some inherently better than others. It is not just the children of the enslaved that are made shadows but the entire nation. James Baldwin famously wrote, "We cannot be free until they are free."[10] *Ghosts of Atlanta* allows us to see how the three cases discussed here differ from others in that they summarize the cultural issues at stake when we commit to the claim that our lived experience of collective belonging, as coded by race, is subject to change because it can be spatially constructed. The ultimate significance of this book is that it demonstrates that when we consider that space and place act rhetorically to forge identification with or against a thing or a person, we can make use of our landscape and built environment as a witness and storyteller that mediate our differences, teach the lesson to be learned, and provide visibility for all of our cultures and historical trajectories.

Gentrification, a social and economic process that renders change, presents an exigence where rhetoricians, developers, planners, residents, and other scholars can begin reexamining how we design our neighborhoods and cities. Considering that gentrification particularly forces displacement of the lower class and people of color from locations they call home, the exigence of gentrification also gives us a chance to examine how we redefine spaces rhetorically to forge identification of home with the people who are threatened to be displaced and the gentry entering the community. When we speak of revitalizing spaces and places that make up the American landscape, government officials, planners, and residents might ask, "What makes a place home?" Is it the sanctuary of grandma's house,[11] walkable streets,[12] place-based public art and culture (e.g., AoAB),[13] access to amenities and utilities, or the aesthetic? It might be reasonable to inquire about the parts of the locations that capture our attention. What name best represents this neighborhood and the people we want here? Are we adding public art, museums, and commemorations of history? Are the buildings, parks, and trails accessible, safe, and pleasing?

But what's more, the question I pose here is, Do the people who have lived, worked, and played in these spaces see themselves, their values, their culture, and their history there? In this book, I take on the concern beyond the physical appearance of the environment to understand how the way we narrate our spaces affects our connection to them and our collective witnessing of the people that traverse(d) them. I ask, How does culture produce spaces? And how is culture produced by space? Further, I ask, How is Atlanta—the landscape and the people—produced by its spaces?

Intentionally, my question of culture production focuses on Black people as it is a unique identification forged not out of the sharing of known physical origins but from the sharing of trauma that forced the production of metaphorical roots of connectivity. Noting the instability of symbolic origins within spaces of white hegemony, I consider the fragility of space due to displacement and cultural gentrification as detrimental to African American identity in affinity to being both American and Black. This requires us to consider how African American historical trajectories are denied and repressed by the neoliberal hegemony. To ponder this issue, I used the more specific case concerning Atlanta as the Black Mecca and asked, How is Black culture in Atlanta disrupted along Atlanta BeltLine's path?

My "how" question focused solely on the process of identification by communication between physical elements of the space and the people that traverse them: the dialogic discourse between African Americans and places that harbor cultural narratives of collective identity. To present the results of this case, the book was intentionally organized to provide a view of time that is both retrospective and proleptic, a picture of landscape narration in three different modes (place-name, public art, and the built environment), and an introductory view of the usefulness of African American musical forms as a means for understanding the reality of America's identity. Through this analysis, we learn that cultural gentrification occurs when urban redevelopment is used to establish white culture-lands, mask immorality, and support individualism. These acts erase Black existence and continuously reconstruct white dominant power structures.

I believe the Black Mecca, Atlanta, is necessary for America's survival. I'm convinced the white rage-filled racial conflict that continues in the nation will lead to destruction. You may have picked up this book thinking it was just information on gentrification in Atlanta, but hopefully, you've found that it is more than that. Cultural gentrification is just another format of America showing itself in the worse ways. One of my interviewees said it best regarding Blandtown, and I reiterate his articulation for all of Atlanta: Atlanta is not being renovated; it is being desecrated. This is a "desecration" of the memories that would make Atlanta home for Black people residing in and outside of the central city.

From the beginning, I also declared that Atlanta was worthy of saving because it's been identified as a Black Mecca. I noted that three things make Atlanta a Black Mecca and an apt metaphorical origin for Black collective identity, which is that it (1) harbors the memories of collective trauma, (2) provides an origination story for Black homeland post–Civil War, and (3) conceptualizes a hope for a utopian future of racial peace and prosperity. Atlanta brings the blues, freedom songs, and trap music—bringing voice to the marginalized and vision to the blind. If the problems of America's identity and the issue of cultural gentrification lie in the persistent actions that seek to cover up and conceal trauma, immorality, and guilt, then visibility is its remedy. By installing constructions of the blues, freedom songs, and trap music in the narrative of our spaces, Atlantans are playing the most constructive role in America's becoming. Trump said that the 1619 Project and critical race theory were un-American and showed a lack of patriotism. Tell me, what's more patriotic than playing out your most incredible trauma over and over and making yourself vulnerable in places that are not safe so your country doesn't fall in on itself? As my husband reminds me, there is no instance in America where a Black person can benefit by going backward in time. Yet we do it to save the nation to which our fate has been bound.

What I hope I have revealed is that we—the audience of readers addressed by this text—are left with "something-to-be-done" to rectify the cultural gentrification and displacement of Black lifeworlds perpetuated by the neoliberal and racist ideologies endemic to white hegemony in the United States. This book is placed as not only a work of critical rhetorical analysis of the romanticizing features of space but also a rhetorical address in and of itself. I stand as both rhetorical critic and rhetor, seeking my readers to participate in efforts to reconstruct Atlanta and all our cities formed by diverse groups in such a way that the various spatial narratives can coexist within the places we call home. In this way, my audience may take on the calling to become witnesses, as best described by Karen Cross and Julia Peck in their reflections on Walter Benjamin's writing. They write,

> The Angel of History . . . stands with his face turned towards the past while the wreckage of history grows before him. The storm in which he is caught is called "progress" and the angel is propelled backwards towards the future. A sad figure, he "would like to stay, awaken the dead, and make whole again what has been smashed." But the storm is too violent.
>
> In light of this allegory we might begin to question: what is the use in being turned longingly towards the past? The angel is not able to breathe life into the debris and reassemble the wreckage that is left behind but can at least be a witness to the past and its destruction. But there are other possibilities. The historical materialist, unlike the angel, is turned towards the future in the hope of change to come. The aim is not to reassemble the past as it was but rather to "seize hold of a memory as it flashes up at a moment of danger" and arrest the image of the past in order to confront the past with its own creations. The task of the historical materialist, having witnessed the "barbarism" of the document and its transmission, is to "brush history against the grain."[14]

Thus far, my three cases placed me as the "historical materialist." I have attempted to be a witness to the past by excavating it within the spatial, racial, and neoliberal context of the Atlanta BeltLine formation. But rather than staying in the past, I have looked at the present and sought to capture the areas of the present where our past faults are set to reappear. In this way, I have sought change for our future.

As a step in the direction toward relieving the detrimental effects of cultural gentrification to diverse collective identities, I consider the methods used in this book as critical for community engagement in urban-redevelopment processes as they allow designers and researchers to position themselves as witnesses seeking to expose the historical narratives for a revisioning of a collective future toward moral reckoning.

Rhetoricians should follow the ghosts, working to identify the intersecting cultural groups that currently and historically reside(d) in the space. Once identified, the critic can use an integrative approach to develop a method for uncovering the spatial narrative. This can be unique to each case as it will be necessary to determine the visual, textual, archival, and demographic data available for critique. In some cases, the people may have been displaced, thus requiring the critic to utilize the things they left behind as resources for uncovering the narrative. For instance, in the case of Blandtown, the only symbolic relic of the past community was in the name it left behind, making an excavation of the narrative associated with the neighborhood name the most apt text for analysis. Since the public history of the name was erroneous, it was necessary to use archival data from newspapers, censuses, and deeds to fill in the gaps. In addition, I had to use the oral history of living residents to get access to the individual narratives that made Blandtown home to the group. What I seek to articulate here is that rhetoricians will need to use nontraditional and diverse means to uncover and access the spatial narrative. It is a nonlinear process requiring creativity and attention to the symbols of culture available.

Rhetorical scholars should be prepared to provide suggestions and insights to developers, designers, and planners. As we seek to take rhetorical scholarship outside of the marls of university bookshelves and paid-subscription online journals, we should consider how to present our research to change makers and decision makers. This requires involvement in local projects, seeking grants, and joining grassroots organizations. It also entails strategically communicating your work to a new audience without the requirements of academic, theoretical, and rhetorical jargon. Rhetoricians can learn to make their work palatable to a larger audience and engage them in using these practices in their community-facing projects.

With that in mind, I encourage us to think about these methods beyond Atlanta and the BeltLine. *Ghosts of Atlanta* began with two goals: (1) to explore the importance of narrating metaphorical spaces for African American identity and (2) to determine how we—scholars, planners, tour guides, historians, architects, officials, and residents—can make diversely shared spaces articulate and be articulated by the diverse historical trajectories that reside in them. The project found itself in Atlanta but claims that these spatial-analysis methods and recommendations regarding spatial narration in neighborhood design can be used beyond the Atlanta BeltLine and African American histories.

In my final remarks, I submit that the past—including its failures and successes, traumas and healings—cannot just be witnessed once but requires a continual enactment of remembrance. Perpetual remembering is an act of constant learning, requiring each generation to recognize the ghosts of the past and simultaneously seek the spiritual calling of the future. By doing so, we don't simply claim history as "nice to know." Memory work is essential, but it is insufficient on its own.[15] We must build and narrate a shared past, as well as organize processes "aimed at accounting for collective harms, identifying" a responsible party, and establishing accountability mechanisms.[16] All are necessary for the laying down of the veil. I consider history as a starting point for change and a mandate to stop repeating the faults of the past and instead let go of those destructive practices to move toward a future where everyone belongs. James Baldwin wrote in *The Fire Next Time* that "if the word integration means anything, this is what it means: that we with love, shall force our brothers to see themselves as they are, to cease fleeing from reality and begin to change it." This is the goal of witnessing. This is the something-to-be-done. This is the fire this time. This is our role in making "America what America must become."[17]

NOTES

INTRODUCTION

1. *Saturday Night Live*, "Mr. Robinson's Neighborhood 2019," December 22, 2019, YouTube video, 4:22, https://www.youtube.com/watch?v=whfQf3Pd5bU.

2. The proper noun "the Culture" is a popular refrain in the Black community used to specifically reference shared Black symbols of communication, language, thought, art, history, music, dance, and other modes of social production that often face co-optation, or appropriation, in the dominant society.

3. Phyl Garland, "Atlanta: Black Mecca of the South," *Ebony Magazine*, August 1971, 157.

4. David Jacobson, *Place and Belonging in America* (Baltimore: Johns Hopkins University Press, 2002).

5. Doreen Massey, *For Space* (London: Sage, 2005).

6. Parker Shipton, "Land and Culture in Tropical Africa: Soils, Symbols, and the Metaphysics of the Mundane," *Annual Review of Anthropology* 23, no. 1 (1994): 349.

7. Shipton, "Land and Culture," 349–50.

8. Stephanie Smallwood, *Saltwater Slavery: A Middle Passage from Africa to American Diaspora* (Cambridge, MA: Harvard University Press, 2007).

9. Ralph Ellison, *Invisible Man*, 2nd ed. (New York: Vintage Books, 1995), 8.

10. Paul Taylor, "Black Aesthetics," *Philosophy Compass* 5, no. 1 (January 2010): 1–15, https://doi.org/10.1111/j.1747-9991.2009.00263.x.

11. Avery F. Gordon, *Ghostly Matters: Haunting and the Sociological Imagination*, new ed. (Minneapolis: University of Minnesota Press, 2008), 8.

12. W. E. B. Du Bois, *The Souls of Black Folk* (1903; repr., n.p.: Millennium Publications, 2014).

13. Gordon, *Ghostly Matters*, 58.

14. Du Bois, *Souls of Black Folk*, 4.

15. Gordon, *Ghostly Matters*, xv–xx.

16. Ellison, *Invisible Man*, 4, 5, 3.

17. Ellison, *Invisible Man*, xv.

18. Toni Morrison, *Playing in the Dark: Whiteness and the Literary Imagination* (New York: Vintage Books, 1992), 33.

19. Put another way, according to Kobena Mercer, Stuart Hall suggests that "in calling vast numbers of disparate people into a shared identification," the freeborn Englishman's

discursive configuration of identity required "his difference from colonial and enslaved others who were excluded from any 'natural rights.'" Hall suggests that this narrative identification with a nation-state recognizes a dependence on space and time to create a sense of place, anchoring point, or home. See Kobena Mercer, "Introduction," in *The Fateful Triangle: Race, Ethnicity, Nation*, by Stuart Hall (Cambridge, MA: Harvard University Press, 2017), 6, EBSCOhost.

20. Ellison, *Invisible Man*, 94.

21. Thomas K. Nakayama and Lisa N. Peñaloza, "Madonna T/Races: Music Videos through the Prism of Color," in *The Madonna Connection: Representational Politics, Subcultural Identities, and Cultural Theory*, ed. Cathy Schwichtenberg (New York: Routledge, 1993), 54. See also Thomas K. Nakayama and Robert L. Krizek, "Whiteness: A Strategic Rhetoric," *Quarterly Journal of Speech* 81, no. 3 (August 1995): 291–309, https://doi.org/10.1080/00335639509384117.

22. Morrison, *Playing in the Dark*, 33.

23. Morrison, *Playing in the Dark*, 33.

24. Akira Drake Rodriguez, "Remaking Black Political Spaces for Black Liberation," Metropolitics, December 1, 2016, https://metropolitics.org/Remaking-Black-Political-Spaces.html.

25. Avery F. Gordon, "Some Thoughts on Haunting and Futurity," *Borderlands* 10, no. 2 (2011): 3.

26. Gordon, *Ghostly Matters*.

27. The phrase "feeling some type of way" is used in informal language to mean "I'm unable to express the complexity of the emotion at the moment." This phrase "can be used seriously or in jest." See "Some Type of Way," Urban Dictionary, accessed February 8, 2022, https://www.urbandictionary.com/define.php?term=some%20type%20of%20way.

28. Brandi Thompson Summers, *Black in Place: The Spatial Aesthetics of Race in a Post-Chocolate City* (Chapel Hill: University of North Carolina Press, 2019), 15, EBSCOhost.

29. Regarding that conclusion, see Michelle Boyd, "Defensive Development: The Role of Racial Conflict in Gentrification," *Urban Affairs Review* 43, no. 6 (2008): 751–76. Regarding the stereotypes, see Caitlin Cahill, "Negotiating Grit and Glamour: Young Women of Color and the Gentrification of the Lower East Side," *City and Society* 19, no. 2 (2007): 202–31.

30. Stuart Hall, "Cultural Identity and Diaspora," in *Identity: Community, Culture, Difference*, ed. Jonathan Rutherford (London: Lawrence and Wishart, 1990), 222–37, Project MUSE. The concepts described here come from Stuart Hall's designation of the "Presence Africaine," "Presence Europeenne," and "Presence Americain" in the cultural life of Black people across the African diaspora. The African presence is the culture that was forcefully repressed during enslavement yet remains the "unspoken, unspeakable" present "in the stories and tales told to children, in religious practices and beliefs, in the spiritual life, the arts, crafts, musics and rhythms of slave and post-emancipation society." The European presence is "about exclusion, imposition and expropriation." It presents in Black culture as a "dialogue of power and resistance, of refusal and recognition, with and against" European domination. The American presence is "ground, place, territory." It is the symbol of juncture where the different cultures—American, European, and

African—meet and have their creolization, assimilation, and syncretism negotiated. "It also has to be understood as the places of many, continuous displacements." Ibid., 230, 233, 234.

31. bell hooks, *Yearning: Race, Gender, and Cultural Politics* (Boston: South End Press, 1990), 384.

32. Morrison, *Playing in the Dark*, 39.

33. Morrison, *Playing in the Dark*, 38.

34. Haunting is "one way in which abusive systems of power make themselves known and their impacts felt in everyday life, especially when they are supposedly over and done with (such as with transatlantic slavery, for instance) or when their oppressive nature is continuously denied (such as with free labor or national security)." See Janice Radway, "Foreword," in *Ghostly Matters: Haunting and the Sociological Imagination*, by Avery F. Gordon, new ed. (Minneapolis: University of Minnesota Press, 2008), loc. 186.

35. Avery F. Gordon, "Some Thoughts on Haunting and Futurity," *Borderlands* 10, no. 2 (2011), 2–3.

36. Gordon, *Ghostly Matters*, 8.

37. Gordon, *Ghostly Matters*, 8.

38. Maurice J. Hobson, *The Legend of the Black Mecca* (Chapel Hill: University of North Carolina Press, 2017).

39. hooks, *Yearning*, 384.

40. US Office of Management and Budget, "29-County Metropolitan Statistical Area (MSA)," Metro Atlanta Chamber, 2021, https://dch.georgia.gov/sites/dch.georgia.gov/files/Atlanta%20Service%20Area%20Map.pdf.

41. Robert D. Bullard, Glenn S. Johnson, and Angel O. Torres, "Atlanta Megasprawl," *Forum for Applied Research and Public Policy* 14, no. 3 (Fall 1999): 18.

42. Ryan Austin Gravel, "Belt Line - Atlanta: Design of Infrastructure as a Reflection of Public Policy" (master's thesis, Georgia Institute of Technology, 1999), https://beltline.org/wp-content/uploads/2012/04/Ryan-Gravel-Thesis-1999.pdf.

43. Nick Van Mead, "A City Cursed by Sprawl: Can the BeltLine Save Atlanta?," *The Guardian*, October 25, 2018, https://www.theguardian.com/cities/2018/oct/25/cursed-sprawl-can-beltline-save-atlanta.

44. James C. Fraser, "Beyond Gentrification: Mobilizing Communities and Claiming Space," *Urban Geography* 25, no. 5 (July 2004): 443, https://doi.org/10.2747/0272-3638.25.5.437.

45. *Saturday Night Live*, "Mr. Robinson's Neighborhood."

46. Summers, *Black in Place*, 15.

47. As Neil Smith attests, "public policy and the private market are conspiring against minorities, working people, the poor and homeless. . . . Gentrification has become part of this policy of revenge." Neil Smith, *The New Urban Frontier: Gentrification and the Revanchist City* (New York: Taylor and Francis, 1996), "Introduction," n.p.

48. Rodriguez, "Remaking Black Political Spaces."

49. The debate over the economic versus cultural understandings of gentrification has been ongoing in gentrification studies. To combine the economic and the cultural, Sharon Zukin links capitalist development to historic preservation, noting that the gentrifying

class's investment in culture through cultural appropriation has an economic rationality, helping them to "valorize their investment," "satisfy civic pride," and "profit from appropriated goods." Sharon Zukin, "Gentrification: Culture and Capital in the Urban Core," *Annual Review of Sociology* 13 (1987): 143. *Ghosts of Atlanta* recognizes the truth of this argument but focuses on cultural understanding rather than attempting to combine the economic and the cultural, which can lead to superimposing the economic over the cultural.

50. Mercer, "Introduction," 4.

51. Mercer, "Introduction," 10.

52. Hall, "Cultural Identity," 223.

53. Mercer, "Introduction," 11.

54. Mercer, "Introduction," 4.

55. Karl Marx and Frederick Engels, *The German Ideology*, ed. C. J. Arthur (1845–1846; repr., New York, NY: International Publishers, 1972), cited in George Yudice, "Culture," in *Keywords for American Cultural Studies*, ed. Bruce Burgett and Glenn Hendler, 3rd ed. (New York: New York University Press, 2020), 78.

56. Stuart Hall, "Encoding, Decoding," in *The Cultural Studies Reader*, ed. Simon During, 2nd ed. (London: Routledge, 1993), 507–17.

57. The term "hegemony" as used here comes from the work of Antonio Gramsci. Thomas R. Bates explains that the basic premise of Gramsci's concept of "hegemony" is that "man is not ruled by force alone, but also by ideas." The ideas of the ruling class are also the ruling ideas of the age. Further, ideas have "the vital function of preserving the 'ideological unity of a whole social bloc.'" Antonio Gramsci, *Il materialism storico e la filosofia di Benedetto Croce* (Turin: G. Einauldi, 1966), 75, quoted in Thomas R. Bates, "Gramsci and the Theory of Hegemony," *Journal of the History of Ideas* 36, no. 2 (June 1975): 351. Hegemony "means political leadership based on the consent of the led, a consent which is secured by the diffusion and popularization of the world view of the ruling class." Bates, "Gramsci," 351–52.

58. Capitalist economic activities move rapidly, reducing the time it takes to move goods, people, and discourse around the world. David Harvey describes this as "time-space compression." It's an acknowledgment that the rapidity at which it takes to move capital across space compresses space and accelerates social life. One of the consequences of time-space compression is the loss of the relevance of place. Unique identities and cultures of places soon become indistinguishable from other places as they are homogenized in the search for cheap labor and resources. Yet "the diminution of spatial barriers has provoked an increasing sense of nationalism and localism, and excessive geopolitical rivalries and tensions, precisely because of the reduction in the power of spatial barriers to separate and defend against others." David Harvey, "Between Space and Time: Reflections on the Geographical Imagination," *Annals of the Association of American Geographers* 80, no. 3 (September 1990): 427. See also Doreen Massey, *Space, Place and Gender* (Minneapolis: University of Minnesota Press, 1994) 146–56.

59. Massey, *For Space*, 4–5.

60. Massey, *For Space*, 12.

61. Exploring European discourses on "body" in the eighteenth and nineteenth centuries, Jayna Brown discusses that Georg Hegel, in his "Geographical Basis of History," used

the guise of science and philosophy to justify racial hierarchies and claimed, "the white races, from the northern climates, were the creators of civilization, while 'the Negro' remained incapable of historical change." Georg Wilhem Friedrich Hegel, *The Philosophy of History*, trans. John Sibree, rev. ed. (1837; repr., New York: Colonial Press, 1899), 93, quoted in Jayna Brown, "Body," in *Keywords for African American Studies*, ed. Erica R. Edwards, Roderick A. Ferguson, and Jeffrey O. G. Ogbar (New York: New York University Press, 2020), 30.

62. Ellison, *Invisible Man*, 3.

63. Ellison, *Invisible Man*, 3.

64. Craig Evan Barton, "The Mnemonic City: Duality, Invisibility and Memory in American Urbanism," in *Constructions of Tectonics for the Postindustrial World: ACSA European Conference; Proceedings of the 1996 ACSA European Conference, Royal Danish Academy of Fine Arts, May 25–29, 1996, Copenhagen, Denmark* (Washington, DC: Association of Collegiate Schools of Architecture, 1997), 223.

65. Robert W. McChesney, "Global Media, Neoliberalism, and Imperialism," *Monthly Review: An Independent Socialist Magazine* 52, no. 10 (March 2001): 1.

66. Deepa Kumar, "Media, Class, and Power: Debunking the Myth of a Classless Society," in *Class and News*, ed. Don Heider (New York: Rowman and Littlefield, 2004), 6–21.

67. Summers, *Black in Place*, 6.

68. Joe R. Feagin, *Systemic Racism: A Theory of Oppression* (New York: Routledge, 2006).

69. Wendy Cheng and Rashad Shabazz, "Introduction: Race, Space, and Scale in the Twenty-First Century," *Occasion* 8 (August 2015): 4.

70. Ralph Ellison, *The Collected Essays of Ralph Ellison*, ed. John F. Callahan, Modern Library paperback ed. (New York: Modern Library, 2003), 575.

71. Katherine McKittrick and Clyde Woods, "No One Knows the Mysteries at the Bottom of the Ocean," in *Black Geographies and the Politics of Place*, ed. Katherine McKittrick and Clyde Woods (Cambridge, MA: South End Press, 2007), 3, 6.

72. Summers, *Black in Place*, 13.

73. Melissa Oyler, "New Developments in Historically Black Neighborhoods: Will a New Mixed-Use Development Ease the Pain of the Past in Charlotte's Second Ward?," *Bisnow*, February 5, 2018, https://www.bisnow.com/charlotte/news/neighborhood/will-a-new-mixed-use-development-ease-the-pain-of-second-wards-past-84490.

74. Miriam Hall, "Harlem's 125th Street Grapples with History amid Retail Transformation," *Bisnow*, February 28, 2018, https://www.bisnow.com/new-york/news/neighborhood/harlem-whole-foods-125th-street-85546.

75. John Banister, "Renewed Activity Reminds U Street Residents of Historic Past, but Many Cannot Afford to Stay," *Bisnow*, February 27, 2018, https://www.bisnow.com/washington-dc/news/neighborhood/developmentwave-has-brought-historic-u-street-back-to-life-but-at-what-cost-85416.

76. Kwame Holmes, "Not in the Family Way: Urban 'Life Cycles' and the Culture of Black Displacement," *Occasion* 8 (August 2015): 1–9.

77. Summers, *Black in Place*, 12.

78. Gordon, *Ghostly Matters*, 97.

79. Eminent domain is the power of the government to expropriate private property for public use in exchange for compensation. Eminent domain has been a recent

hot-button issue in Atlanta. For example, in Peoplestown, a predominantly African American neighborhood in Atlanta, the city under Mayor Kaseem Reed proposed a park and retention pond as a solution to flooding in the area that started in 2012. In order to construct the park and retention pond, they sought to use eminent domain to acquire the houses of about twenty-four families. While most residents left, a few long-time residents refused. See Katie Leslie, "In Peoplestown, Proposal to Fix Flooding Leads to Displacement," *Atlanta Journal-Constitution*, October 5, 2014, sec. News, https://www.ajc.com/news/peoplestown-proposal-fix-flooding-leads-displacement/Q2dvGiTWypxQwQ7lH6VGmL/. See also J. D. Capelouto and Wilborn P. Nobles III, "On Eve of Election, Peoplestown Housing, Flooding Dispute Takes Center Stage," *Atlanta Journal-Constitution*, November 1, 2021, sec. Local News, https://www.ajc.com/news/atlanta-news/on-eve-of-election-peoplestown-housing-flooding-dispute-takes-center-stage/KIOGPU7RQRAV5D7FDQ7FKI333Q/.

According to Cliff Albright, "Community members suspect the flooding is being used as a pretext to facilitate private development in the neighborhood" and as a way to "accelerate the gentrification and displacement that is already affecting low-income black and brown communities." See Cliff Albright, "Gentrification Is Sweeping through America: Here Are the People Fighting Back," *The Guardian*, November 10, 2017, sec. US News, https://www.theguardian.com/us-news/2017/nov/10/atlanta-super-gentrification-eminent-domain.

80. Ellison, *Collected Essays*, 406.

81. Gravel, "Belt Line - Atlanta."

82. Gravel, "Belt Line - Atlanta," 1.

83. Hobson, *Legend*, 73.

84. Larry Keating, *Atlanta: Race, Class, and Urban Expansion*, Comparative American Cities, ed. Joe T. Darden (Philadelphia: Temple University Press, 2001), 93.

85. Gravel, "Belt Line - Atlanta," 15.

86. Dan Immergluck, Ann Carpenter, and Abram Lueders, "Declines in Low-Cost Rented Housing Units in Eight Large Southeastern Cities," *Community and Economic Development Discussion Paper* 3, no. 16 (May 2016): 1–32.

87. Willoughby Mariano, Lindsey Conway, and Anastaciah Ondieki, "How the Atlanta Beltline Broke Its Promise on Affordable Housing," *Atlanta Journal-Constitution*, July 13, 2017, https://www.ajc.com/news/local/how-the-atlanta-beltline-broke-its-promise-affordable-housing/oVXnu1BlYCoIbA9U4u2CEM/#:~:text=Journal%2DConstitution%20found.-,Beltline%20Inc.,of%20dollars%20of%20potential%20funds.

88. This calculation is based off a home that increases from $100,000 to $150,000 over four years at a millage rate of 0.0430 and a homestead exemption of $30,000. See Dan Immergluck and Tharunya Balan, "Sustainable for Whom? Green Urban Development, Environmental Gentrification, and the Atlanta Beltline," *Urban Geography* 39, no 4 (2017): 1–17.

89. Immergluck and Balan, "Sustainable for Whom?," 14.

90. A tax allocation district (TAD) is a "redevelopment and financing tool by which governments can provide financial assistance to eligible public and private redevelopment efforts within an officially designated area or TAD. Increases in property tax revenues, which

are generated primarily from new investment in the district, are allocated to pay infrastructure costs or certain private development costs within TAD." The BeltLine TAD was created on December 31, 2005, set to extend for twenty-five years. See "Tax Allocation District (TAD)," City of Atlanta, GA, accessed May 18, 2020, https://www.atlantaga.gov/government/departments/city-planning/office-of-zoning-development/plans-and-studies/tax-allocation-district-tad. See also BeltLine Ordinance, Atlanta City Council, ordinance 05-O-1733 § 8(d) (2005); Dan Immergluck, *Red Hot City: Housing, Race, and Exclusion in Twenty-First-Century Atlanta* (Oakland: University of California Press, 2022), 59–94.

91. "Glossary of Terms to Affordable Housing," US Department of Housing and Urban Development, Archives, accessed February 10, 2022, https://archives.hud.gov/local/nv/goodstories/2006-04-06glos.cfm.

92. "Atlanta City Design Housing," Development of City Planning, March 15, 2021, https://storymaps.arcgis.com/stories/e91c43ad299a4634add2bed4cf2eca9d.

93. City of Atlanta, *Equitable Housing Assessment: City of Atlanta; Final Briefing Book* (Atlanta: HR&A Advisors, Fall 2018), 8, https://drive.google.com/file/d/11qN-vHLINeXkW7JIcWDMBC4OmfHSjLa_/view.

94. Development of City Planning, "Atlanta City Design Housing."

95. City of Atlanta, *Equitable Housing Assessment*, 8.

96. Immergluck, *Red Hot City*, 60–61.

97. Abraham Harold Maslow, "A Theory of Human Motivation," *Psychological Review* 50, no. 4 (1943): 370–96.

98. Deirdre Oakley, Erin Ruel, and Lesley Reid, "Atlanta's Last Demolitions and Relocations: The Relationship Between Neighborhood Characteristics and Resident Satisfaction," *Housing Studies* 28, no. 2 (2013): 207.

99. Maurice Halbwachs, *The Collective Memory* (New York: Harper and Row, 1980), 1–15.

100. Eun Young Lee, "Looking Forward: Decentering and Reorienting Communication Studies in the Spatial Turn," *Women's Studies in Communication* 39, no. 2 (2016): 133.

101. On the notion of the veil, see Du Bois, *Souls of Black Folk*.

102. Ellison, *Collected Essays*, 492.

103. Kenneth E. Foote and Maoz Azaryahu, "Toward a Geography of Memory: Geographical Dimensions of Public Memory and Commemoration," *Journal of Political and Military Sociology* 35, no. 1 (2007): 127.

104. David J. Bodenhamer, "Narrating Space and Place," in *Deep Maps and Spatial Narratives*, ed. David J. Bodenhamer, John Corrigan, and Trevor M. Harris (Bloomington: Indiana University Press, 2015), 7–27.

105. Annette Kuhn, "Photography and Cultural Memory: A Methodological Exploration," *Visual Studies* 22, no. 3 (2007): 283.

106. Kent A. Ono and John M. Sloop, "The Critique of Vernacular Discourse," *Communication Monographs* 62, no. 1 (1995): 19–46.

107. Richard Delgado and Jean Stefancic, *Critical Race Theory: The Cutting Edge* (Philadelphia: Temple University Press, 2013), 5.

108. I use Audre Lorde's definition of poetry. She writes, "I speak here of poetry as a revelatory distillation of experience, not the sterile word play that, too often, the white fathers distorted the word poetry to mean—in order to cover a desperate wish

for imagination without insight." See Audre Lorde, *Sister Outsider: Essays and Speeches* (Berkeley, CA: Crossing Press, 1984), 37.

109. Lorde, *Sister Outsider*, 53.

110. For the quotes, see Lorde, *Sister Outsider*, 55.

111. Lorde, *Sister Outsider*, 39.

112. Lorde, *Sister Outsider*, 38.

CHAPTER 1: "BACK TO WHERE THEY COME FROM, OF COURSE—ATLANTA"

1. Patrick Phillips, *Blood at the Root: A Racial Cleansing in America* (New York: W. W. Norton, 1923), 178, 173.

2. Phillips, *Blood at the Root*, 203.

3. "QuickFacts: Forsyth County, Georgia," US Census Bureau, accessed June 1, 2022, https://www.census.gov/quickfacts/forsythcountygeorgia.

4. Lori I. Coleman, "Our Whole Future Is Bound Up in This Project: The Making of Buford Dam" (master's thesis, Georgia State University, 2008).

5. Deanna M. Gillespie, "'Revolutionize Life in the Chattahoochee River Valley': Buford Dam and the Development of Northeastern Georgia, 1950–1970," *Georgia Historical Quarterly* 100, no. 4 (2016): 417.

6. Gillespie, "'Revolutionize Life,'" 425.

7. Phillips, *Blood at the Root*, 76.

8. Phillips, *Blood at the Root*, 78.

9. Phillips, *Blood at the Root*, 184.

10. Phillips, *Blood at the Root*, 183.

11. Phillips, *Blood at the Root*, 184.

12. Phillips, *Blood at the Root*, 119.

13. Gillespie, "'Revolutionize Life,'" 432.

14. Phillips, *Blood at the Root*, 182.

15. According to Dan Immergluck, Atlanta established a comprehensive class-based zoning system as a "legally defensible tool of racial exclusion." Under class-based zoning, groups were segregated based on their social class rather than race. However, "when the Black middle class was quite small, it would be generally effective, at least in excluding Black people from middle- and upper-income neighborhoods," Immergluck explains. Immergluck, *Red Hot City*, 20.

16. Phillips, *Blood at the Root*, 290.

17. Phillips, *Blood at the Root*, 217.

18. US Census Bureau, "QuickFacts."

19. David W. Noble, *Death of a Nation* (Minneapolis: University of Minnesota Press, 2002), cited in George Lipsitz, "Space," in *Keywords for American Cultural Studies*, ed. Bruce Burgett and Glenn Hendler, 3rd ed. (New York: New York University Press, 2020), 229.

20. Morrison, *Playing in the Dark*, 33.

21. Morrison, *Playing in the Dark*, 35.

22. Morrison, *Playing in the Dark*, 25.

23. Lipsitz, "Space," 230.

24. Frederick Douglass, "'What to the Slave Is the Fourth of July?' 1852," in *Let Nobody Turn Us Around: Voices of Resistance, Reform, and Renewal; An African American Anthology*, ed. Manning Marable and Leith Mullings (Lanham, MD: Rowman and Littlefield, 2000), 90.

25. Ellison, "Commencement Address," 404.

26. Ellison, "Commencement Address," 406.

27. Gordon, *Ghostly Matters*, 168.

28. Gordon, *Ghostly Matters*, 168.

29. Gordon, *Ghostly Matters*, 168.

30. Lipsitz, "Space," 230.

31. Du Bois, *Souls of Black Folk*, 38.

32. Du Bois, *Souls of Black Folk*, 38.

33. Garland, "Atlanta," 157.

34. Edward S. Casey, "Public Memory in Place and Time," in *Framing Public Memory*, ed. Kendall R. Phillips (Tuscaloosa: University of Alabama Press, 2004), 17–44.

35. Jan Assman and John Czaplicka, "Collective Memory and Cultural Identity," *New German Critique*, no. 65 (Spring–Summer 1995): 127.

36. Ron Eyerman, *Cultural Trauma: Slavery and the Formation of African American Identity* (Cambridge, UK: Cambridge University Press, 2001), 1–10.

37. John H. Johnson, "Publisher's Statement," *Ebony Magazine*, August 1971, 33.

38. Halbwachs, *Collective Memory*, 1–15.

39. Akhil Gupta and James Ferguson, "Beyond 'Culture': Space, Identity, and the Politics of Difference," *Cultural Anthropology* 7, no. 1 (1992): 11.

40. Gupta and Ferguson, "Beyond 'Culture,'" 11.

41. Clyde Woods, *Development Drowned and Reborn: The Blues and Bourbon Restorations in Post-Katrina New Orleans*, ed. Laura Pulido and Jordan T. Camp (Athens: University of Georgia Press, 2017), 26.

42. Johnson, "Publisher's Statement," 33.

43. "Black Voices of the South," *Ebony Magazine*, August 1971, 50.

44. "Black Voices," 52.

45. William H. Frey, "The New Great Migration: Black Americans' Return to the South, 1965–2000," Brookings Institution, May 1, 2004, https://www.brookings.edu/articles/the-new-great-migration-black-americans-return-to-the-south-1965-2000/.

46. Lerone Bennett Jr., "Old Illusions and New Souths: Second Reconstruction Gives New Meaning to the Failures and Promises of the Past," *Ebony Magazine*, August 1971, 34.

47. Garland, "Atlanta."

48. "Black Voices," 52.

49. Woods, *Development Drowned and Reborn*, 28.

50. Halbwachs, *Collective Memory*, 1–15.

51. Kodwo Eshun, "Further Considerations of Afrofuturism," *New Centennial Review* 3, no. 2 (2003): 287–302.

52. In 1929, Atlanta University established an economic and finance department with graduate studies. In 1946, the university established the Atlanta University Graduate School

of Business Administration. In 1988, Atlanta University and Clark College consolidated to form Clark Atlanta University (CAU), combining both schools' business programs to make the CAU School of Business.

53. Simeon Booker, "Black Business Is Tops in South: Banks, Savings and Loan, and Insurance Firms Total $1/2 Billion," *Ebony Magazine*, March 2002, 56–63.

54. Garland, "Atlanta."

55. Garland, "Atlanta."

56. Jacobson, *Place and Belonging.*

57. Hobson, *Legend*, 13.

58. Andy Ambrose, "Atlanta," *New Georgia Encyclopedia* (blog), July 26, 2017, https://www.georgiaencyclopedia.org/articles/counties-cities-neighborhoods/atlanta.

59. After the Civil War, the convict-leasing system formed, allowing the states' convicts to be leased to private parties. The Thirteenth Amendment allowed slavery in the case of punishment for a crime, which spurred the increased imprisonment of Black people. This allowed slavery to persist in another form. Through the convict-leasing system, Black prisoners were used to industrialize the city, working in mines and rock quarries and building railroads and roads, among other things. After 1908, the system was replaced by already-established state-run chain gangs. See "The New South and the New Slavery," Georgia Exhibits, accessed February 8, 2022, https://georgia-exhibits.galileo.usg.edu/spotlight/convict-labor.

Beginning in 1866 and lasting legally until 1908 (though there are reports into the 1920s that the system continued illegally), the state of Georgia became one of the first to use a convict-leasing system. Reporting on one such lease agreement, A. Elizabeth Taylor says that in 1869, "the entire penitentiary was leased to Grant, Alexander and Company, a construction company engaged largely in railroad building." The convicts' quarters "were often too small for the number of men required to sleep in them, . . . too few hours were allowed for sleep during the short nights of the summer months. Religious services were neglected in all of the lessee camps. Water facilities were inadequate in many camps, and the personal cleanliness of the convicts were generally neglected. Cruel and inhuman punishment was inflicted on the prisoners sometimes." See A. Elizabeth Taylor, "The Origin and Development of the Convict Lease System in Georgia," *Georgia Historical Quarterly* 26, no. 2 (1942), 114, 115. See also Audrey Vila, "Convict Leasing in 1920s Georgia," Prison in the Western World, Duke University, accessed February 8, 2022, https://sites.duke.edu/history190s_02_ss22020/2020/08/06/convict-leasing-in-1920s-georgia-by-audrey-vila/.

60. Hobson, *Legend*, 17.

61. Radical Reconstruction was a period lasting roughly from 1866 to 1877, when freedmen saw moves toward equal rights in voting and political office. During this time, the Fourteenth and Fifteenth Amendments to the US Constitution were ratified, sixteen Black Congressmen served in the US Congress, and two Black senators served in the US Senate. This period ended when Rutherford B. Hayes was elected to the presidency in 1877 and the federal troops were removed from the South.

62. Hobson, *Legend*, 17.

63. William H. Frey, *Diversity Explosion: How New Racial Demographics Are Remaking America* (Washington, DC: Brookings Institution Press, 2015), 131–48, Project MUSE.

64. "History," Atlanta University Center Consortium, accessed August 8, 2023, https://aucenter.edu/history/.

65. Emmet John Hughes, "The Negro's New Economic Life," *Fortune* 54 (September 1956): 248, quoted in Clifford Kuhn, Harlon E. Joyce, and E. Bernard West, *Living Atlanta: An Oral History of the City, 1914–1948* (Athens: University of Georgia Press, 1990), 39.

66. Hobson, *Legend*, 162.

67. Richard Rothstein, *The Color of Law: A Forgotten History of How Our Government Segregated America* (New York: Liveright, 2017).

68. Irene V. Holliman, "Techwood Homes," *New Georgia Encyclopedia* (blog), August 26, 2020, https://www.georgiaencyclopedia.org/articles/arts-culture/techwood-homes/.

69. Holliman, "Techwood Homes."

70. Akira Drake Rodriguez, *Diverging Space for Deviants: The Politics of Atlanta's Public Housing* (Athens: University of Georgia Press, 2021).

71. Holliman, "Techwood Homes."

72. Hobson, *Legend*, 179.

73. Hobson, *Legend*, 183.

74. Hobson, *Legend*, 190.

75. As discussed by Alex Schwartz, the HOPE VI program was launched in 1993 by Congress "to demolish and redevelop distressed public housing." The National Commission on Severely Distressed Public Housing completed research revealing that approximately "6% of the nation's public housing was severely distressed." This was approximately 86,000 units. "From 1993 through 2010, HOPE VI funded the demolition of more than 150,000 units of distressed public housing and invested $6.2 billion in the redevelopment of 262 public housing projects in 34 states, plus the District of Colombia and Puerto Rico." See Alex Schwartz, *Housing Policy in the United States: An Introduction*, 3rd ed. (New York: Routledge, 2014), 183, 184.

76. Katherine Hankins, Mechelle Puckett, Deirdre Oakley, and Erin Ruel, "Forced Mobility: The Relocation of Public-Housing Residents in Atlanta," *Environment and Planning A* 46, no. 12 (December 2014): 2932–49, https://doi.org/10.1068/a45742.

77. Frey, *Diversity Explosion*, 131–48.

78. "1990–2020 Population Change (State of Georgia, Multiple Geographies)," Georgia Association of Regional Commissions, November 5, 2021, https://opendata.atlanta regional.com/maps/59dd97445d884cd6998336f84ba6ba77.

79. Karen Pooley, "Segregation's New Geography: The Atlanta Metro Region, Race, and the Declining Prospects for Upward Mobility," *Southern Spaces*, April 15, 2015, https ://southernspaces.org/2015/segregations-new-geography-atlanta-metro-region-race-and -declining-prospects-upward-mobility/.

80. "White rage" was described by Carol Anderson as retaliation against Black people triggered by Black advancement. She writes, "White rage is not about visible violence, but rather it works its way through the courts, the legislatures, and a range of government bureaucracies. It wreaks havoc subtly, almost imperceptibly. Too imperceptibly, certainly, for a nation consistently drawn to the spectacular—to what it

can see. It's not the Klan." See Carol Anderson, *White Rage: The Unspoken Truth of Our Racial Divide* (New York: Bloomsbury, 2016), 3.

81. Condé Nast, "The 'Atlanta' Season 3 Premiere Is Based on a Real-Life Tragedy," *GQ*, March 25, 2022, https://www.gq.com/story/atlanta-season-3-premiere-three-slaps-devonte-hart.

CHAPTER 2: "POOF! ALL THE BLACK PEOPLE ARE GONE," OR AN AMERICAN HAUNTING

1. Catherine Fox, "10 Years of ArtsATL: The Humble Beginnings of the Goat Farm Arts Center," *ARTS ATL* (blog), October 11, 2019, https://www.artsatl.org/10-years-of-artsatl-the-humble-beginnings-of-the-goat-farm-arts-center/.

2. The Goat Farm Art Center is located at 1200 Foster Street NW, Atlanta. It is housed at the original location of E. Van Winkle Gin and Machine Works built between the 1880s to the 1930s. Edward Van Winkle opened the complex in 1889 to produce cotton-related machinery. It was bought by the Murray Company of Texas in 1912. Then the plant was used to manufacture ammunition during World War II. See "E. Van Winkle Gin and Machine Works—Atlanta: A National Register of Historic Places Travel Itinerary," National Park Service, accessed April 6, 2021, https://www.nps.gov/nr/travel/atlanta/gin.htm.

3. Keating, *Atlanta*, 45.

4. Star Medzerian Vanguri, ed., *Rhetorics of Names and Naming* (New York: Routledge, 2016).

5. Derek H. Alderman, "Street Names as Memorial Arenas: The Reputational Politics of Commemorating Martin Luther King Jr. in a Georgia County," *Historical Geography* 30 (2002): 99–120.

6. Derek Handley, "'The Line Drawn': Freedom Corner and Rhetorics of Place in Pittsburgh, 1960s–2000s," *Rhetoric Review* 38, no. 2 (2019): 173–89.

7. Morrison, *Playing in the Dark*, 17.

8. Du Bois, *Souls of Black Folk*, 43.

9. Erin McElroy and Alex Werth, "Deracinated Dispossessions: On the Foreclosures of 'Gentrification' in Oakland, CA," *Antipode* 51, no. 3 (2019): 878–98.

10. Du Bois, *Souls of Black Folk*, 43.

11. "1900 United States Federal Census," US Census Bureau, 1900, roll 97, p. 25, Cooks, Fulton, GA, enumeration district 28, Ancestry.com, https://www.ancestry.com/imageviewer/collections/7602/images/4120058_00744?pId=77146392. Additional information on land purchases and sales by Samson Booth (sometimes "Sampson" or "Sam" Booth) completed in Blandtown (District 17, Lot 188 of Fulton County) is available at the Fulton County Deeds and Records Room. See, e.g., "Grantee Index: A–G," April 30, 1901, Fulton County Deeds and Records Room, Fulton County, GA; "Property Deed - Smith Irving to Sam Booth," April 1897, book 122, p. 293, Fulton County Deeds and Records Room, Fulton County, GA; "Property Deed - Winnie Alexander Harrison, et al. to Sam Booth," January 15, 1901, Fulton County Deeds and Records Room, Fulton County, GA.

12. Morrison, *Playing in the Dark*, 17.

13. For the quotes, see Morrison, *Playing in the Dark*, 25.

14. Anyka Barber comments from an unpublished meeting, cited in McElroy and Werth, "Deracinated Dispossessions."

15. Cydney Alexis, Scott Barnett, and Eric Leake, "Composing Place, Composing Las Vegas," in *Rhetorics of Names and Naming*, ed. Star Medzerian Vanguri (New York: Routledge, 2016), 13–32.

16. Alexis, Barnett, and Leake, "Composing Place," 27.

17. Sara Safransky, "Land Justice as a Historical Diagnostic: Thinking with Detroit," *Annals of the American Association of Geographers* 108, no. 2 (2018): 502.

18. Frantz Fanon, *Black Skin, White Masks* (New York: Grove Press, 1967), 117.

19. Cheng and Shabazz, "Introduction," 1–7.

20. McKittrick and Woods, "No One Knows," 3.

21. "1880 United States Federal Census," US Census Bureau, June 16, 1880, roll 147, p. 46C, Caseys, Fulton, GA, enumeration district 082, Ancestry.com, https://www.ancestry.com/imageviewer/collections/6742/images/4240140-00554?pId=8586334.

22. "Property Deed - Francis Kimball to Samuel Bland (Colored)," October 2, 1872, box 75, book T3, p. 696, Georgia Archives, Fulton County, GA.

23. "Property Deed - Samuel Bland to Viney Bland," October 14, 1873, box 76, book U, p. 184, Georgia Archives, Fulton County, GA.

24. Mabelle Pickert, *History of Cook's District in Fulton County, Atlanta, Georgia* (Atlanta: Evan P. Howell School, 1956).

25. "Property Deed - Viney Bland to Southern National Building and Loan Association," July 5, 1892, box 65 (92–93), book I4, pp. 709–10, Georgia Archives, Fulton County, GA.

26. "Property Deed - Felix Bland to Winnie Alexander," June 24, 1892, box 65, book I4, pp. 639, 710, Georgia Archives, Fulton County, GA.

27. "Property Deed - Viney Bland to Viney and Felix Bland," 1901, Georgia Archives, Fulton County, GA; "Property Deed - Viney Bland to Felix Bland," 1901, book 164, p.139, Fulton County Deeds and Records Room, Fulton County, GA.

28. "Property Deed - Felix Bland to RA Sims and Mrs. RA Sims," 1916, book 189, pp. 674–75, Fulton County Deeds and Records Room, Fulton County, GA.

29. "Felix Bland to RA Sims and Mrs. RA Sims," deed; "Property Deed - Cherry Osborn to Blandtown Christian Church," 1918, book 502, p. 417, Fulton County Deeds and Records Room, Fulton County, GA.

30. "Property Deed - Nancy Russell and Viney Woodard to James Irwin," November 9, 1923, book 198, pp. 296–97, Fulton County Deeds and Records Room, Fulton County, GA.

31. The details on Rocky Mountain Christian Church are unclear and unverified. Deeds between Cherry Osborn, Felix Bland, and James Irwin only note the name "Blandtown Christian Church." However, one unverified primary source, "Some Pictures from 1947 Homecoming at Greater Bethel AME Church," a document saved from an attendee at the event, cites that the Rocky Mountain Christian Church was established by John James Irwin and "the church housed the first school." Another account from Mabelle Pickert states that Felix Bland came to the Rocky Mountain Christian Church and that he was the reverend. It also notes that the church stopped operating in 1951. Pickert, *History of Cook's District.*

32. District 17, Lot 188, Fulton County Board of Assessors, 1970–1980, book 186, Kenan Research Center, Atlanta History Center, Atlanta, GA.

33. Historical records and interview data contradict the number of churches. In some cases, the discrepancy may be because of church name changes. The following churches are cited as having been in Blandtown: Rocky Mountain Christian Church (ceased operation in 1951 according to Pickert, *History of Cook's District*), Greater Bethel African Methodist Episcopal Church, Blandtown Christian Church, and St. Peter's Baptist Church. It is unclear whether Rocky Mountain Christian Church and Blandtown Christian Church are the same.

34. This data is based on census tract 89.02, which includes some neighborhoods outside of central Blandtown. The term "nonwhite" is used here as it is in the 1960 US census data. See US Census Bureau, *Atlanta, Ga.: Standard Metropolitan Statistical Area; Census Tracts* (Washington, DC: US Government Printing Office, 1962), https://www.census.gov/library/publications/1961/dec/population-and-housing-phc-1.html. See also Pickert, *History of Cook's District*.

35. "Colored School Offered County in Blandtown," *Atlanta Constitution*, September 2, 1920, 18.

36. Anderson, *White Rage*, 29.

37. Pickert, *History of Cook's District*.

38. Johnny Lee Green, interview by author, March 9, 2018.

39. LeeAnn B. Lands, *The Culture of Property: Race, Class, and Housing Landscapes in Atlanta, 1880–1950* (Athens: University of Georgia Press, 2009), 34.

40. "Terror-Stricken Residents Flee Flaming Homes," *Atlanta Constitution*, March 14, 1938, 1, 8.

41. "Auction Sale: Beautiful Shaded Lots and One 5 Room New House," April 22, 1911, VIS 290.002.032, FF 528, folder 1, Map Collection, Kenan Research Center, Atlanta History Center, Atlanta, GA.

42. L. U. Kauffman, "Kauffman's Map of the Borough of Atlanta and Adjacent Territory," 1938, in Jason Rhodes, "Geographies of Privilege and Exclusion: The 1938 Home Owners Loan Corporation 'Residential Security Map' of Atlanta," Atlanta Studies, September 7, 2017, https://atlantastudies.org/2017/09/07/jason-rhodes-geographies-of-privilege-and-exclusion-the-1938-home-owners-loan-corporation-residential-security-map-of-atlanta/.

43. "Map of Atlanta: Negro Residential Areas," 1952, Planning Atlanta: A New City in the Making, 1930s–1990s; City Planning Maps, Digital Collections, Georgia State University Library, Atlanta, GA, https://digitalcollections.library.gsu.edu/digital/collection/PlanATL/id/145/rec/8.

44. *Atlanta Constitution*, September 6, 1906, 4, unsigned, untitled newspaper snippet.

45. "Lad Shunned Church, Jailed: Charge against Patrolmen," *Atlanta Constitution*, September 4, 1948, 10.

46. Robert D. Bullard, "Environmental Justice in the 21st Century: Race Still Matters," *Phylon* 49, no. 3–4 (2001): 151–71.

47. "Blandtown Not on Howell Mill Road," *Atlanta Constitution*, August 2, 1914, 4.

48. Ellison, *Invisible Man*, 94.

49. Morrison, *Playing in the Dark*, 44.

50. "Atlanta Police Make Changes to Four Zone Boundaries as Part of Beat Redesign," Atlanta Police Department, March 12, 2019, https://www.atlantapd.org/Home/Components/News/News/190/.

51. Renee Wright, interview by author, July 11, 2019. The city of East Cobb is within metro Atlanta but north of the central city. It is known for its majority white and affluent population.

52. "Community Profile," Association of Religion Data Archives, US Census Bureau, ACS 2017 5-year estimates, accessed January 2, 2020, http://maps.nazarene.orgARDAD emographics/summary.html?y=4001507.0515619386&x=-9398094.724389998&b =.42&denom=.

53. Wright, interview.

54. Association of Religion Data Archives, "Community Profile."

55. Keating, *Atlanta*, 7–40.

56. William B. Hartsfield, "Letter from William B. Hartsfield to Select Residents of Buckhead," January 7, 1943, box 10, Stuart A. Rose Manuscript Archives and Rare Book Library, Emory University, Atlanta, GA.

57. Du Bois, *Souls of Black Folk*, 44.

58. Georgia State University Library, "Map of Atlanta."

59. "Industrial District Plan," 1954, Planning Atlanta: A New City in the Making, 1930s–1990s; City Planning Maps, Digital Collections, Georgia State University Library, Atlanta, GA, http://digitalcollections.library.gsu.edu/cdm/ref/collection/atlmaps/id/2547.

60. Jesse A. Gibson, "Atlanta Urban League Neighborhood Information Data Sheet—Blandtown," December 1953, Atlanta Urban League Papers, Robert W. Woodruff Library Digital Exhibits, Atlanta University Center, Atlanta, GA, https://digitalexhibits.auctr.edu/items/show/746.

61. Keating, *Atlanta*, 46.

62. Seth Coleman, "Residents of Industrial Area Waging Quixotic Zoning Fight," *Atlanta Constitution*, May 5, 1994, 32.

63. Bullard, "Environmental Justice."

64. Coleman, "Residents of Industrial Area."

65. Keating, *Atlanta*, 41–68.

66. Keating, *Atlanta*, 47.

67. Hess Denmark Jr., "Your Government: City of Atlanta," *Atlanta Voice*, August 6, 1994, 1, 15.

68. Bullard, "Environmental Justice."

69. Sean Richard Keenan, "West Midtown Residents Worry a New Concrete Plant Will Hurt Environment, Snarl Traffic," *Curbed Atlanta*, December 10, 2018, https://atlanta.curbed.com/2018/12/10/18133814/beltline-west-midtown-concrete-mixing-facility-blandtown.

70. Daniel Alvarado, "Proposed Blandtown Concrete Plant Fails to Secure Agreement in Mediation with City," *What Now Atlanta* (blog), accessed June 8, 2022, https://whatnowatlanta.com/proposed-blandtown-concrete-plant-fails-to-secure-agreement-in-first-mediation-meeting-with-city/; Sean Richard Keenan, "Battle over Blandtown Concrete Plant Fizzles, but Legal Melee Could Ensue," *Curbed Atlanta*, April 23, 2019, https://atlanta.curbed.com/2019/4/23/18511697/west-midtown-blandtown-concrete-plant-smryna-ready-mix.

71. Bullard, "Environmental Justice," 158.

72. Bullard, "Environmental Justice," 158.

73. Bullard, "Environmental Justice," 159.

74. Lisa Chamberlain, "Building a City within the City of Atlanta," *New York Times*, May 24, 2006, https://www.nytimes.com/2006/05/24/realestate/commercial/24atlanta.html.

75. An Amended Ordinance, Atlanta City Council, ordinance 18-O-1289 (2018).

76. David Pendered, "From Industrial . . . to Residential," *Atlanta Journal-Constitution*, December 15, 2003, F5.

77. Diane Glassi, "Housing Boom Erasing Country Feel," *Atlanta Constitution*, August 20, 2001, 6.

78. John McCosh, "Urban Pioneers Recasting Old Industrial Zone," *Atlanta Constitution*, August 20, 2001, 25.

79. Sara Safransky, "Greening the Urban Frontier: Race, Property, and Resettlement in Detroit," *Geoforum* 56 (2014): 237–48.

80. Safransky, "Greening the Urban Frontier."

81. Summers, *Black in Place*, 67.

82. "Visit the West Midtown Atlanta Neighborhood," Discover Atlanta, accessed September 30, 2019, https://www.atlanta.net/explore/neighborhoods/midtown/west-midtown/.

83. Summers, *Black in Place*, 66.

84. AECOM, *Atlanta BeltLine Master Plan: Subarea 8; Upper Westside-Northside Plan Recommendations*, prepared for Atlanta BeltLine (Atlanta: Atlanta City Council, March 19, 2012), 6, https://beltline.org/wp-content/uploads/2012/05/ABI-Subarea-8-Master-Plan.pdf.

85. Anonymous, interview by author, July 18, 2019.

86. Wright, interview.

87. Anonymous, interview by author, July 19, 2019.

88. Anonymous, interview, July 19, 2019.

89. Anonymous, interview by author, August 1, 2019.

90. Sara Safransky, "Grammars of Reckoning: Redressing Racial Regimes of Property," *Society and Space* 40, no. 2 (2022): 296.

91. Safransky, "Grammars of Reckoning," 296.

92. Fanon, *Black Skin*, 91.

93. Summers, *Black in Place*, 69.

94. Du Bois, *Souls of Black Folk*, 44.

95. Fanon, *Black Skin*, 14.

96. Fanon, *Black Skin*, xii, xv.

97. Fanon, *Black Skin*, 1.

98. Alexis, Barnett, and Leake, "Composing Place," 26.

99. Alexis, Barnett, and Leake, "Composing Place," 26.

100. See, respectively, Woods, *Development Drowned and Reborn*, 28; Ralph Ellison, "Richard Wright's Blues," *Antioch Review* 50, no. 2 (1945): 491.

101. Ellison, "Richard Wright's Blues," 491.

102. Bessie Smith, "Poor Man's Blues," single, Columbia, 1928, 14399-D, vinyl.

103. Woods, *Development Drowned and Reborn*, 29.

104. Anonymous, interview, July 18, 2019.

105. Gregor Turk, interview by author, September 4, 2019.

106. Anonymous, interview, July 19, 2019.

107. Fanon, *Black Skin*, xii.

108. Fanon, *Black Skin*, 118.

109. Fanon, *Black Skin*, 107.

CHAPTER 3: "THE WHITE PEOPLE CAME, AND CHANGED EVERYTHING," OR A BATTLE FOR A NATION'S SOUL

1. Use of the phrase "predominantly white upper-ability classroom" comes from Brittney Cooper, *Eloquent Rage: A Black Feminist Discovers Her Superpower* (New York: Picador, 2018), 41.

2. Richard Wright, "Blueprint for Negro Writing," in *Within the Circle: An Anthology of African American Literary Criticism from the Harlem Renaissance to the Present*, ed. Angelyn Mitchell (Durham, NC: Duke University Press, 1994), 99.

3. Wright, "Blueprint for Negro Writing," 100.

4. Wright, "Blueprint for Negro Writing," 101.

5. Fanon, *Black Skin*.

6. Fanon, *Black Skin*, 107–8.

7. Gordon, *Ghostly Matters*, 66.

8. Gordon, *Ghostly Matters*, 66.

9. Karcheik Sims-Alvarado, *Atlanta and the Civil Rights Movement: 1944–1968* (Charleston, SC: Arcadia Publishing, 2017), 68.

10. Morrison, *Playing in the Dark*, 36.

11. Morrison, *Playing in the Dark*, 36.

12. Morrison, *Playing in the Dark*, 37.

13. Morrison, *Playing in the Dark*, 64.

14. Ellison, *Collected Essays*, 119.

15. Ellison, *Collected Essays*, 119.

16. Fanon, *Black Skin*, 168, 169.

17. Fanon, *Black Skin*, 170.

18. Ellison, *Collected Essays*, 119.

19. According to historian Carol Anderson, as the Ku Klux Klan rose and began terrorizing freed African Americans after the Civil War, Congress provided some protection by issuing the Enforcement Acts of 1870 and 1871, which protected Black people's right to vote, serve on juries, and hold office by making private criminal acts a federal crime. The Enforcement Acts paired with the Fourteenth Amendment (citizenship) and Fifteenth Amendment (voting rights for Black men) hindered the KKK's mission for a time. The Enforcement Acts were difficult to enforce as the Supreme Court argued such laws violated state's rights. See Anderson, *White Rage*, 31–34.

20. Under President Calvin Coolidge, in 1925, the US Congress provided assistance to the Stone Mountain carving project by "authorizing the United States Mint's coinage of five million silver half dollars" to be designed by Gutzon Borglum (the artist commissioned for the project) "to raise funds." See Grace Elizabeth Hale, "Granite Stopped Time: The Stone Mountain Memorial and the Representation of White Southern Identity," *Georgia Historical Quarterly* 82, no. 1 (1998): 30. See also Bruce Stewart, "Stone Mountain," *New Georgia Encyclopedia* (blog), October 21, 2016, https://www.georgiaencyclopedia.org/articles/geography-environment/stone-mountain.

21. Patrick Burkhardt, "The Lost Cause Ideology and Civil War Memory at the Semicentennial: A Look at the Confederate Monument in St. Louis," *The Confluence* 2, no. 2 (Spring–Summer 2011): 16–25.

22. Alan T. Nolan, "The Anatomy of the Myth," in *The Myth of the Lost Cause and Civil War History*, ed. Gary W. Gallagher and Alan T. Nolan (Bloomington: Indiana University Press, 2000), 16, 18.

23. Morrison, *Playing in the Dark*, 55.

24. W. E. B. Du Bois, *Black Reconstruction in America: An Essay toward a History of the Part Which Black Folk Played in the Attempt to Reconstruct Democracy in America, 1860–1880*, ed. Henry Louis Gates Jr. (New York: Oxford University Press, 2007), loc. 13696.

25. Du Bois, *Black Reconstruction in America*, loc. 17028.

26. Du Bois, *Black Reconstruction in America*, loc. 17028.

27. Nolan, "Anatomy of the Myth," 14.

28. Mark Pendergrast, "Stone Mountain, Mount Rushmore, Donald Trump, and the KKK," SaportaReport, August 30, 2020, https://saportareport.com/stone-mountain-mount-rushmore-donald-trump-and-the-kkk/columnists/david/.

29. Pendergrast, "Stone Mountain."

30. "Armed Demonstrators Clash at Stone Mountain During Tense Protests," WSB-TV 2, August 15, 2020, https://www.wsbtv.com/news/dozens-protesters-counter-protesters-face-off-defend-stone-mountain-rally/JBMRHJCD2ZAFDBCWTS6UIBGI5M/.

31. Hale, "Granite Stopped Time," 32–33.

32. The Stone Acres Plantation that opened in 1963 was renamed Antebellum Plantation and is now known as the Historic Square. "Stone Mountain Antebellum Plantation," Stone Mountain Guide, accessed April 9, 2021, https://www.stonemountainguide.com/Plantation.html. See also Hale, "Granite Stopped Time," 39–44.

33. Gordon, *Ghostly Matters*, 63.

34. Ersula J. Ore, *Lynching: Violence, Rhetoric, and American Identity* (Jackson: University Press of Mississippi, 2019), 3–30.

35. Ellison, *Collected Essays*, 119.

36. Holmes, "Not in the Family," 2.

37. Holmes, "Not in the Family."

38. Miranda Kyle, interview by author, October 28, 2020.

39. Kyle, interview.

40. Atlanta BeltLine Inc., *Art on the Atlanta BeltLine: Atlanta BeltLine Inc.'s Public Art Program* (Atlanta: Atlanta BeltLine Inc., January 2018), https://beltline.org/wp-content/uploads/2018/03/Art-on-the-BeltLine-Policy-Document.pdf.

41. Atlanta BeltLine Inc., *Art*, 21.

42. Martin Luther King Jr., *Why We Can't Wait* (New York: Signet Classics, 1963), 90.

43. Hayden White, "The Value of Narrativity in the Representation of Reality," *Critical Inquiry* 7, no. 1 (1980): 20.

44. Michael Warner, *Publics and Counterpublics* (New York: Zone Books, 2002).

45. Holmes, "Not in the Family."

46. Karen Cross and Julia Peck, "Editorial: Special Issue on Photography and Memory," *Photographies* 3, no. 2 (September 2010): 127.

47. Marita Sturken, *Tangled Memories: The Vietnam War, the Aids Epidemic, and the Politics of Remembering* (Berkeley: University of California Press, 1997), 19.

48. Gordon, "Some Thoughts."

49. White, "Value of Narrativity," 5–27.

50. "Booker T. Washington Delivers the 1895 Atlanta Compromise Speech," History Matters, accessed February 12, 2024, http://historymatters.gmu.edu/d/39/.

51. Georgia African American Historic Preservation Network, "Changing Settlement Patterns in an Atlanta Neighborhood: The Reynoldstown Historic District," *Reflections* 5, no. 2 (July 2005): 1–8, https://gadnr.org/sites/default/files/hpd/pdf/AfricanAmericanHistoricPlaces/July%202005.pdf.

52. Bill Torpy, "Torpy at Large: What Reynoldstown's 50–50 Split Says about 'One Atlanta,'" *Atlanta Journal-Constitution*, January 11, 2018, sec. Local News, https://www.ajc.com/news/local/torpy-large-what-reynoldstown-split-says-about-one-atlanta/R2XIZInV9l2vmCW52RruSP/.

53. Mosaic Group, *Atlanta BeltLine Westside Impact Neighborhood Analysis: Demographic, Health and Community Asset Report* (Atlanta: Mosaic Group, August 2015), https://beltline.org/wp-content/uploads/2019/03/BeltLine-Westside-Impact-Neighborhood-Analysis.pdf.

54. "Our History," *Historic West End* (blog), August 24, 2014, https://atlantawestend.com/our-history/.

55. As reviewed by Dan Immergluck, Atlanta passed a racial segregation rule in 1913 that prohibited Black families from residing in properties "previously occupied by whites or next to white residences." In 1915, the state supreme court overturned the ordinance. In 1916, it approved legislation prohibiting Black residents from residing in a neighborhood with a white majority. It was not enforceable due to a 1917 US Supreme Court decision. The city established "white single-family zones and Black single-family zones" in 1922. It was ruled unconstitutional by the state supreme court. The city passed a law in 1929 prohibiting citizens from living on a street where the majority of the population were of a race with which "the citizen was forbidden to intermarry." It was also struck down. However, class-based ordinances survived as a "legally defensible tool of racial exclusion." Immergluck, *Red Hot City*, 19–20.

56. Mosaic Group, *Atlanta BeltLine Westside Impact*.

57. Sociologist Glenn Bracey defines the phrase "rescuing whites" as a framing device that saves white people "from direct criticism for racism." Bracey specifically targets scholars that use absenting whites, personification, and narrative bracketing to "temper" their language and "make it palatable to whites." Because such acts remove white people as agents of racism and white supremacy, they romanticize the events that occur. Glenn Bracey, "Rescuing Whites: White Privileging Discourse in Race Critical Scholarship" (unpublished manuscript, 2017), PDF.

58. The quote comes from the exhibition's sign.

59. Morrison, *Playing in the Dark*, 67.

60. The Columbians were a fascist group that was organized in 1946 in response to increased Black electoral power after the US Supreme Courts struck down the white democratic primary in *Smith v. Allright* (1944). The Columbians considered themselves to be defending their communities from Black intrusion. See also Immergluck, *Red Hot City*, 21.

61. Sims-Alvarado, *Atlanta*, 98.

62. Sims-Alvarado, *Atlanta*, 53.

63. Sims-Alvarado, *Atlanta*, 53.

64. Ellison, *Collected Essays*, 110.

65. Morrison, *Playing in the Dark*, 68.

66. Ellison, *Collected Essays*, 110.

67. Kevin Rinker, "City Lights: Atlanta Opera and Civil Rights on the BeltLine; Donald Runnicles; And More," *90.1 FM WABE* (blog), October 26, 2018, https://www.wabe.org/episode/city-lights-atlanta-opera-and-civil-rights-on-the-beltline-donald-runnicles-and-more/.

68. Rinker, "City Lights."

69. Lorde, *Sister Outsider*, 112.

70. Woods, *Development Drowned and Reborn*, 34, 35.

71. Woods, *Development Drowned and Reborn*, 35–36.

72. Woods, *Development Drowned and Reborn*, 2.

73. King, *Why We Can't Wait*, 64.

74. King, *Why We Can't Wait*, 53.

75. Fanon, *Black Skin*, 107.

76. King, *Why We Can't Wait*, 64.

77. Julius Lester, "Freedom Songs in the North," *Sing Out* 42 (1964): 1–2, quoted in Elizabeth Ellis Miller, "Remembering Freedom Songs: Repurposing an Activist Genre," *College English* 81, no. 1 (September 2018): 53.

78. Miller, "Remembering Freedom Songs," 55.

79. Miller, "Remembering Freedom Songs," 54.

80. "Soundtrack for a Revolution: Lyrics of the Freedom Songs," PBS, accessed February 10, 2024, https://www.pbs.org/wgbh/americanexperience/features/soundtrack-lyrics/.

81. Gordon, *Ghostly Matters*, 65.

82. The Freedom Singers, "Which Side Are You On?," track 13 on various artists, *Sing for Freedom: The Story of the Civil Rights Movements through Its Songs*, Smithsonian Folkways Recordings, Washington, DC, 1990, https://smithsonianfolkways.bandcamp.com/track/which-side-are-you-on.

83. Freedom Singers, "Which Side."

84. Clarence N. Stone, *Regime Politics: Governing Atlanta, 1946–1988* (Lawrence: University Press of Kansas, 1989), 59.

85. Freedom Singers, "Which Side."

CHAPTER 4: SO, THE BLACK MECCA TURNED TO BEER TOWN, OR AMERICAN TRAPPIN'

1. Malachy Browne, Christina Kelso, and Barbara Marcolini, "How Rayshard Brooks Was Fatally Shot by the Atlanta Police," *New York Times*, June 14, 2020, https://www.nytimes.com/2020/06/14/us/videos-rayshard-brooks-shooting-atlanta-police.html.

2. Browne, Kelso, and Marcolini, "How Rayshard Brooks"; Aimee Ortiz, "What We Know about the Death of Rayshard Brooks," *New York Times*, September 10, 2020, https://www.nytimes.com/article/rayshard-brooks-what-we-know.html.

3. Shaddi Abusaid and Jozsef Papp, "Officers Charged in Rayshard Brooks' Killing File Federal Lawsuits," *Atlanta Journal-Constitution*, June 10, 2022, sec. Crime and Public

Safety, https://www.ajc.com/news/crime/officers-charged-in-rayshard-brooks-killing-file-federal-lawsuits/YHEIVE43WZGNVGBJVWIGXX4R5I/.

4. Newspapers have varying accounts of the total killed and injured. Gregory Mixon, *The Atlanta Riot: Race, Class, and Violence in a New South City*, Southern Dissent Series (Gainesville: University Press of Florida, 2005), 110.

5. Mixon, *Atlanta Riot*, 116–27.

6. Christopher Mele, "Neoliberalism, Race and the Redefining of Urban Redevelopment," *International Journal of Urban and Regional Research* 37, no. 2 (2013): 598–99, https://doi.org/10.1111/j.1468-2427.2012.01144.x.

7. Businesses referenced here include Monday Night Garage (brewery), Best End Brewing Company (brewery), Wild Heaven West End Brewery and Gardens (brewery), ASW Whiskey Exchange (distillery), Boxcar at Hop City West End (restaurant), Hop City Beer and Wine (store), and Cultured South (kombucha taproom).

8. Shanequa Gay, interview by author, August 11, 2022.

9. David Schlussel, "'The Mellow Pot-Smoke': White Individualism in Marijuana Legalization Campaigns," *California Law Review* 105, no. 885 (2017): 893.

10. "Dry" is a term used to describe a municipality that banned the production, distribution, import, and sale of alcoholic beverages. "Wet" is a term used to describe a municipality without such prohibition.

11. Lisa McGirr, *The War on Alcohol: Prohibition and the Rise of the American State* (New York: W. W. Norton, 2015), 71.

12. Morrison, *Playing in the Dark*, 52.

13. Jack Turner, "American Individualism and Structural Injustice: Tocqueville, Gender, and Race," *Polity* 40, no. 2 (April 2008): 199.

14. Mark Pendergrast, *City on the Verge: Atlanta and the Fight for America's Urban Future* (New York: Basic Books, 2017), 206.

15. Jamiles Lartey, "Nowhere for People to Go: Who Will Survive the Gentrification of Atlanta?," *The Guardian*, October 23, 2018, https://www.theguardian.com/cities/2018/oct/23/nowhere-for-people-to-go-who-will-survive-the-gentrification-of-atlanta.

16. Van Mead, "City Cursed by Sprawl."

17. Bob Townsend, "First Look: New Realm Debuts Atlanta's First Beltline Brewery Restaurant Tonight," *Atlanta Journal-Constitution*, January 8, 2018, https://www.ajc.com/blog/atlanta-restaurants/first-look-new-realm-debuts-atlanta-first-beltline-brewery-restaurant-tonight/wQhs4ZKo2bZmi9fk9oTXlL/.

18. Van Mead, "City Cursed by Sprawl."

19. Gordon, *Ghostly Matters*, 67.

20. Gordon, *Ghostly Matters*, 64.

21. "Atlanta—Gentrification and Displacement," Urban Displacement Project, accessed April 10, 2021, https://www.urbandisplacement.org/atlanta/atlanta-gentrification-and-displacement.

22. According to communication theorist Mark P. Orbe, marginalized cultures, or "co-cultural groups," respond to the dominant culture through aggressive, assertive, or nonassertive forms of assimilation, accommodation, and separation. "Assimilation" is fitting in. "Accommodation" is trying to change the rules of the environment to make it

conducive to their life experiences. And "separation" is maintaining a distinct identity from the dominant group. Mark P. Orbe, *Constructing Co-cultural Theory: An Explication of Culture, Power and Communication* (Thousand Oaks, CA: Sage, 1998), 86–120.

23. Woods, *Development Drowned and Reborn*, 1–2.

24. Ryan Gravel, *Where We Want to Live: Reclaiming Infrastructure for a New Generation of Cities* (New York: St. Martin's Press, 2016), 78.

25. Rashawn Ray, Andre M. Perry, David Harshbarger, Samantha Elizondo, and Alexandra Gibbons, "Homeownership, Racial Segregation, and Policy Solutions to Racial Wealth Equity," Brookings Institution, September 1, 2021, https://www.brookings.edu/essay/homeownership-racial-segregation-and-policies-for-racial-wealth-equity/.

26. From Burke's perspective, the individual is a person who rejects social constructs and seeks personal advantage. The universal is a shift from the individual to communal, in which the individual identifies herself with the environment and translates her identity into that scene. By doing so, the individual shifts from thoughts of self to thoughts of universal effects. Where individualism requires division, universality occurs by identifying yourself as being of the same substance, made of the same things (ideals, language, characteristics, etc.) as your environment. Kenneth Burke, *A Rhetoric of Motives* (Berkeley: University of California Press, 1969), 16, 23.

27. Lawrie Balfour, "Unreconstructed Democracy: W. E. B. Du Bois and the Case for Reparations," *American Political Science Review* 97, no. 1 (February 2003): 33.

28. Maria Saporta, "Ryan Gravel and Nathaniel Smith Resign from BeltLine Partnership Board over Equity Concerns," SaportaReport, September 26, 2016, https://saportareport.com/ryan-gravel-nathaniel-smith-resign-beltline-partnership-board-equity-concerns/sections/reports/maria_saporta/.

29. Mele, "Neoliberalism," 599.

30. Atlanta BeltLine, "Westside Study Group Virtual Public Meeting - Special Services District (SSD): Building the BeltLine for All," Facebook, February 15, 2021, https://www.facebook.com/atlantabeltline/videos/5121566391251398.

31. Summers, *Black in Place*, 62, 69.

32. Pendergrast, *City on the Verge*, 206.

33. According to the study by the Housing Justice League and the Research|Action Cooperative of "long-time, low-income residents" in "three historic Black neighborhoods on the Southside" affected by BeltLine construction, residents want to stay in their neighborhoods, have already felt the effects of displacement and gentrification, and do not feel that they are a part of the development process. See Housing Justice League and Research|Action Cooperative, *BeltLining: Gentrification, Broken Promises, and Hope on Atlanta's South Side* (Atlanta: Housing Justice League and Research|Action Cooperative, October 2017), 1, https://researchaction.net/wp-content/uploads/2017/10/HJL-RA-Beltlining-Exec-Sum-FINAL-10-17.pdf.

34. For instance, the West End, a Black neighborhood along the Westside Trail, is categorized as experiencing "early/ongoing gentrification," with a home value change of 78.4 percent from 2000 to 2018. Urban Displacement Project, "Atlanta."

35. Balfour, "Unreconstructed Democracy," 36.

36. Du Bois, *Souls of Black Folk*, 86.

37. See, respectively, Alexis de Tocqueville, *Democracy in America*, ed. Olivier Zunz, trans. Arthur Goldhammer (New York: Library of America, 1835), 2:394, quoted in Turner, "American Individualism," 213; Turner, "American Individualism," 213.

38. Turner, "American Individualism," 214.

39. Brene Brown, *Daring Greatly* (New York: Penguin Random House, 2012), 33.

40. Du Bois, *Souls of Black Folk*, 44.

41. Fanon, *Black Skin*, 216–17.

42. Original unfound. Quoted in Ellison, *Collected Essays*, 147–50.

43. Ellison, *Collected Essays*, 147–50.

44. Variety, "Issa Rae – 'I'm Rooting for Everybody Black' - Full Emmys Red Carpet Interview," September 19, 2017, video, 3:02, https://www.youtube.com/watch?v=WafoKj6MzcU.

45. B. Cooper, *Eloquent Rage*, 185–86.

46. Fanon, *Black Skin*, 195.

47. Fanon, *Black Skin*.

48. Gay, interview.

49. Turner, "American Individualism," 197–215.

50. Summers, *Black in Place*, 65.

51. Frantz Fanon, *The Wretched of the Earth* (New York: Grove Press, 1963), 5.

52. Lawrence Bobo, James R. Kluegel, and Ryan A. Smith, "Laissez-Faire Racism: The Crystallization of a Kinder, Gentler, Antiblack Ideology," in *Racial Attitudes in the 1990s: Continuity and Change*, ed. Steven A. Tuch and Jack K. Martin (Westport, CT: Praeger, 1997), 17.

53. Bobo, Kluegel, and Smith, "Laissez-Faire Racism," 21.

54. According to a 2018 report from the Brookings Institution, "homes in neighborhoods where the share of the population is 50 percent Black are valued at roughly half the price as homes in neighborhoods with no Black residents," and "structural characteristics of homes and neighborhood amenities do not fully explain the absolute difference in home value." Andre M. Perry, Jonathan Rothwell, and David Harshbarger, "The Devaluation of Assets in Black Neighborhoods," Brookings Institution, November 27, 2018, https://www.brookings.edu/research/devaluation-of-assets-in-black-neighborhoods/.

55. Turner, "American Individualism," 209.

56. Summers, *Black in Place*, 3.

57. Summers, *Black in Place*, 3.

58. William Teasley, interview by author, July 11, 2022.

59. Bryan Crable, *Ralph Ellison and Kenneth Burke: At the Roots of the Racial Divide* (Charlottesville: University of Virginia Press, 2012), 64.

60. Crable, *Ralph Ellison*, 64.

61. Crable, *Ralph Ellison*, 64.

62. Nakayama and Krizek, "Whiteness."

63. Nakayama and Krizek, "Whiteness," 299.

64. B. Cooper, *Eloquent Rage*, 53.

65. Massey, *Space, Place and Gender*, 146–56.

66. Fanon, *Wretched of the Earth*, 11.

67. Fanon, *Wretched of the Earth*, 9.

68. Wilbur G. Kurtz, "Whitehall Tavern," 1931, ahc.MSS130, box 49, folder 13, Wilbur G. Kurtz, Sr. Papers, Kenan Research Center, Atlanta History Center, Atlanta, GA.

69. Timothy J. Crimmins, "West End: Metamorphosis from Suburban Town to Intown Neighborhood," *Atlanta Historical Journal* 26, no. 2–3 (Summer–Fall 1982): 33–50.

70. Kurtz, "Wilbur G. Kurtz."

71. Ron Smith and Mary O. Boyle, *Atlanta Beer: A Heady History of Brewing in the Hub of the South* (Charleston, SC: American Palate, 2013).

72. Crimmins, "West End."

73. Cornelia E. Cooper, "History of West End 1830–1910," *Atlanta Historical Bulletin* 8, no. 31 (January 1947): 67.

74. C. Cooper, "History of West End."

75. Gregory Clark, *Rhetorical Landscapes in America: Variations on a Theme from Kenneth Burke* (Columbia: University of South Carolina Press, 2004), 73.

76. Kurtz, "Wilbur G. Kurtz," 4.

77. Kurtz, "Wilbur G. Kurtz," 4.

78. Kurtz, "Wilbur G. Kurtz."

79. R. Smith and Boyle, *Atlanta Beer*.

80. Kurtz, "Wilbur G. Kurtz."

81. C. Cooper, "History of West End."

82. R. Smith and Boyle, *Atlanta Beer*.

83. Crimmins, "West End."

84. Crimmins, "West End," 43.

85. C. Cooper, "History of West End."

86. Crimmins, "West End."

87. Crimmins, "West End," 41.

88. Crimmins, "West End."

89. Kevin M. Kruse, "How Segregation Caused Your Traffic Jam," *New York Times*, August 14, 2019, https://www.nytimes.com/interactive/2019/08/14/magazine/traffic-atlanta-segregation.html.

90. R. Smith and Boyle, *Atlanta Beer*, 38.

91. Gregory Lamont Mixon, "The Atlanta Riot of 1906" (PhD diss., University of Cincinnati, 1989), 1.

92. Mixon, "Atlanta Riot of 1906," 521–84.

93. Mixon, "Atlanta Riot of 1906," 524.

94. Mixon, "Atlanta Riot of 1906," 521–84.

95. R. Smith and Boyle, *Atlanta Beer*, 38.

96. Mixon, "Atlanta Riot of 1906," 521–84.

97. Mixon, "Atlanta Riot of 1906," 531.

98. There are varying estimates in newspaper records.

99. Mixon, *Atlanta Riot*, 86.

100. Mixon, "Atlanta Riot of 1906," 539.

101. Mixon, *Atlanta Riot*, 88.

102. Mixon, "Atlanta Riot of 1906," 567.

103. Mixon, *Atlanta Riot*, 123.

104. Walter White, *A Man Called White: The Autobiography of Walter White* (Athens: University of Georgia Press, 1948), 11.

105. Mixon, "Atlanta Riot of 1906," 521–84.

106. Mixon, "Atlanta Riot of 1906," 521–84.

107. Mixon, "Atlanta Riot of 1906," 521–84.

108. Mixon, "Atlanta Riot of 1906," 643–706.

109. J. Nikol Beckham, "The Value of a Pint: A Cultural Economy of American Beer" (PhD diss., University of North Carolina at Chapel Hill, 2014), 41.

110. R. Smith and Boyle, *Atlanta Beer.*

111. Burke, *Rhetoric of Motives.*

112. Cecil W. Dugger, "West End Shows Signs of Rebirth," *Atlanta Constitution*, November 7, 1982, 47.

113. Crimmins, "West End."

114. "The Mall-West End," *Atlanta Voice*, February 6, 1971, 3.

115. "Dent to Manage West End Mall," *Atlanta Constitution*, May 22, 1972, sec. People and Events, 28.

116. Crimmins, "West End."

117. Clark, *Rhetorical Landscapes in America*, 31.

118. Sharon Bailey, "Name Change Lands in Briar Patch," *Atlanta Constitution*, February 19, 1982, 20.

119. "Payroll Tax Would Catch Outsiders, Vandiver Says," *Atlanta Constitution*, May 26, 1959, 1.

120. Bailey, "Name Change," 20.

121. Waights G. Henry Jr., "No Peoples Should Bury Past," *Atlanta Constitution*, March 26, 1982, sec. Another Voice, 5.

122. Bailey, "Name Change," 20.

123. Keith Graham, "Harris' Tales Re-Evaluated by Academia," *Atlanta Constitution*, August 25, 1983, 41, 44–45.

124. Keith Graham, "A New Life for the Wren's Nest: Bad Times Befall Uncle Remus Home," *Atlanta Constitution*, August 25, 1983, 44.

125. Graham, "Harris' Tales."

126. Graham, "New Life."

127. Jim Auchmutey, "Uncle Remus: Time Takes Toll on Film, Author's Legacy," *Atlanta Journal-Constitution*, November 12, 2006, K10.

128. Clark says that religious theology works as a constitution that "establishes the common ground upon which people can interact." Clark, *Rhetorical Landscapes in America*, 127.

129. "New West End Theater Is to Open Tonight," *Atlanta Constitution*, August 30, 1940, 21.

130. Edward B. Fiske, "Black Theology Now Evolves," *Atlanta Constitution*, November 28, 1968, 167.

131. Nat Sheppard, "Drop White Concepts, Blacks Urged," *Atlanta Constitution*, March 6, 1970, 21.

132. Alexis Grace, "Artists, Supporters Gather to Celebrate 30th Anniversary of Hammonds House Museum," *Atlanta Voice*, October 12, 2018, 9–10.

133. Clark, *Rhetorical Landscapes in America*, 68.

134. Jewel Wicker, "How Atlanta's Clubs Fueled the City's Budding Hip-Hop Scene in the '90s," *VICE*, May 11, 2019, https://www.vice.com/en_us/article/vbwqzb/deep-dive-atlanta-hip-hop.

135. Wicker, "How Atlanta's Clubs."

136. Dennis McCafferty, "Few Rooms to Be Had for Tired Celebrators," *Atlanta Journal-Constitution*, August 20, 1995, sec. Local, 33.

137. Cameron Hightower and James C. Fraser, "The Raced-Space of Gentrification: 'Reverse Blockbusting,' Home Selling, and Neighborhood Remake in North Nashville," *City and Community* 19, no. 1 (March 2020): 225, https://doi.org/10.1111/cico.12444.

138. Mosaic Group, *Atlanta BeltLine Westside Impact.*

139. Tony Phillips, "The Beginning of the End for West End," *Atlanta Voice*, February 22, 1992, 1, 10.

140. Hightower and Fraser, "Raced-Space of Gentrification," 17. Hightower and Fraser write, "urban pioneers—a colloquial phrase based on the problematic conception of space being uninhabited—are defined as those who move into a newly gentrifying area surrounded by neighbors who are members of the original, lower class community." Ibid., 239.

141. Tinah Saunders, "Home Sales in the City Last Year Rose 8 Percent," *Atlanta Journal-Constitution*, August 7, 1997, sec. City Life, 337.

142. H. M. Cauley, "AJC 2003 Home Sales Report: Older Homes Snapped Up," *Atlanta Journal-Constitution*, May 15, 2003, JD1, JD4.

143. Cameron McWhirter, "The Crooks Are Afoot and So Are the Police," *Atlanta Journal-Constitution*, August 22, 2007.

144. Hightower and Fraser, "Raced-Space of Gentrification," 224–25.

145. Gay, interview.

146. Tunnell-Spangler-Walsh and Associates, Grice and Associates, and Smith Daila Architects, *Atlanta BeltLine Master Plan: Subarea 1*, prepared for Atlanta BeltLine (Atlanta: Atlanta City Council, December 6, 2010), 21, https://beltline.org/wp-content/uploads/2012/05/Atlanta-BeltLine-Subarea-1-Master-Plan-All.pdf. The 2010 *Atlanta BeltLine Master Plan: Subarea 1* was updated in 2021.

147. Tunnell-Spangler-Walsh and Associates, Grice and Associates, and Smith Daila Architects, *Atlanta BeltLine Master Plan*, 23.

148. Gay, interview.

149. Hightower and Fraser, "Raced-Space of Gentrification," 226.

150. "Ackerman & Co. and MDH Partners Acquire 433,204 SF Lee + White Project in Atlanta," 24-7 Press Release, September 20, 2019, https://www.24-7pressrelease.com/press-release/466217/ackerman-co-and-mdh-partners-acquire-433204-sf-lee-white-project-in-atlanta.

151. Du Bois, *Souls of Black Folk*, 86.

152. Beckham, "Value of a Pint," 12.

153. Alison E. Feeney, "The History of Beer in Pennsylvania and the Current Growth of Craft Breweries," *Pennsylvania Geographer* 53, no. 1 (2015): 25–43.

154. R. Smith and Boyle, *Atlanta Beer.*

155. Georgia General Assembly, Malt Beverages, S. 85 2017–2018 (2017), https://dor.georgia.gov/senate-bill-85.

156. Teasley, interview.

157. Teasley, interview.

158. Teasley, interview.

159. Feeney, "History of Beer," 31.

160. Feeney, "History of Beer," 31.

161. Bob Townsend, "Beer Town: Lee + White Development in West End Is Poised to Become 'Malt Disney,'" *Atlanta Journal-Constitution*, March 6, 2019, https://www.ajc.com/entertainment/dining/lee-white-development-west-end-poised-become-malt-disney/y4TQIIu6zz57UlyWwf3SRI/.

162. Ignazio Cabras and David M. Higgins, "Beer, Brewing, and Business History," *Business History* 58, no. 5 (2016): 609–24.

163. Amy Wenk, "New Law Means Dozens of New Breweries in Atlanta," *Atlanta Business Chronicle*, February 23, 2018, https://www.bizjournals.com/atlanta/news/2018/02/23/new-law-means-dozens-of-new-breweries-in-atlanta.html.

164. Tyler Estep, "Gwinnett Beer: Ordinance Changes Open Door for More Craft Brewers," *Atlanta Journal-Constitution*, April 22, 2019, https://www.ajc.com/news/local/new-laws-designed-attract-more-craft-breweries-gwinnett/3C44Y7ToRcX3GJYxcXWqUL/.

165. Feeney, "History of Beer"; Ralph B. McLaughlin, Neil Reid, and Michael S. Moore, "The Ubiquity of Good Taste: A Spatial Analysis of the Craft Brewing Industry in the United States," in *The Geography of Beer: Regions, Environment, and Societies*, ed. Mark Patterson and Nancy Hoalst-Pullen (Dordrecht: Springer, 2014), 131–54.

166. Vaughn Stafford Gray, "How Black Brewers Are Decolonizing the Craft Beer Industry," Toast, accessed August 4, 2022, https://pos.toasttab.com/blog/on-the-line/black-owned-breweries.

167. Gray, "How Black Brewers."

168. Beckham, "Value of a Pint," 165.

169. Beckham, "Value of a Pint," 212.

170. Beckham, "Value of a Pint," 213.

171. Beckham, "Value of a Pint."

172. William Moore, interview by author, July 13, 2022.

173. Teasley, interview.

174. Massey, *Space, Place and Gender*, 146–56.

175. Feeney, "History of Beer."

176. Beckham, "Value of a Pint," 45.

177. Beckham, "Value of a Pint," 48.

178. Feeney, "History of Beer."

179. Feeney, "History of Beer."

180. Townsend, "Beer Town."

181. "Stuckey's and Wild Heaven Beer Collaborate on Pecan Log Roll Beer," Brewbound, November 25, 2020, https://www.brewbound.com/news/stuckeys-and-wild-heaven-beer-collaborate-on-pecan-log-roll-beer/.

182. Gay, interview.

183. Fanon, *Black Skin*, 188.

184. Fanon, *Wretched of the Earth*, 6.

185. Fanon, *Wretched of the Earth*, 11.

186. Fanon, *Black Skin*, 197.

187. Fanon, *Black Skin*, 192.

188. Fanon, *Black Skin*, 193.

189. Fanon, *Black Skin*, 193.

190. Woods, *Development Drowned and Reborn*, 2.

191. "Lambo" is short for "Lamborghini."

192. Laura Pulido and Jordan T. Camp, "Introduction," in *Development Drowned and Reborn: The Blues and Bourbon Restorations in Post-Katrina New Orleans*, by Clyde Woods (Athens: University of Georgia Press, 2017), xxvii.

193. Rhana A. Gittens, "Atlanta's Pink Trap House: Reimagining the Black Public Sphere as an Aesthetic Community," *Theory and Event* 24, no. 2 (2021): 434–55, https://doi.org/10.1353/tae.2021.0021.

194. Regina N. Bradley, *Chronicling Stankonia: The Rise of the Hip-Hop South* (Chapel Hill: University of North Carolina Press, 2021), 91.

195. Bradley, *Chronicling Stankonia*, 89.

196. Ellison, *Collected Essays*, 94.

197. Ellison, *Collected Essays*, 150.

198. Jernej Kaluza, "Reality of Trap: Trap Music and Its Emancipatory Potential," *IAFOR Journal of Media, Communication and Film* 5, no. 1 (August 2018): 30.

CHAPTER 5: "BUT I AM STILL YOUR NEIGHBOR"

1. James Baldwin, *The Fire Next Time* (New York: Vintage Books, 1962), 10.

2. Victoria Lemos, "Westview Cemetery," Archive Atlanta Podcast, February 1, 2019, audio, 22:24, https://www.archiveatlantapodcast.com/e/episode-21-westview-cemetery/.

3. "Self-Guided Tour Map at Oakland Cemetery," Historic Oakland Foundation, accessed February 12, 2024, https://oaklandcemetery.com/downloads/oakland-cemetery-self-guided-tour-map/.

4. John Ruch, "Complicated History Lives at Oakland Cemetery's Restored African American Grounds," SaportaReport, June 13, 2022, https://saportareport.com/complicated-history-lives-at-oakland-cemeterys-restored-african-american-grounds/columnists/johnruch/.

5. "HOF Holds Ribbon-Cutting for African American Burial Grounds," Historic Oakland Foundation, June 14, 2022, https://oaklandcemetery.com/hof-holds-ribbon-cutting-for-african-american-burial-grounds/.

6. Crable, *Ralph Ellison*, 138–39.

7. Crable, *Ralph Ellison*, 173.

8. Crable, *Ralph Ellison*, 138.

9. Burke, *Rhetoric of Motives*, 195.

10. Baldwin, *Fire Next Time*, 21.

11. In her essay, hooks recollects on the fear of being Black in a public space being mediated by her grandmother creating a sense of safety in the home. She writes, "Oh! That feeling of *safety*, of *arrival*, of *homecoming* when we finally reached the edges of her yard, when we could see the soot-black face of grandfather, Daddy Gus, sitting in his chair on the porch, smell his cigar, and rest on his lap. Such a contrast, that feeling of arrival, of homecoming this sweetness and the bitterness of that journey, that constant reminder of white power and control." hooks, *Yearning*, 383. See also ibid., 382–90.

12. Gravel, *Where We Want*.

13. Atlanta BeltLine Inc., *Art*.

14. Cross and Peck, "Editorial," 12; Walter Benjamin, "Theses on the Philosophy of History," in *Illuminations: Essays and Reflections*, ed. Hannah Arendt, trans. Harry Zohn (London: Pimlico, 1999), 249, 248, 247, quoted in ibid.

15. Safransky, "Grammars of Reckoning," 292–305.

16. Safransky, "Grammars of Reckoning," 298–99.

17. Baldwin, *Fire Next Time*, 10.

INDEX

ABOUT THE AUTHOR

Photo courtesy of the author

RHANA GITTENS WHEELER is assistant professor of communication and coordinator of the African American Studies Program at Oglethorpe University. Originally from Lauderdale Lakes, Florida, she earned her bachelor's in journalism and MBA from the University of Florida. She completed her PhD at Georgia State University. Her research centers on critical rhetoric, critical rhetoric studies, identity, public memory, and space and place. She currently resides in Atlanta with her husband, Brian, and their miniature schnauzer, Pearl.

Printed in the United States
by Baker & Taylor Publisher Services